OTHER P[...]

Other People's Worlds

An Introduction to Cultural and Social Anthropology

Joy Hendry

NEW YORK UNIVERSITY PRESS
Washington Square, New York

First published in the U.S.A. in 1999 by
NEW YORK UNIVERSITY PRESS
Washington Square
New York, N.Y. 10003

This book is printed on paper suitable for recycling and
made from fully managed and sustained forest sources.

Library of Congress Cataloging-in-Publication Data
Hendry, Joy.
Other people's worlds : an introduction to cultural and
social anthropology / Joy Hendry.
p.   cm.
Includes bibliographical references (p.) and index.
Filmography: p.
ISBN 0–8147–3601–7 (cloth : alk. paper). — ISBN 0–8147–3602–5
(pbk : alk. paper)
1. Ethnology.   I. Title.
GN316.H46   1999
306—dc21   98–53610
                                                CIP

Printed in Great Britain

To my Mother,
who worried and waited

Contents

List of Figures and Maps

Figures

Maps

List of Photographs

Acknowledgements

I must first of all acknowledge an enormous debt to the 'other people' whose worlds I have been privileged to share. These include some who barely receive a mention in the text, for I did not eventually choose to pursue further the study of their worlds, but they undoubtedly influenced my initial discovery of the subject. First, the various people of Morocco among whom I lived and travelled in 1966–7 and the French family to whom I became attached on that occasion and which has made me welcome ever since in Paris and les Alpes Maritimes; secondly, the again various people I encountered while living in French Canada in 1967–8, including a Canadian godfather who happened to visit my father, his wartime friend, at the time I was born, and the staff and pupils of Beth Jacob School in Outremont where I taught for the last two-thirds of an academic year which included the Six Days War in Israel and introduced me to the (female) world of a highly protected orthodox Jewish community. In Mexico, where I lived and worked from 1968–70 and again in 1972, I discovered the subject of anthropology, which I pursued formally with a period of fieldwork in Texcoco and the formerly Nahuatl community of San Nicolas Tlaminca. Finally, I have shared in many worlds in Japan over the years, but of these I have published: a farming community in Yame, Kyushu, a seaside community in Tateyama, Chiba, and many friends and colleagues in Tokyo and other university cities. To all these and many more casual 'other' acquaintances, I record a deep gratitude for allowing me to share their lives.

More people than I can possibly list have influenced my understanding of the subject I present here, and some may anyway feel that I have over-simplified it in an attempt to make social anthropology accessible to anyone who feels inclined to pick up the book. However, I must at the very least mention my own first supervisor, Peter Rivière, whose words have undoubt-edly appeared inadvertently in these pages, so firmly ingrained were some of them in the recesses of my mind, and Rodney Needham, whose work on symbolic classification clearly inspired the whole basis of the original lecture course and therefore the approach of the book. I hope that neither will feel I have moved so far from their original inspiration that they are totally misrepresented.

For more practical help, with reading, suggestions and comments on the student guide, which formed the original draft of the book, I am indebted to

Ross Bowden, Jeremy MacClancy, Howard Morphy and Mike O'Hanlon for help with Chapter 6, Nazia Tenvir and Haroon Sarwar with Chapter 11, and, more generally, to Renate Barber, Genevieve Bicknell, Annabel Black, Paul Collinson, Martin Flatman, Ian Fowler, David Gellner, Clare Hall, Renée Hirschon, Tammy Kohn, Chris McDonaugh, Diana Martin, Lola Martinez, Peter Parkes, Bob Parkin, Sue Pennington, Josephine Reynell, Peter Rivière (again!), Alison Shaw, Cris Shore and Felicity Wood. Students over the years have also added their helpful comments, and Peter Momtchiloff at Oxford University Press kindly read and commented on a draft when he took on the anthropology list. I must also acknowledge the incisive comments of several anonymous readers, and thank them for some of the examples I have incorporated into the final text.

Thanks, too, to various friends and colleagues for the generous loan of their photographs, which are credited individually, but especially to the Pitt Rivers Museum, University of Oxford, for allowing me, first, to publish my snapshot of the totem pole, and secondly, to Michael O'Hanlon, the director, and Jeremy Coote, curator, who have allowed me to use formerly published photographs. For technical support, I would like to thank Bob Pomfret, who prepared the prints of the photographs, Gerry Black, who made the diagrams and world maps, and Bev Massingham and other Social Sciences secretarial staff for general secretarial support.

Finally, I would like to thank my father and mother, whose pleasant but unashamedly chauvinistic bickering about their respective origins in Scotland and Yorkshire made me aware of cultural boundary-marking before I had any idea what it was, and helped me to keep at bay the tendency to exoticise anthropology long before it became politically important to do so.

JOY HENDRY

Introduction

A New Encounter

Social anthropology is one of those fields which many people have vaguely heard of, but few know how to define. Even students of the subject dread that inevitable party-stopping question, 'just what is it you are doing at university?' and several rather pat answers have been invented to snuff out the interest. Once started on an explanation, however, an enthusiastic student may be hard to stop, and for many, social anthropology comes to change their lives in a profound and irreversible way. It may still be difficult to say quite why, but they will share an understanding of life with others who have ventured into the same pastures, an understanding which will also stand them in good stead in all kinds of future endeavours, despite the blank looks their employers may give them when they ask about the precise content of their degree.

Social anthropology is not an esoteric, difficult subject, however. Quite the contrary, it is concerned with the most mundane aspects of everyday life and it should, up to a fairly advanced point, be relatively plain sailing. There are one or two mind-bending exercises in which one must engage to cross the threshold of initial understanding, however, and a few problems may arise for those who, for whatever reasons, find it hard to suspend deeply ingrained ideas and values. Those who have been brought up bilingual or bicultural, or in a society different from that of their parents, often have an initial advantage in this respect, and social anthropology may help them to find a niche of their own in the world. Others just need a little more time.

This book is written to help with this initial experience. It does not claim to be comprehensive, or even to give a broad summary of the basic works in the field. References to the anthropology discussed are provided at the end of each chapter, along with further reading, and together these should offer a sound introduction to anyone embarking on the study of the subject. The later chapters also cover several of the traditional sections into which it is divided. The main aim, however, is to help **initiates** over some of the first hurdles they are likely to encounter, and to make this process an enjoyable one. My own first tutor warned me to expect to be confused for the best part of a year, and some difficulty may be inevitable because of the very nature of the subject, but this book aims to smooth the way.

1

The text is written primarily for students taking up the study of social anthropology, or thinking about taking it up, but it is also written for their mothers, brothers and friends, for their future employers and any number of other sundry people who feel bemused by the name. It is written (I hope) in a style open to any to follow, making no assumptions about prior knowledge or background, and it is written in such a way that one can use it to refer back to the parts one feels unsure about later. Most of all, however, it is written in an effort to make the whole venture enjoyable. It is a subject I discovered almost by chance when, during my youth, I was setting out to enjoy myself. Imagine my delight when I found I could spend the rest of my life doing just that for a career.

This book is based on a series of lectures presented annually to my first year students at Oxford Brookes University, and the lectures are only part of the experience we inflict upon those students. They also play games, watch films, read other books and articles, and write about what they are learning in missives which are (rather boringly) called essays. During the later part of their university career we send out some of the students into Oxford, or further afield, to carry out their own investigations. In a cosmopolitan society, there are plenty of 'other people's worlds' to investigate, and over the years these have included studies of greyhound racing, public houses, churches, witches' covens and college dinners.

What Social Anthropologists Do

Since it is difficult to say in a few words what social anthropology is, and, indeed, this whole book is dedicated to answering that question, let us start by looking at what people who call themselves social anthropologists do, or have done to achieve that title. As a social anthropologist myself, I know for a fact that most people I mention it to glaze over in a haze of incomprehension. Even those who nod knowledgeably may well be labouring under a complete misapprehension about what the subject is – in Mexico, for example, the words are well known, but they generally refer to archaeology rather than what we, in Britain, call social anthropology.

What social anthropologists generally share is an interest in different ways people have of looking at the world they live in. These different ways are not individual idiosyncrasies, but different views of the world learned as people grow up in different societies, or within different groups which make up one larger society. It may be the differences between people who live in Birmingham and Glasgow, or between those in Paris and Bangkok, or even the variety of views across a number of diverse groups within one of those places. There is an almost unlimited variety of world views for anthropologists to look at, and each social anthropologist tends to specialize, at least for a time, in looking at one of them.

Most social anthropologists gain their specialist knowledge by going to live in the society of their choice. They do not just go there for a week or two with an interpreter and a set of questionnaires. They go for a year or more, set up home with the people they are interested in, and try to live as far as possible as those people do – in every respect. The idea is to find out exactly what it is like to be a member of the society in question, and they operate on the assumption that the best way to do this is to live with them and share their lives. This form of investigation is called **participant observation**, because the observer finds out what he or she wants to know by participating in the lives of the people under study.

He or she participates in the routines of everyday life, perhaps trying out the activities of a number of different members of the society, practising their customs, taking part in their rites, and observing as far as possible their most intimate ceremonies. If the people concerned get up early, the anthropologist gets up early; if the people stay up all night, the anthropologist should do the same. If the people take hallucinogenic drugs, so might the anthropologist; if they stand for long periods of the night in a freezing stream, again, so should the observer (this example may sound far-fetched, but it was part of a study carried out in the Andes on which a book called *The Coming of the Sun* is based (Tayler, 1997). The idea is to experience what it is like to be a member of that world, for otherwise one could not begin to understand how it looks and feels.

An important part of this exercise, more technically though rather quaintly known as **fieldwork**, is to learn the language of the people concerned. This was absolutely vital in the case of far-flung tribes with whom the outside world had previously had little contact, for otherwise communication would have been well-nigh impossible, but it is essential anywhere to gain an understanding of the way the world is seen and described by the people concerned. Anthropologists have found that working with interpreters gives a wholly inadequate view, for first-hand knowledge of a language is the only way to become fully aware of the meanings and implications of the words used, which might be very different from straight dictionary translations.

This concern with language is important even for anthropologists who choose to work in a society where their own idiom is the native tongue, for there are many versions of any particular language. Teenagers who claim that their parents do not understand them, for example, are not merely being adolescent and rebellious. They are also usually quite accurately referring to differences in language (and values) which have developed between genera-tions. Within the English language there are also clear regional differences, and differences based on other allegiances such as class and occupation. An anthropologist working in his or her own language must be especially careful to look out for these sometimes rather fine distinctions.

Sometimes anthropologists experience great difficulties in finding ways to fit into the society of their choice. People may be very suspicious of a stranger whose main aim in life seems to be to poke their nose into the affairs of those around them, and considerable ingenuity may be required in order to allay the reservations they encounter. In remote areas, anthropologists have even been killed, and one I know, who went to work in the South American rain forest, claimed he had spent several weeks living off food thrown out for dogs. It may be necessary to carry quantities of gifts or medicines to make an initial bid for acceptance, or to arrange to be adopted as a fictitious relative of a member of the society so that others know how to relate to you.

Many have found it useful to arrive with their whole family, for this helps to overcome problems of crossing local barriers of age and gender. In some parts of the world men and women lead very separate lives, and a man may find it virtually impossible to investigate the lives of women, and vice versa. A female anthropologist who worked in Mexico reports that she found it essential to adopt an 'anomalous sexless' role so that women would not be jealous of her talking to men, and men would not misinterpret her intentions. In rural Japan, at gatherings where men and women sat separately, but in age order, I used to be seated between the youngest man and the oldest woman so my role must have been ambiguous in this respect too. Working with my children in Japan opened doors to subjects I had never even anticipated.

My own experiences have been relatively easy: first in Mexico, where anthropologists are thick on the ground even if the local population is not always clear about their intentions, and then in Japan, where the pursuit of academic inquiry of any kind is regarded with great respect. In both cases, I received much co-operation from the start, but each had its own problems too. In Mexico, people would sometimes express their suspicion of outsiders asking questions by telling quite blatant lies, even in matters as basic as the number of their children. In Japan, people were more likely to tell me things they thought I'd like to hear, a more subtle form of deception.

Both of these problems, and indeed many others encountered by anthropologists, are solved at least to some extent by the fact that the study is carried out over a longish period of time. A year is regarded as a bare minimum, in order to see the complete cycle of annual events, seasons and so forth, but many spend much longer, especially if they are starting from scratch with a new language. Thus the initial reservations of the **informants**, which is the word used for members of the society under study, are usually dispelled, and their views become more transparent as they relax and operate in normal everyday life. It also proves beneficial to anthropologists to return to the place of their research after some years have elapsed and place their findings in a long-term context.

Other aspects of the method of investigation help too, for it is usual to choose a relatively small group of people so that the anthropologist can get to know everyone well, and observe their relationships at first hand, as well as being told about them. The group may be a village, a school, perhaps an occupational unit such as a factory, bank or advertising agency, or a large extended family. One of my acquaintances in Oxford took up the study of a group of criminals, whom he used at first to meet largely in public houses, although later he had to spend a lot of his time in prisons. Another decided to observe an enclosed order of nuns. The authors of two PhD theses I examined recently on Japan worked in a bridal parlour (see Goldstein-Gidoni in the references to Chapter 12) and a regional museum.

In all such cases, the anthropologist is observing people in what we call **face-to-face** relations. This is a great advantage, not least because such people will talk of each other as well as of themselves, and this offers sources of information which reinforce each other and go deeper than a few one-to-one interviews might. More importantly still, members of such groups are likely to share a system of values, and although they might disagree with one another on specific issues, there will certainly be a set of underlying assumptions which they will draw upon in their communication with each other. It is this set of shared assumptions which defines in broad terms the language they use and the way they see the world through that language.

Anthropologists learn that language, and that world view, by living among the people. They may start out by asking questions, indeed must do, for there are a lot of practical details to amass. Later, however, they may find they learn more by sitting quietly and listening, by joining in with the work of the day, or even by simply observing the activities of others. In Japan, as elsewhere, much is communicated at a non-verbal level, perhaps in silence, in slight movements of the body, or by exchanging gifts or other material goods such as plates of food. Too much verbosity could blind the investigator to this level of interaction.

Listening also allows one a chance to check the validity of statements made in answer to questions. In Japan, for example, there is something of a controversy about whether love marriages are better than those arranged by elders. One old man told me how much he approved of love marriages, winking and confiding that his own had been such. Later I learned that he had refused to consent when his own daughter wanted to have such a marriage, and, even later, I heard him telling one of his friends how dangerous he thought it was for young people to initiate their own relationships. This man was often sought as a go-between, as it turned out, undoubtedly because of his charm and diplomacy – the same qualities which probably lay behind his initial reaction to my investigations, since he knew love marriages were the norm where I came from.

It is this kind of information which adds an extra dimension to the findings of social anthropologists who carry out long-term participant observation, and it goes beyond the more limited fieldwork or statistical surveys of the sociologist or economist. There are of course drawbacks in the case of social anthropology, because much depends on the character and interests of the investigators, and their own cultural background, but the depth of under-standing which can penetrate the cool front of a diplomat has a value which should not be underestimated, especially in the multicultural world in which most of us now live. To respond to criticisms about the personal element involved, anthropologists now usually provide information about their own background and experience when they write up their work. This subject is discussed again in Chapter 1.

Translation is the anthropologists' next task. After learning how to live with the people under study, they must come back to their own cultures and explain what they have found in their own languages. They must discover ways to analyse and make sense of their findings that are comprehensible to their colleagues and compatriots, which is not as easy as it may sound. Other anthropologists who have parallel experiences are usually sympathetic and encouraging, and provide models in their own work for the subsequent reports from the returned fieldworker. These basic accounts are called **ethnography**, literally writings about a particular 'ethnic' group of people, though ethnicity has been defined in different ways (see Banks, 1996 for further detail), and groups may anyway be characterized in other ways, as we saw for the criminals and nuns mentioned above (and see MacClancy, 1996, in relation to sport).

Comparisons are usually made with previous work, and much time may be spent trying to assess the extent to which areas of apparent similarity are comparable with phenomena observed elsewhere. Findings which seem to be peculiar to a particular group may be especially interesting, but they may also dissolve into general features of society which are manifested under a different guise in other places. The more accomplished scholars among these returned fieldworkers will use their material to contribute to or to formulate general theories about social life and human behaviour, and this venture has been one of the most important aims of social anthropology.

It should be emphasized straight away, however, that these theories do not always build upon one another. Indeed, many set out to contradict the theories of previous anthropologists. There are some classic works, which are accepted by most people in the field, and these will be discussed quite early on in this book. There are also several areas where different interpretations exist side by side, and there is no consensus about which is better than another. Some of these will be mentioned too. This book is inevitably informed by the British anthropological traditions which exist in Oxford, where I was trained, but the book is intended as an introduction to the subject that is accessible and engaging no matter what the reader's background. An important thing to remember, however, is that the study of society is not simply the learning of a body of facts. The study of ourselves and our social worlds is an area of much interpretation and many differing views.

Writing for the general public, on the one hand, or working with them, on the other, is less often the aim of social anthropologists, at least at first, for colleagues share much of the same background and they have parallel experiences on which to draw. This book is an attempt to bridge the first of those gaps. A growing number of anthropologists afterwards bridge the second by putting their new understanding into practical applications in the wider world, an area known as **applied anthropology**, which we shall consider in the last section of this introductory chapter. Some also make, or advise on, TV documentaries about the area where they worked, and there is now a superb worldwide collection of visual ethnography. Reference to some of the classic films is made at the end of each chapter of this book, and their availability is listed in a 'Filmography' at the end.

Other students of anthropology go out into the world to do quite unrelated tasks, but always informed by the knowledge that *their* world, *their* way of thinking, is only one of many. They are equipped with the skill to see the other's point of view, whether the other be Chinese, Czech or from Church Hanborough, and it is this skill which can be acquired through the study of social anthropology. Even without becoming a professional anthropologist, students of the subject can gain a great deal from at least a smattering of practical experience, carrying out a project in a 'world' different from their own. This book offers only the first key to the first door to this experience, but it is a door that many people fail ever to open.

A History of Social Anthropology

The subject of social anthropology as it is practised today has developed only within this century, and some of the stages in its development will be illustrated in the chapters which follow. However, its intellectual foundations go back much further and it is useful before embarking on these chapters to have an idea of the background to the inquiries discussed. A thorough history of the subject would form the subject matter of a book in its own right, and indeed, several have been written (see for example Kuper, 1983, listed under 'Further Reading'), but this section will summarize some of the issues which have been addressed and help enthusiastic new devotees to avoid trying to reinvent the wheel.

People have probably speculated about their strange neighbours since time immemorial, but the European interest in social life became more focused when travellers' tales began to show striking similarities between societies found in different parts of the world. Some of them, described as 'primitive', were at a much earlier stage of technological development, and these were at one time thought to shed light on the prehistorical past of the investigators' so-called 'civilized' worlds. In the eighteenth century, when the natural sciences were becoming established, various theories were advanced in France and Britain that society should be regarded as a natural system, subject to laws like the objects of study of the other sciences.

In France, for example, Montesquieu set out in the eighteenth century to discover laws of social life by analysing and comparing various types of political institutions, and examining religious beliefs as social phenomena, which he argued were usually suited to the society in which they were found and therefore difficult to transport. In Scotland, during the same period, David Hume was investigating the origin of religion in human nature, and he posited a development from polytheism through monotheism to the inevitable decline of religion. He was part of the school of Moral Philosophers which included Adam Smith and Adam Ferguson, one of the early thinkers to argue that contemporary 'primitive' society could throw light on the past history of 'higher' societies.

It was in France, though, that a science of society was seriously proposed, first by Saint-Simon, who followed Condorcet's assertion that social phenomena were just as natural as those of organic and inorganic sciences and should therefore be studied by the same methods. The subject was named *sociology* by Comte, who drew up a ranking of sciences ranging from mathematics and astronomy as the most general, through to psychology and sociology at the extreme of greatest complexity. His laws of social life were based on the assumption that all societies evolved through the same stages, and that the human species has a fundamental tendency to ameliorate itself.

This evolutionary approach characterized the thinking of the nineteenth century, when several systematic attempts were made to trace the development of social institutions through different stages. A study of marriage was made by J. F. McLennan, for example, and one of law by Henry Maine. In Britain the most influential theoretical writer of the time was probably Herbert Spencer, whose ideas about the 'survival of the fittest' were later attributed to that other great evolutionist of the nineteenth century, Charles Darwin. Spencer made many biological analogies in his consideration of society as 'superorganic', and he also advocated looking at how the parts of a society related to one another rather than taking them out of context as others were wont to do.

This was later to be the cornerstone of two schools of anthropology known as **functionalism** and **structural functionalism**, led by twentieth-century scholars, Malinowski and Radcliffe-Brown, respectively. These approaches, each seeking an explanation of social behaviour within a particular society at a particular time, were something of a reaction to the previous evolutionary method, and were later criticized for neglecting history. They entailed spending a long time with a particular people and really learning their language in all its complexity, and this was what came to distinguish social anthropology from sociology.

Bronislaw Malinowski, the Polish-born anthropologist who was the first major proponent in Britain of the value of this long-term study, was interned in Australia at the start of the First World War, and spent several years in the Trobriand Islands, where he discovered the great advantages of time for properly understanding the ways of thinking of another people. The **functionalist** approach he advocated was grounded in the idea that all social and cultural behaviour could be explained as responding to various human needs. He taught social anthropology at the London School of Economics on his return to Europe, and inspired a cohort of anthropological fieldworkers who produced a body of detailed ethnography. Some of Malinowski's work will be discussed in Chapters 3 and 7.

Radcliffe-Brown's long-term fieldwork was carried out in the Andaman Islands (Bay of Bengal) from 1906 to 1908, but it was less intensive than that of Malinowski, and his interests were in the value of social behaviour for the maintenance and well-being of a network of social relations he called the **social structure** – hence the phrase **structural functionalism**. He taught in Sydney, Cape Town and Chicago, so his work was very influential around the world, though it has remained known as British social anthropology. We will look at an example of Radcliffe-Brown's work in Chapter 9.

In the United States the emphasis on intensive fieldwork dates back to the earlier work of Franz Boas, a German immigrant of Jewish origin, who argued in 1896 that all cultures were equal but different, and a great deal of work needed to be applied to each one. He spent long periods of time studying with groups of native Americans, and trained his followers to collect detailed empirical data about their material culture, as well as language and social behaviour. His work became known as cultural anthropology, and he introduced the idea of **cultural relativism**, which argues that because cultures are based on different ideas about the world, they can only be properly understood in terms of their own standards and values.

In Europe, a French sociologist who had a profound influence on the subject of social anthropology, particularly when Radcliffe-Brown returned to lead the profession from a chair in Oxford, was Emile Durkheim, whose concerns were still evolutionary, but who insisted that society must be looked at as more than the sum of individuals who make it up. He advocated the identification of **social facts** which exist outside the individual and exercise constraint 'like moulds in which our actions are inevitably shaped'. Examples are legal and moral regulations, religious faiths, financial systems, and taste in art, all of which form part of our socialization and education in a particular society. He led a group of scholars who were largely wiped out in the First World War. Some work which he wrote with another member, Marcel Mauss, will be discussed in Chapter 1. Mauss will reappear in Chapter 3.

The first chair in anthropology was created in Oxford at the turn of the twentieth century, and it was held by Edward Tylor, who reacted to the idea that 'savages' were somehow different from 'civilized' people. He had travelled in Mexico as a young man and he continually argued that 'human nature is everywhere similar'. He encouraged the comparison of 'primitive' and 'civilized' practices, but he was still an evolutionist. Another school of thought argued for a cradle of civilization from which practices had spread or *diffused* around the world, as people influenced and copied one another, but eventually another influential Oxford professor of anthropology, Edward Evans-Pritchard, pointed out the futility of speculation about how societies had developed, or evolved, and even rejected the idea of social laws.

He argued that societies are systems only because human beings need to order the world rationally, and anthropologists should study this **structural** order, and seek *meaning* in the context of a particular society. He advocated representing a particular society by establishing sets of related abstractions which could then be compared with those of other societies. These structures could undergo transformations, which would represent change, an advance on the earlier structural functional explanations which seemed to ignore history. Evans-Pritchard worked in British colonies, as did many of the British anthropologists of his time, which inevitably imposed change on the people they studied. Some examples of Evans-Pritchard's work are discussed further in Chapter 7 and Chapter 10 of this book.

Perhaps the most influential anthropologist in Britain this century has been another Frenchman, Claude Lévi-Strauss, whose brand of **structuralism** is a little different from that of Evans-Pritchard and Radcliffe-Brown. We shall discuss his work in Chapter 7. Throughout the chapters of this book the work of many anthropologists will be discussed, and other influential characters from the history of the subject will be introduced. As this book goes to press, the International Union of Anthropological and Ethnological Sciences is preparing for a conference in Williamsburg, Virginia, entitled 'The 21st Century: The Century of Anthropology'. Clearly this international body feels that our history is still short.

The Contemporary Importance of Social Anthropology

It is now quite unacceptable to talk of 'savages' or 'primitive people', because all people, whatever their stage of technological achievement, have been shown to have complex, rational systems of thought and valuable contributions to make to the knowledge and wisdom of the world. This understanding is in no small part due to the work of anthropologists, who still have important roles to play in facilitating communication between indigenous people and representatives of the 'developments' of multinational enterprise, whose views of the world are so different. Anthropologists can help at both ends, and their contemporary roles are by no means limited to the study of distant tribes.

Another big conference, this time of the Association of Social Anthropologists, held in Oxford in 1993, addressed the theme, 'Globalization and Localization', which neatly summarizes the contemporary potential for anthropologists to contribute to an understanding of what has become known as 'the global village'. Developments in communication technology, the products of multinational companies, and television advertising have permeated the world at large with an apparently shared culture of Coca-cola, sushi and brand-name trainers, to name but a few of the material markers. In local contexts, however, this global culture is interpreted and used in quite different ways (for some examples see Howes (ed.), 1996), though its apparent uniformity tends to mask these differences.

Anthropologists are therefore at last making some impact in the arenas of big business and finance, which until recently resisted our insistence on **cultural relativism** in the mistaken belief that the world was converging towards a kind of global homogenization. The so-called 'tiger economies' have illustrated forcibly that it is possible to contribute both successfully and less successfully to world markets, with many of their cultural differences firmly in place. Likewise, the oil barons of the Middle East retain their own distinctive views of the world. Anthropologists are now not only called upon to help companies set up outlets in foreign countries, but also to understand their own corporate culture from a social point of view.

Other features of the phenomenon of **globalization** are the increased numbers of people who travel outside their own home territories, whether for business or pleasure, and the increased tendency for individuals to grow up in one place and settle in another, and for children to be born and raised in a mixture of cultural arenas. Schools around the world are realizing the advantages of employing teachers whose anthropological training will help them to understand the plurality of backgrounds of the members of their multicultural classes. At a local level, anthropologists can help schools reach the children of isolated or itinerant groups – even in Oxford, some of my ex-students play such roles in building good relations with Traveller Gypsies, for example.

Health workers, carers and counsellors are also taking time and trouble to find out about the variety of attitudes and beliefs which exist among their patients and other clients, so that these may be taken into consideration in the treatment and advice they offer. Medical anthropology is a thriving branch of the subject, and many universities now offer one-year courses to train health professionals in the contribution the subject may make to their work, as well as opening their eyes to the values of indigenous methods of coping with ill health. Anthropologists have also had an important contribution to make to world health programmes, especially, for example, where the administration of inoculations may offend local cultural values.

Anthropologists are also now employed to advise on the realization of development projects, whose administrators have gradually come to appreciate the advantages of taking into consideration the views of the people they are aiming to help before imposing expensive projects on recipients whose unwillingness has rendered them useless and wasteful. There have been some classic cases of misunderstanding, dotting the underdeveloped 'third' world with crumbling constructions, rusting machinery, and local boycotting of perfectly good health measures, simply because the people they were designed for were neither consulted, nor their views of the world taken into consideration.

The application of anthropology is not new, but sometimes the subject has become associated with endeavour which is now politically unacceptable at a local level. Some early anthropologists were expected to help colonial administrators rule the peoples in their charge, for example, so they set out to understand the customs, language and political systems of aboriginal or tribal people so that their compatriots could subdue them. Anthropologists also adopted a role of advocacy, helping the people they knew so well to represent their own interests comprehensibly to the outside world; but local people have also complained about feeling patronized and diminished by such help, so the aid situation is not without complications.

One of the most famous studies of Japan – *The Chrysanthemum and the Sword*, by American anthropologist Ruth Benedict (1954), grew out of an assignment for the United States' Office of War Information during the Second World War, when she was commissioned to help the Allied Forces to understand their most threatening enemy. Benedict's book was translated into Japanese after the war ended, and it became very popular there, as she impressed local people with her level of understanding; but some objected to being represented in this way, reading expressions of superiority into the American cultural examples she used to compare with those found in Japan. The book is still widely read, but it also still causes controversy, some 50 years later (see Hendry, 1996).

One of the problems at the time of Benedict's writing was that anthropologists had tended to study people who were called 'primitive' and underdeveloped, and some Japanese readers felt that they were, by implication, being classed in this way, despite her use of America as a comparative base. Since then there have been great changes in the focus of social and cultural anthropology, which is now applied to any part of the globe, including the most industrialized nations. In 1982, for example, Anthony Cohen published a collection of papers by anthropologists who had worked in British communities, defined geographically, and there have been many studies of North American cultural forms.

Another problem, especially from a British perspective, was a legacy of biases and assumptions left over from our own colonial history, and it has taken the anthropology of scholars from some of those former colonies to make clear the way their compatriots felt to be the objects of outside studies. Residents of our former colonies have now settled in Britain, too, and some of the most exciting new studies for students of anthropology here concern the *contested* nature of social and cultural identity in just one location. Gerd Baumann's (1996) study in Southall, a multi-ethnic area of West London, draws on the lives of young people born in Sikh, Muslim, Afro-Caribbean and Irish families, all as English as members of the white minority who would appear to have few 'cultural' features to distinguish them.

The phenomenon of multiculturalism is of course already familiar in other parts of the world, and anthropologists may have another role to play where inter-ethnic relations have broken down in contemporary war zones, such as Serbia and Mozambique. They are not in a position to wave a magic wand, of course, and there is undoubtedly a limit to the value of mutual understanding in resolving disputes. Continuing difficulties in the Middle East and Northern Ireland provide an almost continual poignant reminder of the expression of deep rifts, couched in ethnic and religious terms, cited to underpin issues of political history. Anthropologists have also addressed the subject of disputes in areas where there are a variety of cultural influences, however, and this is a subject to which we shall return, in Chapter 9.

Politicians in the new European Community, set up as a long-term solution to the terrible results of war, find themselves regularly in situations of difficult intercultural encounter. The solutions they have devised to deal with this situation have become the subject of recent anthropological study, and this interest has apparently coincided with a realization on the part of the European leaders of the advantage of anthropological knowledge. For some of the fieldworkers, remuneration for their advice has helped them to afford the expensive life-style of cities such as Brussels and Strasbourg where they carry out their research. The study of intercultural communication of this sort can also be carried out among, and be of help to diplomats, international business people and a multitude of other citizens of the world.

With the speed and efficiency of electronic communications of one sort or another, some anthropologists are able to specialize in a completely new way on religious and cultural **diasporas**, people scattered geographically, but now easily able to keep in touch. One of my colleagues seems to be following up his initial fieldwork in Africa with a second bout on his computer, keeping up with Cameroonians living in different parts of the world. Other diaspora studies involve examining the plight of cultural refugees. The term was originally used for Greeks living abroad, but other examples are the communities of Chinese and Jews who maintain to different degrees their internal associations over their integration, or otherwise, to the outside world they occupy physically.

My own upbringing was as part of a Scottish community only as far away from the homeland as central England, but it is said that there are 20 million people around the world who describe themselves as Scots, while the population of Scotland is less than six million. In Chapter 4, we will consider one of the ways in which Scottish celebrations are held abroad, but here we encounter another interesting anthropological subject, for it seems that many of the people who recently enjoy (or try to enjoy) eating haggis on Burns Night (see Photograph 0.1) are actually not Scottish at all. Nor were there many Chinese people at a Chinese New Year party to which I was recently invited. In other words, 'culture' has become a kind of theme for leisure activities, and people not only seek food from cultures other than their own when they eat out in restaurants, but organize whole events around cultural themes.

This phenomenon may be related to the relatively recent propensity for large numbers of people to travel outside their own countries for holidays, which introduces them to cultural difference when they are relaxing, away from their usual lives. The anthropology of tourism is another new and exiting branch of the subject, which addresses the problems tourists bring for local people, as well as the issues associated with 'representing' cultural forms

Photograph 0.1   Piping in the haggis on Burns Night, in the heart of England. The chef, carrying the haggis, is English, as is the piper, whose name is Shakespeare (photograph: Joy Hendry)

in special shows. Young travellers, known as 'backpackers', apparently vie with one another to find 'real' people in 'real' situations, tramping through fields and villages, while those for whom resources are relatively abundant watch shows of dancing and singing, selected for them and brought to their expensive hotels.

Around the world, leisure parks choose culture as their theme, sometimes to represent images and experiences of local culture for the visitor to enjoy in a kind of encapsulated form, elsewhere they choose foreign countries. In Florida there is the Disney-dream Epcot Centre, for example, where displays from a series of countries may be visited, and their food tasted, but in Japan whole days may be spent apparently visiting foreign lands such as Canada, Spain and Germany, without leaving Japan's shores. These parks have imported houses, streets and museums from the countries concerned, as well as employing artists to demonstrate the skills associated with the area, performers to entertain, and a huge range of goods to be purchased.

Clearly the excitement of cultural difference is now shared beyond anthropological circles, and such positive attitudes are infinitely preferable to the fights and wars which break out because of such difference, but there is a danger in making cultural variety appear too trite and shallow. Increasingly, a person is likely, wherever they live, to encounter people from backgrounds different from their own, and they may find themselves in situations which conflict with the expectations of their own upbringing. The study of social anthropology is an important step towards breaking down prejudices and misunderstandings about strangers we encounter, at home or abroad, and it provides a basis for the deep understanding of other people and their worlds. Let us build on the excitement, but remember the depths when we return home.

References

Baumann, Gerd (1996) *Contesting Culture: Discourses of Identity in multi-ethnic London* (Cambridge University Press).

Benedict, Ruth (1954) *The Chrysanthemum and the Sword* (Tokyo: Tuttle).

Hendry, Joy (1996) 'The chrysanthemum continues to flower: Ruth Benedict and some perils of popular anthropology', in Jeremy MacClancy and Chris McDonaugh (eds), *Popularizing Anthropology* (London: Routledge), pp. 106–21.

MacClancy, Jeremy (ed.) (1996) *Sport, Identity and Ethnicity* (Oxford: Berg).

Tayler, Donald (1997) *The Coming of the Sun: A Prologue to Ika Sacred Narrative* (Oxford: Pitt Rivers Museum Monograph Series, no. 7).

Further Reading

Banks, Marcus (ed.) (1996) *Ethnicity: Anthropological Constructions* (London: Routledge).

Cohen, A. (ed.) (1982) *Belonging* (Manchester University Press).

Howes, David (ed.) (1996) *Cross-Cultural Consumption: Global Markets, Local Realities* (London: Routledge).

Kuper, Adam (1983) *Anthropology and Anthropologists: The Modern British School* (London: Routledge & Kegan Paul).

Willigen, John van (1993) *Applied Anthropology: An Introduction* (Westport, Conn. and London: Bergin & Garvey).

Novels

Lodge, David, *Nice Work* (Harmondsworth, Penguin, 1989) is an amusing fictional account of an anthropologist and a business man who trail each other at work.

Tan, Amy, *The Joy Luck Club* (London: Minerva, 1994) is a novel touching on problems of cultural identity in the relationship between Chinese women and their Chinese–American daughters.

CHAPTER 1

Seeing the World

Souvenirs and Handkerchiefs

Visitors to foreign countries very often return with a selection of objects collectively known as souvenirs. These are items acquired on the journey. They may be received as gifts, purchased in a tourist shop, or even just picked up on the beach. Their economic value is not necessarily important, for these objects are not usually for resale. Instead, they are essentially material reminders of the experience of the traveller. The objects may also be chosen for a variety of other reasons – for some perceived intrinsic beauty, to show off to friends, to give as a gift, or just to stand on the windowsill and bring out one of the colours in the curtains. However, all will be chosen because they are in some way remarkable, and because they stand for the place in which they were acquired.

The same objects, taken individually, will have different meanings to the people for whom they are a part of everyday life. In tourist resorts local business people become astute at anticipating the interests of visitors, and many secure their living by making available a range of local goods. Some goods may be designed for the purpose, but the best bargains – or business prospects, depending on who notices first – are those goods which are mundane locally, but unusual and appealing to outsiders. Objects which are taken for granted and perhaps readily produced in one place may be rare and charming in another. They may also have quite different uses.

To take a simple example, there are in Japan some light and relatively cheap souvenirs known as *hankachi*. These are neatly finished squares of soft cloth, often individually packed in cellophane, and characteristically printed with a Japanese motif such as an *ukiyoe* print (see Photograph 1.1), or a local view. These *hankachi* are named after 'handkerchiefs', but they are often so exquisitely soft and beautiful that it would seem a positive injustice to apply them to a runny nose. Indeed, they may well be inadequate for the task, for in Japan 'handkerchiefs' are for delicately dabbing at a sweaty brow on a hot summer's day. In Japan, the whole idea of blowing one's nose into a piece of cloth, and storing the subsequent contents in a pocket, is seen as quite disgusting.

17

Photograph 1.1   This Japanese handkerchief makes a good gift or souvenir, but it would hardly serve for blowing the nose (photograph: Bob Pomfret)

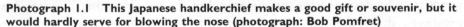

This single example illustrates a basic principle underlying the whole subject of anthropology, namely that different people *see* things – or, in anthropological terms, classify things – in different ways. For a foreign visitor to Japan, the *hankachi* is, at least at first, a member of the **class** of objects known as souvenirs. It may also belong to a class known as gifts, which could be shared at least superficially by both Japanese donor and foreign recipient. Once received, however, the same object may be further **classified** together with other similar objects in several different **categories**, depending on local ideas about usage. Moreover, a possibility among one particular people – that of containing nasal mucus and storing it in a pocket – invokes extremely negative reactions in another people.

The handkerchief continues to be a good illustration of principles under-lying this subject even within one culture, for different segments of the population have different ideas about handkerchiefs. A generation ago in Britain, for example, people were brought up to regard 'a clean hankie' as a vital part of their daily dress. Indeed, we would be chastised by our mothers (or teachers) if we were found to be without one. Thus some older members of the British community continue to carry handkerchiefs, as they were trained, while younger people rarely use more than the paper tissue which has come to be a more convenient, if less environmentally friendly, substitute.

During the heyday of handkerchiefs, there was great variety in the quality, and people would judge one another's taste and affluence according to the type they carried. Perhaps associated with this idea, it used to be part of smart dress among some groups of men to wear a handkerchief peeking out of their top pocket. Others would avoid the custom, seeing it as ostentatious or crude. Some people would carry handkerchiefs made of silk, others would have them embossed with their initial, and some would tie knots in the corners of them and wear them on the beach to keep off the sun. People who thought of themselves as 'ladies' would display the delicate lace edging of their handkerchiefs by wearing them in the front of their low-cut dresses, or by dropping them at strategic moments for passing men to pick up.

Different ideas about these small squares of cloth indicated information about the social allegiances of their owners, and thus provided ways of **classifying** other people according to their upbringing, generation and status. The use of handkerchiefs was thus rather appropriately associated with the **class** system in Britain. Nowadays, they are much less used, but beautiful lace hankies are still a popular gift from Venice or Brussels, and in the airport in Beijing, they come in a range of qualities so that they can be given as change in a country which forbids the export of its currency. In a 'progressive' kindergarten in Japan, which has done away with the use of uniform for its charges, the children who go there must nevertheless wear a hankie pinned to their clothes to indicate their membership of a particular class.

Learning to Classify

We have seen then that **classification** in an anthropological sense is concerned with the way different people *see* the world. This is because people divide up the world into categories of objects and categories of people in ways that differ from other people. It may also be concerned with the way place and time are classified, as we shall shortly illustrate in more detail. A system of classification is something which is shared by members of a particular society. It is among the most fundamental characteristics of that society, and it is acquired by children growing up to be members of that society. It is, indeed, the basis of the **socialization** of a child, the conversion of a biological being into a social one who shares a system of communication with those who surround it.

As babies learn to speak, they learn simultaneously a range of meaning for the words they enunciate. They learn to use the 'label' of each word for a particular 'category' of meaning. Anyone who has spent time with babies will know that this category and its meaning may for some time be rather different from that of the adults around, and mothers are usually required to 'translate' the baby's utterances. A classic and potentially embarrassing example is the way some babies learn the word 'Daddy' and then apply it indiscriminately to sundry other men they meet. The baby has learned the label 'Daddy', which applies to a particular man they probably know rather well, but they are not yet aware of any of the further detail about the meaning of the word. They may have in mind a category closer to 'man', or perhaps 'young man with blond hair', nothing which they could possibly explain, but some part of the world which they can link with that label. Later they will come to associate much more meaning with the label, which they will realize is only appropriate for one particular man. But all this takes time.

In other societies, the label which corresponds to 'daddy' may actually apply to a range of people, as we shall discuss in more detail later on, and the baby in that society will eventually learn who those people are and how they are to be distinguished from other people. In both cases the babies are learning to classify people. They will also learn any number of other terms, together with the characteristics which define them. Just as they learn language, then, they are learning the system of classification shared by the people who use that language. In complex societies, like many of those where English is spoken, there will be variations in both the language and the system of classification, and these may be related, rather appropriately again, to 'class distinctions'.

Our first system of classification is usually learnt so early that it becomes deeply engrained. Until we think about it, it seems as natural as eating and sleeping. We have notions of people, classified as relatives, friends or strangers, with further sub-divisions depending on various other characteristics, and we have ideas about the expectations of those categories; we also classify places, again with expectations about them – for example, we may learn to drop our voices when we enter a church, and salivate for popcorn when we enter a cinema. Things of one sort or another are classified as nice or nasty, clean or dirty, safe or dangerous.

Until we travel outside our own society we tend to take for granted that our system of classification is universal. Even then we may learn differences only rather reluctantly, and some notions are very hard to shift. We may find foreign countries, or even just foreign neighbours, 'smelly', 'dirty', or simply 'strange'. For anthropologists to learn the system of classification of another people, they must first learn to stand outside their own system and to reject notions of revulsion or disapproval based on early upbringing. As a baby learns to classify in its own society, the anthropologist must learn all over again the new system of classification of the people under study.

In the introduction to his translation of a book on the subject of classification, Rodney Needham compares the anthropologist setting out to study a strange people with a person blind from birth who is suddenly given sight. In the latter case, the first impression is apparently of a

> painful chaos of forms and colours, a gaudy confusion of visual impressions none of which seem to bear any comprehensible relationship to the others. (Durkheim and Mauss, 1963, p. vii)

Just as the previously blind person needs to learn to distinguish and classify objects, the 'culturally blind' anthropologist needs to learn to make sense of 'a confusion of foreign impressions, none of which can safely be assumed to be what they appear' (Ibid)

Life, Death and Burial Alive

The task of understanding fully the categories of another society is a very difficult one. Indeed, the whole enterprise is relatively recent, and tended for some time to concentrate on so-called 'primitive' people. In the early twentieth century the French sociologist, Lévy-Bruhl, wrote a book about what he called the mentality of primitive people, which he described as 'pre-logical'. At that time descriptions of people in remote parts of the world were based on limited observation, often without the benefit of language, and their practices sometimes seemed to defy the cherished systems of logic which were held to underpin all civilized thought. At the time Europeans saw themselves at the pinnacle of development, and they saw people who were technologically less advanced as radically different.

In fact, this 'civilized thought' was the thought of Western Europeans. W. H. R. Rivers questioned the idea that there was some fundamental difference between the logic of primitive people and that of their observers. In an essay entitled 'The Primitive Conception of Death' (1926), he suggested that deeper investigation would reveal logic quite recognizable to the Western mind if due consideration was given to the fact that things might be**classified** differently. Drawing on his own experience among Melanesian people in the Solomon Islands, he addressed some apparent contradictions in the use of a local word, *mate*, used to translate 'dead', but also applied to people who by his standards were patently still living.

It might be thought at first sight that the distinction between life and death is rather clear. A person is either alive, or dead. His or her heart is beating or it is not. This is simply one way in which to classify death as a state, however, and even this has been brought into question since the introduction of life support machines. A state of 'brain-death' might now justify the stopping of a heartbeat sustained by such a machine, and this possibility has brought to the surface a degree of woolliness in our own definition of death. Among the Melanesians, Rivers suggested that the category *mate* also included the idea of 'very ill' and 'very old', so that the dividing line between that and the opposite, *toa*, is drawn in a different way from our distinction between life and death.

Our distinction is a biological one, based on certain observations of the body perceived through a fairly sophisticated understanding of its component parts. It probably also involves, more subtly, notions set in a historical and philosophical context about the heart and the soul. Elsewhere, the distinction may be concerned with socioeconomic value, and a scarcity of resources. Japanese folk tales recount a custom of leaving old people up on a mountain once they had reached a certain stage of frailty and inability to contribute to the needs of family life. In Melanesia some people were apparently being buried 'alive', as they were reported to have been in parts of Africa.

Notions of life and death are related to notions of the afterlife, and what becomes of people after they 'die'. Europeans were profoundly shocked in the sixteenth century when they discovered human sacrifice practised among the Aztecs, and they tried immediately to put a stop to it. The Aztec people saw human sacrifice as an essential part of the appeasement of their gods, however, and it was thought to be a noble way to die, which would give one a special, honoured position in the next life. They believed that if they failed to 'feed' their gods in this way, the world would come to an end. As it happened, they were proved right. The Spaniards put a stop to the practice and the Aztec world was indeed destroyed.

Prior to the colonization of the Sudan, when the practice was prohibited, the Dinka people are said to have preferred to bury members of their priestly class while they were still alive. Godfrey Lienhardt, who did not witness the custom, but analysed it in his immensely readable book, *Divinity and Experience*, quotes one of his informants as follows:

When a master of the fishing-spear has fallen sick and is becoming weak, he
will call all his people and tell them to bring his whole camp (tribe or subtribe)
to his home to bury him whilst he lives. His people will obey him and quickly
come, for if they delay and the master . . . dies before they reach him, they will
be most miserable. . .

And he will not be afraid of death; he will be put in the earth while singing his
songs. Nobody among his people will wail or cry because their man has died.
They will be joyful because their master . . . will give them life so that they
shall live untroubled by any evil. (Lienhardt 1961, p. 300)

Lienhardt's book contains much information about these masters, and their
role in performing myth and ritual, when they are seen to embody the
traditions of the Dinka people. He is thus able to interpret this practice as a
representation to the Dinka people of a renewal of their own collective life
(Ibid, p. 301).

In the case of the Melanesians, Rivers puts the distinction between *mate*
and *toa* in the context of different ideas about stages of life, and, again, about
what happens to human beings after death. He also suggests that a clearer
understanding of a different system of classification in this respect could
perhaps explain events which had horrified European travellers and missionaries when they had observed the funerals and burials of people who were
apparently alive.

He also points out, incidentally, that Melanesians use different systems
from Europeans to classify their relatives, applying the term 'father' to the
brothers of their fathers, by his reckoning, and also to the husbands of their
mother's sisters (systems we shall discuss further in Chapter 11). This is
related to a wider system which makes clear distinctions between generations,
and between relatives on the mother's and father's side of the family. Rivers
makes some amusing speculations about what Melanesians might make of
our system of classifying relatives were they to come and study English
people, who apparently apply words (like cousin, uncle and aunt) indiscriminately across these boundaries. He suggests, not altogether frivolously, a
possible native view that 'the hyperdevelopment of material culture has led to
an atrophy of the thought processes' – perhaps a 'post-logical mentality'
(1926, p. 45).

Cultural Relativism and the Anthropologists' Bias

Rivers himself betrays a system of classification common among writers of the
time, describing peoples as 'primitive' or 'savage', as if this in itself allows a

degree of generalization. Although he is arguing against Lévy-Bruhl's ideas of 'pre-logical mentality', he still tends to assume that the Melanesians he describes will share certain forms of classification with other people of 'lower orders'. This broad classification of peoples is related to technological achievements, but it also illustrates an idea of the time that an understanding of earlier stages of development of more 'advanced' peoples could be sought in the practices of the more 'primitive'.

The best-known book which addresses directly the subject of classification, written in French at the turn of the century, reflects this notion that peoples could be fitted onto a scale of civilization, with the European scholarly elite (particularly the French) at one end, and the so-called 'primitive' people at the other. Durkheim and Mauss, in their book entitled *Primitive Classification*, turn to 'primitive' society in an attempt to demonstrate their idea that the origins of mental categories are to be found in society. Nowadays anthropologists are less concerned with origins than they used to be, but they are of necessity concerned with modes of classification, and the book also gives some very good examples of how various these may be.

The first two chapters are concerned in particular with the *classification of other human beings*. They discuss various systems reported from Australian Aboriginal groups which divide themselves into marriage classes and clans associated with animals. The whole society is also divided into two major classes described by the observers as *moieties*. The consequences of such a system for the people concerned are multiple, but major ones include a division of all other human beings into those one may and those one may not marry. Some people also have groups into which marriage is preferred. This will have further ramifications as the system operates to produce relatives of one sort or another, and these will fall into indigenous categories quite impossible to translate accurately into our names for relatives.

We approach a fragment of an understanding of such a system when we prohibit marriage with members of our own families, but otherwise our terms for relations make few distinctions according to the marriage links involved, and these would certainly not affect further decisions about marriage with people to whom we can trace no genealogical link. The Australian groups, on the other hand, classify everybody within the group as part of the overall marriage system, and all must fit into the scheme.

Everyone must also belong to one or other of the animal clans, and both of these allegiances may indicate further rules about what in the environment people may or may not eat. A member of the snake clan may be prohibited from eating snake, or they may be the only people allowed to, either way they are seen as having a special relationship with the snake, just as members of the opossum clan are expected to have a special relationship with opossum. Creatures in the environment may well also be allocated membership of the *moieties*, as may meteorological phenomena such as wind and rain, and distant objects such as the sun and stars. The authors then turn to discuss a system they describe as more complex, which also brings into the arrangement the *classification of space*. This is the system observed among the *Zuñi*, a group of Pueblo Indians of North America, whom they describe, with quotations from Cushing, the original ethnographer, as follows:

> what we find among the Zuñi is a veritable arrangement of the universe. All beings and facts in nature, 'the sun, moon, and stars, the sky, earth and sea, in all their phenomena and elements; and all inanimate objects, as well as plants, animals, and men', are classed, labelled, and assigned to fixed places in a unique and integrated 'system' in which all the parts are co-ordinated and subordinated to one to another by 'degrees of resemblance'.
>
> In the form in which we now find it, the principle of this system is a division of space into seven regions: north, south, west, east, zenith, nadir and the centre. Everything in the universe is assigned to one or other of these seven regions. To mention only the seasons and the elements, the wind, breeze or air, and the winter season are attributed to the north; water, the spring and its damp breezes, to the west; fire and the summer, to the south; the earth, seeds, the frosts which bring the seeds to maturity and end the year, to the east. The pelican, crane, grouse, sagecock, the evergreen oak, etc. are things of the north; the bear, coyote, and spring grass are things of the west. With the east are classed the deer, antelope, turkey, etc. Not only things, but social functions are also distributed in this way. The north is the region of force and destruction; war and destruction belong to it; to the west peace . . ., and hunting; to the south, the region of heat, agriculture and medicine; to the east, the region of the sun, magic and religion; to the upper world and the lower world are assigned diverse combinations of these functions. (Durkheim and Mauss, 1963, pp. 43–4)

This division of the universe into seven classes is also associated with colours, so that, for example, south is red, the region of summer and fire, the north is yellow, and the east is white. A comprehensive system of classification such as this is again learned very early, and an investigator could not expect members of the society necessarily to be able to explain it in an analytical form. It would nevertheless underlie a lot of communication within that society, and until the ethnographer pieced it together much communication could be lost. The use of the word 'yellow' could, for example, have connotations based on other associations with north, so that a person described as 'yellow' could be fierce and destructive, rather than cowardly, as is the case in the English language, though again native speakers may not know why.

In fact, colours themselves are classified differently in different societies, and even by different groups within the same society. Newton's classification of bands of the spectrum into the seven 'colours of the rainbow', identified by scientific measurements, is widely accepted now, but there are different indigenous systems still in existence at a colloquial level. For example, the Japanese word *aoi* may be applied to something described in English as 'blue' (a rather light blue), as 'green' (the colour of pine trees, or a person feeling sick), or as 'pale' (the same person, slightly less sick). The colour blue, even in English, has a huge number of sub-divisions, especially for professional artists or designers.

According to a study by Edwin Ardener (1971), the Welsh language used to have only two words for the colours described in English as grey, brown and black, with *du* for a colour covering part of the range described in English as black and part of 'brown', and *llwyd* covering another aspect of 'brown', and part of grey, which also shaded off into *glas*, a colour including hues described as blue and even green in English. Gradually the Welsh have come to adopt the English word 'brown' into their own language, and the shades covered by the modern colloquial Welsh words are much closer to their nearest English equivalents, probably to avoid confusion, since Welsh speakers are almost always bilingual (see Figure 1.1).

Durkheim and Mauss also bring the *classification of time* into consideration in their description of Chinese ideas collectively known as *taoism*. This is a system of classification independent of social organization, they explain, but it orders and affects many details of daily life. It comprises a division of space into four cardinal points, again associated with animals and colours, a division of objects into associations with five elements, namely earth, water, wood, metal and fire, and a further cycle of twelve signs of the Chinese zodiac. There is also a now widely known huge bipartite division of almost everything into *yin* and *yang*, sometimes also described as female and male, negative and positive, younger and older, or passive and active.

The system is used to classify divisions of time: years, days and even smaller units of two hours within the day, where each is assigned an animal of the zodiac and an element in its *yin* or *yang* form. Taken together with the classification of space into four cardinal points, an immensely complex system of divination (known as *geomancy*), developed in ancient China, was consulted in all kinds of endeavour and influenced much behaviour, particularly of a ritual kind. The system affected many parts of the Far East and even in today's technological super states such as Japan and Hong Kong, activities like choosing sites and times for building, arranging weddings and

ENGLISH	STANDARD WELSH	MODERN COLLOQUIAL WELSH
green	gwyrdd	gwyrdd
blue	glas	glas
grey	llwyd	llwyd
brown		brown
black	du	du

Source: Edwin Ardener (ed.), *Social Anthropology and Language* (1971), p. xxi, by permission of Tavistock Publications.

Figure 1.1   English and Welsh colour classifications

funerals, and investigating unexpected misfortune, will involve consulting almanacs and experts in this ancient lore for advice.

An example quite recognizable to some members of Western societies is the way people's characters are supposed to be related to the year and time at which they were born. The animal associated with a particular year is said to have an influence, so that a person born in the year of the ox is said to be very patient and to speak little, one born in the year of the tiger sensitive, short-tempered and given to deep thinking. Certain pairs of people are also said to be better suited to marriage than others, and a geomancer may advise a change of name to offset a disadvantage of this sort. A Japanese woman born in the year of the horse, which also falls in the active aspect of fire, is said to be a very bad bet for marriage, and a general indication of the seriousness with which these ideas are taken can be found in a sharp drop in the birthrate during those years.

It is clear, then, that technological advance is not necessarily accompanied by a convergence of ideas about the ordering of space, time and social relations. Some elements of systems of classification may be displaced as societies influence one another, such as the example of the use of 'brown' in Welsh, but others persist, and observers of other societies must try to avoid making assumptions based on their own system of thought. The classic work of Durkheim and Mauss not only provides us with examples of widely different systems of classification found in societies relatively untouched by outside influence, it also illustrates a system of classification shared by scholars of the period in which it was written.

Anthropologists have recently been much concerned with examining their own preconceptions, and several works published in the last few years illustrate a concern with the way the background, age, gender and theoretical approach of the ethnographer might affect the results of his or her work. Different ethnographies of the same people were of particular interest, especially where these presented conflicting views, and two studies of the same village in Mexico, by Robert Redfield and Oscar Lewis, provide a classic example. The first study described a positive, cheerful people, with many mechanisms of co-operation; the second concentrated on negative aspects of the same society, illustrating the poverty of the people and a grasping, competitive character.

Various theories were put forward to explain these divergent results, and one put the difference down to changed demographic and economic conditions. Others saw the discrepancy in the character of the ethnographers. A third might be related to the prior interests of each. A more general literary examination of the work of anthropologists suggests that those who made most impact in the subject were simply good writers, and the social and cultural features of the people they chose to study have taken on a disproportionate value in the subject because of the clear and arresting language in which they were described (see, for example, Clifford and Marcus, 1986). This is not necessarily a disadvantage, however, if it helps other people become aware of the relative nature of their own social and cultural assumptions, and therefore to understand the depth of difference which may exist in the views of their neighbours.

In a more recent collection, anthropologists were invited to use autobiography, of themselves and of their informants, as a means to tackle head-on this problem of personal involvement in the research they carry out (Okely and Callaway, 1992), and the resulting book has become a valuable aide to field work. Most anthropological studies make serious attempts to counteract the inevitable bias of the human studying humans – a phenomenon not unlike that known in physics as the Heisenberg uncertainty principle, which recognizes the need to introduce a change to particles of matter in order to observe them. In a similar way, students of anthropology can learn from and about their own experience in the process of understanding people elsewhere.

Changes in Systems of Classification: The Issue of Gender

It was in my view no coincidence that this last collection of papers, about the personal involvement of the ethnographer, was edited by two women, for one of the biases identified in the work of their earlier colleagues was towards allocating much more importance in any society to the activities of men than to those of women. Steps have been taken to rectify this practice in the last few decades, and this reflects an area of quite noticeable change in wider systems of classification with regard to **gender** roles in the so-called 'civilized societies' from which the observers hailed. Indeed, the recognition of 'gender' as a culturally relative notion has added a new dimension to the ideas of 'sex' as a biological feature. Here we can see the role of anthropology as a discipline which forces us to challenge and reconsider our assumptions about everyday life.

This illustrates the way in which changes can be brought about in systems of classification over time within a particular society, or indeed through the influence of one people on another. One of the major distinctions learned is that between men and women, or, more importantly in this context, between the roles assigned to each of the categories. Within only one or two generations, there have been great changes in these roles in Western societies. Women have secured for themselves a much greater part in public life than their mothers and grandmothers played, and men are now much more likely than their fathers were to be found contributing in a significant way in the home.

This has been no mean task, since the pioneers of women's 'liberation' found themselves fighting against the constraints of all sorts of 'social facts', in Durkheim's terms: legal and moral regulations, customs, and other **collective representations** about appropriate attitudes and behaviour. My own maiden aunt lamented the three years she spent waiting to marry and take care of a fiancé who died while they were saving money because, as a teacher in the 1930s, she would have to give up work on marriage. My mother gave up her job to marry, and, at 86, still sees her life in terms of the 'work' of 'running the home'. The men of their generation were expected to provide for the whole family, and for long after women did begin to go out to work, it was still the men who were obliged, by law, to take care of the tax return.

In my own generation, expectations changed markedly, and some women experienced disapproval if they did not keep up their economic activities after marriage and even childbirth. We had been trained in the 'female' roles of housework, caring and comfort, but once we won our places in the wider world, we were expected to maintain them, as well as attend to our homes and children. Some men were overtly supportive, but many found it difficult to do more than 'help' with the household tasks. Outside, men still tended to see other men as appropriate people to promote. Nowadays, men and women do, at least in some families, play an equal part in the rearing of their offspring, children who will be unlikely to carry the same clear ideas in their heads as their grandparents did about 'men's and women's work'.

Anthropologists who noticed the male bias in their colleagues' work, perhaps projecting Western ideas onto the people of their studies, have over the years published a great deal of interesting material about women from different parts of the world, as well as attending to their own roles in society. In the wake of the early feminist works of influential writers such as Simone de Beauvoir, Kate Millet and Germaine Greer, two ground-breaking collections of anthropological articles appeared, first in America in *Women, Culture and Society* (Rosaldo and Lamphere, 1974), and then, shortly afterwards, in *Perceiving Women* (Ardener, 1975) both of which are listed under 'Further Reading'. The latter was the first of a series of publications to come from a group of colleagues in Oxford who eventually founded a Centre for Cross-Cultural Research on Women.

Another of the early titles in this series, *Defining Females: The Nature of Women in Society*, originally published in 1978, examined the way in which even the so-called biological characteristics of women are culturally constructed:

> perceptions of the *nature* of women affect the shape of the *categories* assigned to them, which in turn reflect back upon and reinforce or remould perceptions of the *nature* of women, in a continuing process. (Ardener, 1993, p. 1; for further reading see Caplan, 1987)

Hirschon's paper about a Greek community, for example, explains ideas about the appropriate behaviour for women in terms of beliefs about their sexuality. Only women are thought to be able to control their sexual urges, so both men and women should be married at an early age, and respectable women must be kept out of the way of other men, who might lead them into temptation. If a husband strays from the straight and narrow – in other words, fidelity to his wife – it is the other woman who is blamed. Keeping their houses immaculate, cooking complicated dishes, preserving fruit in sweetmeats and cakes, and sewing and embroidery, are all time-consuming ways of keeping women occupied, and off the street (Hirschon, 1993, pp. 51–72).

Documenting the roles of women, their variety, and sometimes their changes, there is now a veritable plethora of books and articles, although these publications have for long been distinguished from regular anthropology by being called 'women's studies'. Some argued that it was as bad to separate the study of women from the rest of society as it had been to ignore them, but in a Marxist vein, the practitioners retorted that they needed to redress the balance. The subject of their attention has now become known as 'gender', but a book which grew out of a meeting at the first conference of the European Association of Social Anthropologists held in 1990, still addresses the way gender studies are marginalized in anthropology (del Valle, 1993).

In this book, one of the authors puts her finger on the problem when she argues for looking at gender in the context of 'other kinds of social differentiation, such as those based on age, generation, kinship, race, ethnicity, religion, region and social class' (Gullestad, 1993, pp. 128–9). Women concerned with their own liberation from the constraints of Western society have tended to focus overly on their counterparts in other societies, ignoring areas shared by men and women. They have also been accused of imposing, as universal, models subordinating women to men, whereas the situation in any one society might be much more subtle, even lacking hierarchical organization at all, a point conceded by one of the best-known feminist anthropologists, Henrietta Moore, in the same volume (Moore, 1993, p. 194).

Gullestad also advocates looking at gender 'in such a way that it is possible to study changes of cultural categories', pointing out that changes sought by Western women in their roles and definitions of themselves 'will have profound implications for the definitions of masculinity as well' (1993, p. 129). *The Full Monty* (1997), a film which won several Oscars about a group of redundant steel workers seeking to reinstate their self-respect, is a poignant popular representation of this situation in the English city of Sheffield in the late-1990s. Anthropologists have now turned their attention to the new roles of men, and one interesting book, *Dislocating Masculinity: Comparative Ethnographies* (Cornwall and Lindisfarne, 1994), is a re-examination of the notions of masculinity which have been displaced and replaced as women have moved into many of the spheres which were previously closed and almost sacrosanct to men.

In this chapter we have discussed systems of classification which affect and constrain the way in which people 'see' and understand 'the world'. We have considered various examples of difference in modes of classification: of objects, of life and death, of people, of space and time, and we have looked at how these may change. We have identified classificatory constraints (or bias) in the anthropologists as well as in the people they study, and pointed out the inevitability of this when human beings set out to study other human beings. In the next chapter we begin to look at ways in which systems of classification are expressed, and in this and the following two chapters, the various ways in which anthropologists gather information about them.

References

Ardener, Edwin (ed.) (1971) *Social Anthropology and Language* (London: Tavistock).

Ardener, Shirley (ed.) (1993) *Defining Females: The Nature of Women in Society* (Oxford: Berg; first published 1978).

Clifford, James and George E. Marcus (1986) *Writing Culture: the Poetics and Politics of Ethnography* (Berkeley, Los Angeles and London: University of California Press).

Cornwall, Andrea and Nancy Lindisfarne (1994) *Dislocating Masculinity: Comparative Ethnographies* (London: Routledge).

Durkheim, Emile and Marcel Mauss (1963) *Primitive Classification*, trans., with an introduction, by Rodney Needham (London: Cohen & West).

Gullestad, Marianne (1993) 'Home decoration as popular culture. Constructing homes, genders and classes in Norway', in Teresa del Valle (ed.), *Gendered Anthropology* (London: Routledge), pp. 128–61.

Hirschon, Renée (1993) 'Open Body/Closed Space: The Transformation of Female Sexuality', in Shirley Ardener (ed.), *Defining Females: The Nature of Women in Society* (Oxford: Berg), pp. 51–72.

Lienhardt, Godfrey (1961) *Divinity and Experience: The Religion of the Dinka* (Oxford: Clarendon).

Moore, Henrietta L. (1993) 'The differences within and the differences between' in Teresa del Valle (ed.), *Gendered Anthropology* (London: Routledge), pp. 193–204.

Okely, Judith and Helen Callaway (eds) (1992) *Anthropology and Autobiography* (London: Routledge).

Rivers, W. H. R. (1926) 'The Primitive Conception of Death', in *Psychology and Ethnology* (London and New York: Kegan Paul & Trench Trubner).

Valle, Teresa del (ed.) (1993) *Gendered Anthropology* (London: Routledge).

Further Reading

Ardener, Shirley (ed.) (1975) *Perceiving Women* (London: Malaby Press).

Barley, Nigel (1997) *Dancing on the Grave* (London: Abacus).

Caplan, Pat (ed.) (1987) *The Cultural Construction of Sexuality* (London and New York: Tavistock).

Gell, Alfred (1992) *The Anthropology of Time: Cultural Constructions of Temporal Maps and Images* (Oxford: Berg).

Hertz, R. (1960) *Death and the Right Hand*, trans. by R. and C. Needham (London: Cohen & West).

Moore, Henrietta L. (1988) *Feminism and Anthropology* (Cambridge: Polity).

Needham, Rodney (1973) *Right and Left: Essays on Dual Symbolic Classification* (Chicago University Press).

Rosaldo, Michelle Zimbalist and Louise Lamphere (eds) (1974) *Woman, Culture and Society* (Stanford University Press).

Novels

Barker, Pat, *Regeneration* (Harmondsworth: Penguin, 1992), is a trilogy of novels about the First World War, which feature W. H. R. Rivers, although not much direct mention is made of his anthropological work until the third book, the *Ghost Road*, where the effects of a British ban on head-hunting in the Solomon Islands are juxtaposed with reports of the atrocities taking place in war-torn Europe.

Bowen, E. Smith, *Return to Laughter* (London: Victor Gollancz, 1954) is a fictionalized account of fieldwork among the Tiv of Nigeria by Laura Bohannan.

Mahfouz, Naguib, *Palace Walk* (London: Black Swan, 1994), the first of the Cairo Trilogy, illustrates particularly well the contrasting life of men and women in a traditional Egyptian Muslim family.

Films

The 'Strangers Abroad' series (André Singer, 1985) introduces five of the early anthropologists and their influence on the subject. *Off the Verandah*, about Bronislaw Malinowski, demonstrates the value for British colonists of getting down off their verandahs and living with the people they were describing. *Fieldwork*, about Sir Walter Baldwin Spencer, pursues the theme by illustrating his work with the Arunta and other Australian Aboriginal peoples. There are also films about W. H. R. Rivers (see Chapter 11), about Margaret Mead and about Edward Evans-Pritchard.

CHAPTER 2

Disgusting, Forbidden and Unthinkable

Some Areas of Observation

One of the ways in which anthropologists find out about a system of classification is by looking at ideas which are strongly held by the people concerned. These are likely to be ideas learnt early in life, views which are difficult to dislodge even when one becomes aware of the fact that they are culturally relative. They include ideas which would provoke expressions of shock and disgust should they be contravened, ideas which are at the root of prejudice and racial discrimination, for people who engage in practices contradictory to one's own seem barbaric and uncivilized.

In practice, these cherished ideas are usually challenged whenever we travel abroad. From a British perspective, one has only to go as far as France to find toilets which seem not only dirty, but constructed in a fashion we find unpleasant to use, to find people relishing the consumption of creatures we may cringe at the thought of eating, and to encounter customs which appear strange, perhaps even obsessive. We would probably be surprised, at least at first, to discover that friends in France find a number of British habits disgusting too. Further afield, in India, for example, some of the activities taken for granted in Britain are regarded as seriously polluting. A separation of the uses of the right and left hands, for eating and cleaning the body respectively, make passing food with the left hand seem quite disgusting.

Certain practices are also quite simply forbidden in the law and custom of each society. In Britain, again, it is against the law to appear in public in the nude, and 'streakers', who gain a few seconds of attention by running naked across a cricket pitch, or other public place, are promptly arrested. People who wear very few clothes are accepted to different degrees in different places, and company on a beach will be much more tolerant than in a kindergarten, for example. Some London clubs and restaurants have rules about dress, where men may be turned away if they have no jacket and tie; in Oxford, undergraduates are refused entry to the examination hall if they are not wearing the appropriate gowns and black and white clothes; and in my own

London college in the 1960s, women were forbidden from appearing in jeans, or indeed, any trousers – though I found no serious sanctions came into operation when I decided to put the rule to the test.

These regulations may sound quaint and perhaps old-fashioned to foreign visitors, even our former compatriots such as Australians and Americans, but there are conventions of dress everywhere which are difficult for people to break, even if there is no hard and fast rule. It would be 'unthinkable' for a man in most societies to turn up to work in a skirt – even in Scotland, kilts are usually only worn at weddings and other special occasions – and the most ardent feminists, who insist that their girl children wear dungarees, would probably balk at the idea of dressing their boys in little frocks. In some strict Islamic societies, women are expected to veil their faces, elsewhere it is acceptable for them to be quite bare down to the waist.

Men kissing in public is pretty unthinkable in Britain (though this is another area which may be changing, along with new ideas about gender roles), but it is positively expected in greetings in other parts of the world. In most of the Middle East, men are much more free about their bodily interaction than they are in northern Europe, but in the Far East, kissing was not really a custom at all until recently, although men and women might think nothing of falling asleep on strangers in an underground train. In Japan, men and women used to bathe together in public until in the nineteenth century they saw how shocked Western visitors were. Now they bathe on different sides of a partition, but courting couples feel free to cuddle in public places, which they did not previously do, even until the early 1970s.

It is through ideas such as these, which may form the basis of prejudice and suspicion when people from one culture visit, or move to live among members of another, that provide good starting places for anthropological investigation. Notions of **pollution** and **taboo**, which are essentially institutionalized versions of an antipathy towards 'dirt' and the 'unthinkable', are particularly useful in this respect because not only are they firmly held, but they are also greatly concerned with classification. Things which are taboo and things which are regarded as polluted or polluting are very often things which fall between important categories. Thus, by studying the notions a people have about pollution (or dirt), and the things which they regard as taboo (or forbidden), we can learn more about the system of classification of that particular society.

Taboo

Taboo is a word which was brought back by Captain Cook from his voyages in the South Seas. His sailors noticed that in Polynesia the use of this word designated a prohibition and they found it useful themselves when they wanted to keep visitors off the ship, or reserve a particular girl for themselves. It was also a word for which they had an existing category, though they may have found this new word more instantly expressive and appealing than previous ones like 'prohibited' or 'forbidden', just as their countrymen did when they returned to introduce it to the English language. In any society certain things may be regarded as taboo.

In fact there are several possible translations of the word, as was discussed in some detail by Franz Steiner in another classic little book, named simply *Taboo* (1956). Its use in Fiji, for example, had been translated as 'unlawful', '**sacred**' and 'superlatively good', in Malagasy (Madagascar), a closely related word is apparently more like '**profane**d' or 'polluted'. In either case, some special category is indicated, though the translations may seem opposed to English-speakers, and Steiner suggested that the best etymology is one which divides the word into two parts, where *ta* means 'to mark off', and *bu* is simply an emphatic suffix, so that the whole word means 'to mark off thoroughly' or 'to set apart'.

Steiner went on to show that there was a great range of types of taboo. In Polynesia, for example, a close association with political authority meant that the taboos a person could impose provided a measure of their power (or *mana* – see Shore, 1989, and Chapter 3 below). To quote:

> The power to restrict was the yardstick by which power was measured; here was the social manifestation of power. Second, the exercise of this veto was in terms of taboo, that is, the actual sphere of any person's office or office's power was delimited by the kinds of taboos he could impose. Taboo thus provided the means of relating a person to his superiors and inferiors. One can imagine a Chancellor of the Exchequer declaring eight or nine shillings in every twenty taboo as a measure of the power conferred on him. It takes a stretch of the imagination to realize that in the Polynesian system this power could have been conferred on him only by somebody exercising an even more awful taboo, and that the Polynesian chancellor would use the same term for his share in your pound as for the rights of his superiors, because these rights would concern him only as infringements of his own rights, just as taking away eight shillings is a restriction on your use of your twenty shillings. (Steiner, 1956, p. 39)

For a chief or king, this power could be so great and terrible that anything he touched immediately became polluting and dangerous for ordinary people. This explained why people of extremely high rank – including visiting members of the royal family in former British colonies – had to be carried by slaves. As these were owned by the king, polluting them did not cause too much inconvenience, otherwise the visiting dignitaries would pollute for everyone else the ground on which they had walked. Clearly these taboos are helping to delineate categories of social ranking in that particular society. In today's world, when widely shared ideas such as these can be less well relied upon, persons of high status and power are very often separated from their people by a ring of armed body guards to 'set them apart'.

Further powerful examples of distinctions of classification based on taboos of one sort or another are to be found in rules about food. Hindus, for example, are brought up always to use separate pots to cook meat and vegetables, a practice which expresses an idea so strong that many feel they cannot eat at all in non-Hindu restaurants which serve meat in case this rule may have been ignored. Among themselves, Hindus have a variety of food taboos, depending on their caste associations, which affect who cooks the food and who may eat with whom, as well as a series of complicated rules about what may or may not be eaten at any one time. The cow is sacred, so beef is taboo, but a dairy product like butter protects food fried in it, which can then be shared across caste lines. Food distinctions therefore express social divisions within Hindu society (see Photograph 2.1).

Photograph 2.1   The Yakha of East Nepal sacrifice a pig for the Hindu festival of Dasain, though the subsequent feast would be taboo to their Hindu neighbours (photograph: Tamara Kohn)

Muslims, on the other hand, who may live in close proximity to Hindus, have a taboo against eating pork, but this time it is because the pig is regarded as unclean. Although these animals appear to have been forbidden for different reasons from the Hindus' sacred cow, they are both 'set apart' and therefore 'taboo'. In both cases, too, the prohibition makes an important distinction between the categories of people involved. Other peoples have different food taboos. Orthodox Jewish rules prohibit eating meat and dairy products at the same meal, for example, and they also proscribe eating meat which has not been drained of blood, or made kosher. Jeremy MacClancy, in a book entitled *Consuming Culture*, describes these arrangments very colour-fully:

> The Jewish dietary laws do not stop at the curly tail-end of a pig. They are made up of a whole set of kosher dos and don'ts, of which the ban on pork and the separation of meat and milk are merely the most well known. Though these dietary rules are still central in the lives of many Jews, they were even more important in Jesus's time, when each Jewish sect interpreted God's gastronomic intentions in its own way. What foods you ate and with whom you ate them were a key means of saying what particular group you belonged to. The Essenes would only have a meal among themselves, and neither they nor members of the Pharisees, the Maccabees, the Sadducees, the Hasidim, the Sicraii, the Herodians, the Hellenists, or the Therapeutae, would even think of sitting down at the same table with a gentile. For Jews, their food rules came to stand for the whole of their law, and violating any of them was seen as equivalent to leaving the faith. God had founded his Covenant with His chosen people through the medium of food, and His followers were not going to break this holy agreement by nibbling the wrong edible in the wrong company. When forced to eat swine by the Romans, some chose to die rather than pollute themselves and profane their sacred pact with the Almighty. (1992, pp. 33–4)

In many parts of the world there are taboos associated with the body and bodily functions, typically with pregnancy, childbirth and menstruation for women, and illness and death for anyone, regardless of gender. A study of pregnancy and childbirth among the Chinese in Hong Kong, by Diana Martin (1994), describes an abundance of food prohibitions during preg-nancy, even among the most highly educated women. Martin discovered that her informants were quite willing to hand over the care of their babies and tiny infants to others almost as soon as they were born, and also that the food and other taboos are often to be observed in public situations, so she suggests that the prohibitions are an open expression of the fact that the woman is about to become a mother, as well as the only time she has total responsibility for her offspring.

As for menstruation taboos, women in many societies are excluded from certain activities during their monthly periods. They may be required to live in a separate house for the duration, perhaps with other women in the same situation, or they may simply be banned from the fishing boats or not allowed to enter the temple.

In rural Japan, where I did fieldwork in the 1970s, women observed taboos on certain foods, on bathing, and even on watching television for a period of 31–3 days after childbirth. After a death in the family, the bereaved relatives would avoid certain foods for up to 49 days. These customs were explained in terms of the relationship between the soul and the body. The soul of a person who has recently died is said to be prone to stay around the house for a while, and the taboos are concerned with avoiding trouble and seeing that a complete separation occurs. In the case of a baby, the soul is in danger of escaping in the early stages, and the prohibitions are to help avoid this kind of disaster. An examination of these ideas is thus revealing of Japanese notions about the constitution of the person, the relationship of humans with the spiritual world, and, by further examination of the range of people affected by the taboos, of the make-up of the Japanese family.

Pollution

Anthropologists use the word 'pollution' to describe ideas found to be held strongly in various parts of the world about the destruction of a parallel notion of **purity**. In most cases, purity denotes cleanliness, but in many societies there are religious associations with this concept so that it would perhaps be more accurately translated into English as **sanctity**. It may be the case that rituals of purification precede any communication with the spiritual or supernatural world, for example, but in some societies, there are strongly held views about the avoidance of pollution and polluting behaviour for reasons connected with ideas about social relations. In either case these are inevitably concerned with local systems of classification.

In the Japanese case above, taboos related to birth and death may also be explained in terms of the protection they will provide for others, since those observing the taboos may be regarded as polluting at these times. Women after childbirth are thus prohibited from preparing food, entering a public bath, or participating in ritual activities which they may spoil due to their polluted state. Similarly, a girl whose father had recently died had to instruct a group of friends in the plaiting of a straw rope for the shrine festival from a position just over the wall and therefore out of the sacred area which she would defile if she entered. After a death in Japan, a notice is posted on the front door of the house of the deceased to warn visitors of the polluting situation.

In the Indian sub-continent, on the other hand, the food taboos we discussed above express more permanent notions of pollution associated with a caste system which divides all human beings into classes of people conceptually distinguished from one another in such a way that the word 'class' seems inadequate (see Dumont, 1980 and Quigley, 1993 for further reading on two interpretations). The strength of the danger of pollution is evident in the existence of a caste of untouchable people who are employed specifically to protect others. They sweep, clear sewage, deal with dead animals, and make leather goods, all tasks which are thought to be polluting for those of other castes. Brahmins, for example, must have nothing to do with excrement, an idea so firmly engrained that a Brahmin girl in England who was working in a nursery preferred to alienate all her workmates rather than break the taboo and agree to change the nappies of her charges.

Such ideas of pollution demonstrate very clearly ways in which people divide themselves up, in this case initially into castes, an ancient system understood and observed in its own local context, but in practice in another society creating new reasons for emphasizing old divisions. Actually, it is precisely for deeply engrained ideas such as these that foreigners are regarded with suspicion, and often with distaste, wherever they are found. The system of classification, particularly when it is reinforced with taboos associated with ideas of pollution, is very hard to dislodge. It expresses the way the world is perceived, and changes in it can lead to a good deal of confusion, even to shock – that American phrase, culture shock, is no trite description.

The novels of Paul Scott's Raj Quartet, which were televised in Britain under the title of the first in the series, *The Jewel in the Crown*, opened with a forcible illustration of ideas such as these. Hari Kumar, a British public schoolboy of Indian parents, is returned to his relatives in India when his father dies suddenly, leaving no provision for the rest of his education. He finds himself in a society which includes people brought up like himself, but the colour of his skin excludes him from their company. His kinsfolk find his life-style entirely alien and indeed polluting to them, and they force him to drink the urine of the sacred cow, an abhorrence to him, but for them the only way to purge Hari of the pollution he has picked up by living over the sea.

Purity and Classification

Various theories have been advanced to explain particular notions of pollution and taboo, but Mary Douglas has pointed out in her book *Purity and Danger*

(1966), that they all form part of a wider system of classification. The taboos, and the ideas about purity and pollution, are thus themselves fertile areas of investigation for anthropologists, who try to set them in the context of other knowledge about the peoples in question, and about the historical influences they have experienced. The analysis of the 'Abominations of Leviticus' in the same book is one of the best-known attempts to interpret an extremely complex and apparently random system of rules and restrictions of this sort.

The lists of animals which were prohibited in the Biblical Book of Leviticus are many and varied, and previous attempts to make sense of them had been rather unsuccessful, according to Douglas. She argues, however, that they must not be considered piecemeal. Within the context of God's order for the world, laid out in the book of Genesis, important distinctions are to be made between the components of the threefold classification of the world into the earth, the waters and the firmament. Living beings which reside in each medium are described according to their type: flesh, fish and fowl, respectively, and each has an appropriate means of locomotion. In the firmament, for example, two-legged fowl fly with wings, in the water scaly fish swim with fins, and on the earth four-legged animals hop, jump or walk.

Those creatures which are forbidden turn out to be anomalous according to this system, Douglas argues. This includes four-footed creatures which fly, and creatures with two hands and two feet who move about on all fours. It particularly forbids creatures which swarm because these are neither fish, flesh nor fowl. They are matter out of place, and therefore forbidden.

> If the proposed interpretation of the forbidden animals is correct, the dietary laws would have been like signs which at every turn inspired meditation on the oneness, purity and completeness of God. By rules of avoidance holiness was given a physical expression in every encounter with the animal kingdom and at every meal. Observance of the dietary rules would thus have been a meaningful part of the great liturgical act of recognition and worship which culminated in the sacrifice in the Temple. (Douglas, 1966, p. 72)

Mary Douglas's book has become a classic, and it was one of the first works to argue that rituals of purity and impurity create unity of experience in any society, not just those formerly regarded as 'primitive'. It brings the ideas discussed in this chapter right into the most domestic sphere, because in it she writes about *dirt* in a European household, or to be more precise, in *her* type of household, since the ideas may not be shared by Europeans of all classes and ethnic origins; however, this anthropologist provides an excellent example of how the principles learned in exotic places may be most aptly applied in any society, including one's own.

She points out that cleaning is as much concerned with **order** as with hygiene. There is no such thing as absolute dirt, she tells us, 'it exists in the eye of the beholder', and if we abstract pathogenicity and hygiene from our notion of dirt we find it is simply 'matter out of place'. Cleaning expresses our own system of classification so that an object likely to confuse it is regarded as *polluting*, that is *dirty*.

> Shoes are not dirty in themselves, but it is dirty to place them on the dining-table; food is not dirty in itself, but it is dirty to leave cooking utensils in the bedroom, or food bespattered on clothing; similarly, bathroom equipment in the drawing room; clothing lying on chairs; outdoor-things in-doors; upstairs things downstairs; under-clothing appearing where over-clothing should be, and so on. In short, our pollution behaviour is the reaction which condemns any object or idea likely to confuse or contradict cherished classifications. (Douglas, 1966, p. 48)

In Japan, as elsewhere, shoes should not be brought into the house at all, and this is a rule enforced so strictly that even tiny children must obey it as soon as they are able to walk. A foreigner who stepped across a Japanese threshold with shoes on would soon be hustled back out again, for this error would contravene deeply engrained ideas about dirt and cleanliness which further reflect a pervasive Japanese distinction between *inside* and *outside*. Shoes are to be left in the doorway to the outside world where they should be donned before stepping out again. Within the house, itself, there are further distinctions to be made between areas where slippers may be worn, and the fine floor matting which should only be crossed in stockinged-feet.

The force of this distinction was illustrated clearly in the writings of Fukuzawa Yukichi, one of the first Japanese to visit America in the nineteenth century when Japan was opened to the outside world after 200 years of virtual isolation. He was shocked to see people going inside the houses in their shoes, which had come directly in from the outside world, but he was particularly affected to notice them walking on great areas of soft material (carpets) apparently identical to a substance highly valued in Japan for making small purses.

These foreigners seemed dirty to the Japanese just as people in Britain classify 'gypsies' as dirty because they throw rubbish out of their caravan windows and leave it behind when they move on. Judith Okely, who made a study of Traveller Gypsies in Britain in the 1970s, has nevertheless demonstrated forcibly how clean these people are within their own system of classification (Okely, 1983). Again, they make a clear distinction between the inside and the outside, this time of their caravans. Beyond the window is not their world, but within it they have such strict rules about cleanliness that if a dog were to lick a human plate, the owner would feel obliged to break the whole set.

This is part of a strict code of purity and pollution shared by the Traveller Gypsies, who keep their homes immaculate. They separate bowls for washing clothes (outside) from bowls for washing up pots (which hold food which goes inside), and they separate male and female washing as well. For them, cats are regarded as dirty because they lick their own fur and confound the distinction between inside and outside, whereas other members of British society admire cats for keeping themselves clean. Dogs are dirty, too, and should live outside; members of the wider society who allow cats and dogs to live in the house and eat off human plates fill the Travellers with disgust.

It is clear that a look at ideas of dirt and cleanliness, a more domestic way of discussing the notions anthropologists have elsewhere called pollution and purity, opens up avenues to the understanding of different systems of classification, which can evidently exist side by side, even within the same society. It is also clear how strong and powerful these ideas may be. Within one society, where such notions are shared, rules seem natural and normal. To members of other societies, however, the same rules may well appear unnecessarily strict, burdensome barriers to friendship and integration.

Animal Categories and Verbal Abuse

Edmund Leach has written about the role played by tabooed words in language. He is concerned with obscenities – dirty words, blasphemy and words of abuse – words that are unmentionable in some company, and therefore used to shock or impress in other circumstances. He argues that language in general is like a grid, in which words provide labels for important categories and break up the social and physical environment, which would otherwise be a continuum, into discrete, recognizable things. Words which are regarded as taboo help to reinforce this system and prevent confusion by inhibiting the recognition of the parts of the continuum which separate the things.

His first illustration of the argument concerns the boundary of the human being within its environment, particularly important, again, as a baby is learning to see and label the surrounding world. Here taboos are clearly associated with what Leach refers to as exudations of the body – 'feces, urine, semen, menstrual blood, hair clippings, nail parings, body dirt, spittle, mother's milk' is Leach's list (1966, p. 38), although in the case of the baby, vomit and nasal mucus could well be added. In an essay which was initially read to an audience, Leach notes that so strong is the resulting taboo that, even as an adult addressing an adult audience, I cannot refer to these substances by the monosyllabic words which I used as a child but must mention them only in Latin. (Ibid.)

The child is not born with these inhibitions, of course, and it is an important aspect of the training of small children to see that they do not pay inappropriate attention to these same exudations of the body, which are apparently part of them, but which must be carefully separated from them. Failure to learn these practices would be regarded as dirty, although the behaviour regarded as 'clean' and appropriate is of course variable from one society to another. The substances themselves may also be regarded as powerful in some societies, like the cow's urine above, and hair and nail clippings are sometimes the focus of mystical attack. In any case, words for the substances may be used to make a forceful exclamation, and they are also inclined to provoke expressions of disgust.

Leach's second set of tabooed words comprises those which in a religious context would be described as blasphemous. He points out that although life and death are in fact inseparable, religion always tries to separate them, and the gap between this world of 'mortal men' and the next, inhabited by 'immortal nonmen (gods)' is bridged by beings who are ambiguous in terms of such regular systems of classification. Thus we find incarnate deities, virgin mothers and supernatural monsters which may be half-human/half-beast. These ambiguous creatures mediate between the two worlds, but they are also the object of the most intense taboos, and to speak in an inappropriate fashion about them may be regarded as a particularly dangerous endeavour.

The bulk of Leach's essay is about animal categories, and how these relate to categories of human being. Any number of animals are called into play – cow, pig, bitch, cat, rat, filly – but it is worth drawing attention to the fact that all the animal terms which are used to address or describe human beings, either in a derogatory or a familiar fashion, are those for beasts to be found in the households or countryside of Britain. An immediate concern is to distinguish between the human and animal worlds, then, and since it would be impossible to confuse animals from further afield with ourselves, it would therefore be less than forceful, as he points out, to address someone as a polar bear.

Leach chose to focus on the language of British English to illustrate his argument, but he suggests that similar mechanisms operate everywhere, and provides a further example in a consideration of the Kachin language of the people he studied in Southern Burma. Leach's argument was later heavily criticized in an article in the anthropological journal, *Man* (Halverson, 1976), but the ideas do provide a forceful (if inaccurate) linguistic example of the general way in which taboos and ideas of pollution and purity help to delineate systems of classification. In Chapter 4 we shall return to these ideas when we look at ritual activities, but in the meantime, we turn to further aspects of social relations, this time expressed through material objects.

References

Douglas, Mary (1966) *Purity and Danger* (Harmondsworth: Penguin).

Halverson, J. (1976) 'Animal Categories and Terms of Abuse',*Man*, **11**: 505–16.

Hendry, Joy (1984) 'Shoes, the early learning of an important distinction in Japanese society', in G. Daniels (ed.), *Europe Interprets Japan* (Tenterden: Paul Norbury).

Leach, Edmund (1966) 'Animal Categories and Verbal Abuse', in Eric H. Lenneberg (ed.),*New Directions for the Study of Language* (Cambridge, Mass.: MIT Press).

MacClancy, Jeremy (1992) *Consuming Culture: Why You Eat What You Eat* (New York: Henry Holt).

Martin, Diana (1994) 'Pregnancy and Childbirth among the Chinese of Hong Kong', a thesis submitted for the degree o f Doctor of Philosophy in the University of Oxford.

Okely, Judith (1983) *The Traveller Gypsies* (Cambridge University Press).

Shore, Bradd (1989) '*Mana* and *Tapu*', in Alan Howard and Robert Borofsy (eds),*Developments of Polynesian Ethnology* (Honolulu: University of Hawaii Press).

Steiner, Franz (1956) *Taboo* (Harmondsworth: Penguin).

Further Reading

Dumont, Louis (1980) *Homo Hierarchicus: The Caste System and its Implications* (Chicago and London: University of Chicago Press).

Quigley, Declan (1993) *The Interpretation of Caste* (Oxford: Clarendon)

Radcliffe-Brown, A. R. (1952) 'Taboo', ch. in *Structure and Function in Primitive Society* (London: Cohen & West).

Novels

Altaf, Fatima, *The One Who Did Not Ask* (trans. from Urdu by Rukhsana Ahmad (London: Heinemann, 1993), tells poignantly of the problems experienced by the daughter of a well-to-do Indian family when she breaks some of the taboos of her high-class upbringing.

Scott, Paul, *The Jewel in the Crown* (London: Mandarin, 1996) is the first of a series of four novels entitled 'The Raj Quartet' which depict, among other things, reactions to the breaking of unwritten taboos in the life of British India.

Films

Caste at Birth (Mira Hamermesh, 1990) a Sered film, explores the complexities of the caste system in the Indian sub-continent. It illustrates in particular taboos surrounding the 'untouchables'.

The Lau of Malaita (Leslie Woodhead and Pierre Maranda, 1987), a film in the Granada
    'Disappearing World' series, provides information about taboos among a group of Solomon
    Islanders and tells of how their long-standing 'Custom' is being defended (or otherwise) against
    Christian missionaries in the area.
Some Women of Marrakesh (Melissa Llewelyn-Davies, 1977), another 'Disappearing World' film,
    penetrates the enclosed world of female society in the male-orientated Muslim state of Morocco.

CHAPTER 3

Gifts, Exchange and Reciprocity

The Anthropologist's Arrival

With all the complexity of possibility discussed in the last chapter, an anthropologist arriving in a society to make a study might well feel daunted at the task ahead. Where to start? This is a pertinent question and many students worry a great deal about it before they leave for fieldwork. In practice, once they arrive and settle in, there are so many details of daily life to be seen to that the work just seems to take on a pace of its own. In a strange situation, one must first of all learn to cope with very basic needs – eating, of course, but also cooking, bathing, laundry, disposing of rubbish – all these things are highly relevant to an ethnographer, as we have seen, and for the participant observer, the work is begun.

While coping with the mundane, the fieldworker is also bound to enter into communication with other members of the society concerned and this forces an immediate consideration of the nature of social relations. My first days of fieldwork in Japan were greatly eased by the good nature and friendship of my next door neighbour, whom I visited to inquire about refuse collection. To my good fortune, he not only explained carefully about dividing waste into the burnable and the unburnable (which began to indicate information about local systems of classification), but he also instructed me about the more orthodox way of introducing oneself to new neighbours – namely, by calling round with a small gift, such as a towel.

This turned out to be an important custom in a Japanese context, for it allows a relationship to be opened. Some foreigners return from working or studying in Japan complaining sadly that they never made any progress with their neighbours – they had lived there for a year, maybe more, but they had neglected to take that first important step of self-introduction. For an ethnographer, who can only begin to learn properly about the people under study through social interaction with them, the principle of opening relations is a vital one, and if the neighbours are part of the study, as they were in this first fieldwork of mine, it is an advantage to start out in a way that they can comprehend and appreciate.

Social relationships are themselves an important part of the study of social anthropologists, of course, but they are not actually visible without being signified in some way. The presentation of gifts or, indeed, any movement of material objects being passed from one person to another, can provide an observer with information which they can record, if only later to analyse and understand. It gives access to a visible medium of communication, and in the early days of study in a community, when only a limited amount of the spoken language might be understood, details about the movement of objects can help an ethnographer to build up a map of social ties between the people who live there.

Gifts

Gifts are also given at rather specific times, and an examination of the occasions involved may also help to lead to an understanding of important events and stages in the lives of the people concerned. Gifts to individuals may be marking changes of status, exchanges within wider groups may be celebrating occasions important in their society. In many places, presents are given as one grows up and grows old, year by year; they are given as one attains important goals, like entry to a school or university, or achieving a new position at work; many are given if one decides to move from being single to being married, although rather fewer are given if the marriage breaks down; many are also given to mark a new life, and to mark the end of a life.

Gifts are also presented when one couple, or family, visits another, especially if they are to eat together, or to spend a weekend or holiday in the others' home. House-warming presents are made to families who have recently moved in Britain, just as such families are expected to visit their neighbours in Japan. At certain festivals everywhere friends and relations express their relationships by making gifts to each other, or to each others' children, and Christmas has become such a global example of this custom, that non-Christians may join in simply for the purpose of reinforcing their own social relations. This has been described by Baumann in his study of Southall, mentioned in the introduction (see Baumann, 1992).

All this gift exchange must be examined very carefully, however, for things which look familiar may be misleading. In theory, at least in some places, gifts are given voluntarily, but there are always rules and conventions involved. As well as knowing when it is appropriate to give gifts, and to whom, it is important to know how valuable they should be, how they should be received, and how and when they should be repaid. In some societies gifts are ignored by the recipient in front of the donor, in others they must be opened and admired, whether they actually bring pleasure or not. These rules vary from one society to another, and there are also sets of conventions about how the gift should be presented, and what form of words should accompany the presentation.

Another study which has become a classic in the field of social anthropology, and continues to invite comment, addresses precisely this subject. This book, *The Gift*, by Marcel Mauss, was written in 1925, at a time when Europeans still sought to learn about their own past by looking at so-called primitive or 'archaic' people. Mauss was interested in examining 'the realm of contract' and systems of 'economic prestations' by isolating

> one important set of phenomena: namely, prestations which are in theory voluntary, disinterested and spontaneous, but are in fact obligatory and interested. The form usually taken is that of the gift generously offered; but the accompanying behaviour is formal pretence and social deception, while the transaction itself is based on obligation and self-interest. (Mauss, 1970, p. 1)

Through an examination of the practices found in various parts of the world, Mauss suggests that in small scale 'early' societies, gift-exchange is particularly important because it is a **total phenomenon** which may involve simultaneous expressions of a religious, legal, moral and economic nature. He argues further that exchange may often be between whole groups, through their chiefs, and may involve not only goods, wealth and property, but also courtesies, entertainment, ritual, military assistance, women, children, dances and feasts. These '**total prestations**' are again in theory voluntary, but here, more than ever, strictly obligatory, with possible sanctions of private and open warfare.

He proposed that there are three clear obligations involved:

(1)   the obligation to give,
(2)   the obligation to receive, and
(3)   the obligation to repay

and examples of the mechanisms of gift exchange in several different societies illustrate the significance it may hold in the wider arenas of social life. In all cases, ethnographers have returned again and again to the societies he chose, and knowledge about the people concerned has been greatly deepened, but three examples from Mauss's material lay out an agenda for further discussion. They also illustrate principles which arise in all societies in one way or another   quite an achievement.

The first of these is the case of the *kula*, a system of gift-giving found in the Trobriand Islands and described and analysed in detail by Malinowski, of whom we heard in the Introduction. He entitled his first book*Argonauts of the Western Pacific* (1922) after people who build elaborate boats and make long journeys to visit other islands in the area. The ostensible purpose of their voyages is to make gifts: gifts which are passed on to further islanders in time by the recipients, and which continue around in a wide circular progression. The gifts are made of local shells, and in one direction travel necklaces, called *soulava*, and in the other, expressed as a return for the first, according to Malinowski, armbands called *mwali*.

Despite a show of disinterest in the gifts when they arrive, often to be thrown down disdainfully, the *mwali* and *soulava* are greatly prized by the local people. The community as a whole is said to gloat over them while they are in their possession, handing them round with affection, wearing them as adornment, and even placing them over the sick to help them recover. Some of these objects have legends attached to them, and are particularly prized, but it is important not to keep the gifts too long before passing them on. The objects move around a much wider area of the ocean than any of their 'owners', but people gain status by being involved in the*kula*, and they take a lot of trouble to set up the voyages.

In practice, each visit involves considerable preparation, for the elaborate canoes must be built and maintained, and the presentation of gifts is accompanied by the regular exchange and barter of a multitude of other objects, or 'utilities', as Malinowski terms them, which are 'often unprocurable in the district to which they are imported, and indispensable there'.

> The Kula is thus an extremely big and complex institution, both in its geographical extent, and in the manifoldness of its component pursuits. It welds together a considerable number of tribes, and it embraces a vast complex of activities, interconnected, and playing into one another. (1922, p. 83)

Mauss's first example thus demonstrates that this system of ceremonial gift exchange is ensuring **communication** among island people who would otherwise be widely separated. The gifts are surely expressing social relationships.

The second example from Mauss proposes to help understand the force of obligation associated with gift-giving, which he finds lacking in Malinowski's account of the *kula*. He turns to Polynesia to consider practices and ideas of the Maori people, and those of Samoa, where spiritual forces are held to attack a person who fails to repay a gift received. Within the local system of thinking, a person builds up a kind of honour or prestige, known as*mana*, which is conferred by wealth but lost if suitable gifts are not returned. This is said to be because *mana* includes a magical or spiritual element transmitted through the vehicle of *taonga*, which may be property, labour or merchandise, that has the power to turn and destroy the recipient if appropriate repayment is not made.

A part of the giver is thought to be sent with the gift, which gives him or her a kind of a hold over the person who receives it, and also over anyone who may steal it! This view thus represents an explicit expression in spiritual terms of the obligation to repay goods or services received, which Mauss argues exists to some extent everywhere. It also demonstrates very clearly the way those who are unable to repay gifts received, for whatever reason, lose face and prestige within their own society. Indeed, the term *mana*, which is related to ideas of *tabu*, as we discussed in the last chapter, is sometimes translated as 'face'.

This principle is illustrated forcibly in the third example we take from Mauss, namely the case of *potlatch*, originally apparently a Chinook word meaning to 'nourish' or 'consume', but now used to describe competitive feasts which used to be held among peoples of north-west America such as the Tlingit and Haida of Alaska and the Kwakiutl of British Columbia. As elsewhere, the political hierarchy was based on wealth, which indicated proof of favour with the spirits, and people demonstrated their status in this respect by inviting each other to feasts during the cold winter months. Gifts would be handed out, and those who could not afford to repay would lose face, and could even be enslaved for debt.

The chiefs of each group invited would sometimes sit in hierarchical order at these gatherings so that everyone could see their ranking, and trade and marriage arrangements would depend upon an internally recognized relative standing of the groups involved. These people collectively became so rich during the late nineteenth and early twentieth centuries due to their skills at trapping animals with furs highly prized in the wider world, that their winter celebrations became extremely lavish, and they even began to destroy valuable goods to demonstrate their immense wealth. Beautiful blankets would be burned, and huge copper plates hurled over the cliffs, in their agonized efforts to humiliate one another.

This is evidently an exaggerated case, but the principles are quite recognizable. Where wealth is a mark of status, it is not enough to have the resources, others must be made aware of the fact. The notion of **conspicuous consumption** was discussed some time ago by Veblen (1899) for Western societies, and the wanton destruction of valuable goods is an extension of spending wildly to impress. In British society, there are subtle ways to gain status through diverting wealth into children's education, club membership, or perhaps land, sometimes even leaving a shortage of ready cash, a state which may be contrasted snobbishly with an excessively obvious display of wealth.

The Indian Gift

Since Mauss's time, there have been many refinements to the ethnography he used, but his ideas are still discussed, sometimes critically. One important contribution was made by anthropologists who have worked in India, where the obligation to repay gifts received is shown not to be as universal as Mauss seemed to be suggesting. Here a form of gift known as *dân* or *dana*, made to a priest or members of a different caste who can deal with residual pollution, is positively not to be repaid, because it is thought to carry away inauspiciousness and sin, which one would not want back. An interpretation of the Indian situation depends on an understanding of notions of purity and pollution which are inextricably linked with the caste system, as introduced in the previous chapter.

This subject was the focus of a book called *The Poison in the Gift*, by Gloria Goodwin Raheja, who argued that the close examination of gift-giving in the North Indian village where she worked revealed a new theoretical interpretation of caste, based on the centrality of the landowners called Gujars:

> The structural position of Gujars in the caste configuration of the village and the region is dependent not only on their possession of the land, but also on the pattern of their relationships with the other castes in terms of the giving and receiving of specific named prestations, as the 'protectors' . . . of the village.
> . . . Gujars have a 'right' to give *dân* . . . and it is always given in the context of ritual actions that are said to promote the 'well-being [achieved through] gift-giving' (*khairkhairât*) and 'auspiciousness' (*śubh*) of the Gujar donors through the transferral of inauspiciousness (*nâsubh*) to the recipients. (1988, pp. 18–20)

Raheja argues that her observations and analysis of the movement of objects, including gifts, reveals a new understanding of the relations between caste groups, and though she thereby challenges the previous work of both Mauss and Dumont (see Chapter 2) her work is an excellent example of the value of the analysis of material culture for understanding social relations.

Jonathan Parry (1986) also discusses the *dana* gifts which positively reject a return, and he proposes a re-reading of Mauss's ideas, to remind the reader that the ideological distinction between 'free gift' and 'economic self-interest' was part of Mauss's own society, distinguished from the practices of his ethnographic subjects by his choice of the word *prestation* to describe them. In the case of gifts unreciprocated materially, Parry points out that the act of giving builds up not only auspiciousness or status for the donor, but also allows them to accrue credit in their *karmic* destiny:

> I am suggesting, then, that an elaborated ideology of the 'pure' gift is most likely to develop in state societies with an advanced division of labour and a significant commercial sector. But what is also in my view essential to its articulation is a specific type of belief system, as is suggested by the fact that in all of the major world religions great stress is laid on the merit of gifts and alms, ideally given in secrecy and without expectation of any worldly return. (1986, p. 467)

In the world religions mentioned by Parry, teachings suggest that the donors might reasonably expect to build up credit for the afterlife for their generosity, and although the giver may never express things in this way, indeed it may be regarded as counter-productive to do so, the objective possibility of an eventual return of a non-material nature does conserve the principle of reciprocity. Another example of imbalance of this sort is where a person aspiring to leadership may give gifts in order to build up a following, and in this case, loyalty is the return that is expected. Indeed, in this last case, the return must necessarily be blurred to avoid accusations of corruption, although views on what constitutes bribery are culturally variable again, as can often be seen in reports of international politics.

Exchange

In a wider interpretation of social life, gifts may be seen to form just one material part of a complex system of **exchange** which is found in all societies in one form or another. Whether made in material form or not, exchange is an important means of **communication** which expresses social relationships at various levels. Within Western society, some of the ways in which social relationships are fostered are through dropping in to drink cups of tea or coffee together, inviting people to dinner (and other) parties, writing letters, sending Christmas cards, making telephone calls, buying drinks and doing favours.

In each of these cases, a degree of exchange is usually expected, and people would soon become tired of someone who was only on the receiving side, or indeed, only on the offering side. There are exceptions, but generally for a friendship or other relationship to develop, there needs to be a two-way flow. It need not be identical. One person may be better at writing, another at 'phoning, one may enjoy preparing dinners for their friends, another prefer spending time in the pub, but unless an individual has an extraordinarily magnetic personality, or a very depleted bank account, they would usually expect to engage in some level of give and take.

Even at the level of conversation, a social relationship does not usually thrive on one-way flow, and a person who failed to reply to an opening gambit could well be expressing a rejection of the relationship offered. This is of course always a possibility, and unwelcome overtures from strangers may be snuffed out by silence. Greetings are forms of exchange of a very basic kind, and it is not necessary to know someone well to say hello to them on a corridor. Refusal to reply, on the other hand, can be offensive. To try it out with people you see often is an excellent (if unpleasant) way to test the force of exchange in maintaining relationships!

In Japanese, even the smallest 'favours' are expressed in a giving or receiving verb which qualifies the main action verb and makes clear who is obligated to whom. Thus 'I'll carry your bag for you' is literally 'I'll carry-give your bag'; and 'will you hold my books' is difficult to write literally because it asks the other person to hold the books but expresses the obligation using a word more akin to 'receive' in expressing the obligation incurred. Of course it is not necessary to repay exactly every tiny favour in Japan, but the explicit language used is undoubtedly related to the very careful accounting found among Japanese people about the exchange of one sort or another in which they are involved.

Such precise accounting may seem more appropriate for economic transactions, but there is an overlap between the social and the economic in more societies than the so-called primitive ones that Mauss identified. In Mexico and Guatemala, for example, an interesting system developed in some regions which ties a number of villages into a single socioeconomic community. This is achieved by the fact that villages specialize in making only one particular product – bread, pots, woollen goods, flowers, even fireworks. In order to provide for the necessities of life, then, the people of these villages must communicate with each other and this usually takes place at markets. Sometimes these circulate, visiting one village after another, nowadays usually arriving at the same place on a particular day of the week, although the system predates the European calendar. In larger centres, a regular market attracts villagers from the whole area (see Photograph 3.1). In pre-Columbian times, the market day was apparently also a day for sports and festivals, adding to its social function.

In these areas, people tend to marry within the community so that they can use the skills of their own speciality and pass them on to their children. In other parts of the world, a preference for marriage outside the community may provide the means of communication across a wider area, and here

Photograph 3.1 Selling pots from the Mexican village of Santa Cruz de Arriba, at the central market in Texcoco (photograph: Joy Hendry)

marriage is sometimes interpreted as a form of exchange. This is usually described as an exchange of women, perhaps largely because the anthropologists were men and saw the world through the eyes of the men, as we discussed in Chapter 1, but it may also be that this is the way the people (men?) themselves described the situation.

The influential French anthropologist, Claude Lévi-Strauss, identified two main types of exchange of this sort. One he called *restricted (or direct) exchange*, which may be a straight swop between brothers of their sisters, or anyway between women of one community for those of another, and the other he called *generalized (or indirect) exchange*, where women move in one direction only, but several communities are eventually linked into a circle or more complicated arrangement. These different arrangements will be discussed in more detail in Chapter 11. Once marriages have been set up, further communication is effectively maintained through visiting, exchanges of gifts, and probably further marriages in future generations. Again, this is a way in which smaller communities are drawn into larger systems with those around.

Reciprocity

In all the cases of exchange described above, some degree of **reciprocity** is necessary for the communication to continue in an amicable way, and the ultimate sanction for maintaining reciprocity may be, as Mauss predicted, private or open warfare. Warfare is itself a form of exchange, although in this case the reciprocity could be described as negative. Some villages of the Yanomamö Indians (in Brazil and Venezuela) go through cycles where they trade with one another for a while, even arrange marriages, but then relations break down and they go to war. Eventually they may patch up their quarrels and go through the cycle again, and there is even evidence that villages develop specialities and shortages which they did not previously have so that they are forced to look for, or manage without, trading partners (Chagnon, 1983, pp. 149–50).

Reciprocity may be of various kinds, then, with more or less of a time factor involved, and greater or fewer social or moral implications attached. An immediate exchange is less likely to represent a social relationship than a delayed one, since the transaction will be completed on the spot and there is no need for further communication. A small shopkeeper who gives credit is likely to be one with whom customers also have a social relationship of some sort, whereas it is possible to make purchases in a supermarket – an immediately agreed form of reciprocity – without even exchanging greetings with the cashier. Unbalanced reciprocity, on the other hand, is more likely the greater the strength of the relationship.

In another classic piece of work entitled 'On the Sociology of Primitive Exchange', Marshall Sahlins (1974) drew up a typology of reciprocity, according to the social distance represented. Again he is talking of so-called 'primitive people', but there are clear parallels with wider situations, and the article raises a number of examples which are quite transferable to any society. He identifies three main types of reciprocity, but he emphasizes that these are the extremes and the mid-point of a spectrum of possible types to be encountered in practice.

The first type, which he calls **generalized reciprocity**, not to be confused with generalized exchange, as discussed above, is that found at the 'solidary extreme', that is among those with, or wishing to express, the closest social relations. In this case, there is no return stipulated and no definite obligation, indeed the return may never actually be fulfilled. Sharing of goods within a family is the example Sahlins gives as the extreme, where 'the expectation of a direct material return is unseemly. At best . . . implicit' (1974, p. 147). In practice, the return is related to the circumstances of the recipient more than to the value of that received, and failure to reciprocate does not necessarily stop the giving.

The mid-point of the continuum Sahlins calls **balanced reciprocity** and this is where goods of equal worth pass immediately between two parties, with no time-lag and no moral implications. Here we are more in the realm of economic than social transactions 'from our own vantage point', as Sahlins puts it, and while generalized reciprocities are characterized by a material flow sustained by social relations, balanced exchange is where social relations hinge on the material flow. The type of exchange involved will be akin to trade, but may also include peace treaties or alliances, some marital transactions, and compensation payments.

Sahlins' third type, at the 'unsociable extreme' of the spectrum, is **negative reciprocity**:

> the attempt to get something for nothing with impunity, the several forms of appropriation, transactions opened and conducted toward net utilitarian advantage. Indicative ethnographic terms include 'haggling' or 'barter', 'gambling', 'chicanery', 'theft', and other varieties of seizure. Negative reciprocity is the most impersonal sort of exchange. In guises such as 'barter' it is from our own point of view the 'most economic'. The participants confront each other as opposed interests, each looking to maximize utility at the other's expense. Approaching the transaction with an eye singular to the main chance, the aim of the opening party or of both parties is the unearned increment . . . negative reciprocity ranges through various degrees of cunning, guile, stealth, and violence to the finesse of a well-conducted horse-raid. . . . the flow may be one-way once more, reciprocation contingent upon mustering countervailing pressure or guile. (Ibid., pp. 148–9)

Sahlins goes on to argue that the spectrum of reciprocity he has outlined may be related to degrees of social distance within any particular social world. In a well-known diagram which applies to a tribal model of social relations (Figure 3.1), he maps the spectrum of types of reciprocity onto a series of concentric spheres moving out from the home, through to unrelated people from other tribes. Within the home, village, or even lineage, generalized reciprocity is expected, while for the rest if the tribe, a balanced arrangement is sufficient. Outside the tribe, with 'other' tribes or peoples, anything goes, and the moral system is, in effect, suspended. Sahlins' scheme also considers social ranking, relative wealth, and the nature of the goods exchanged.

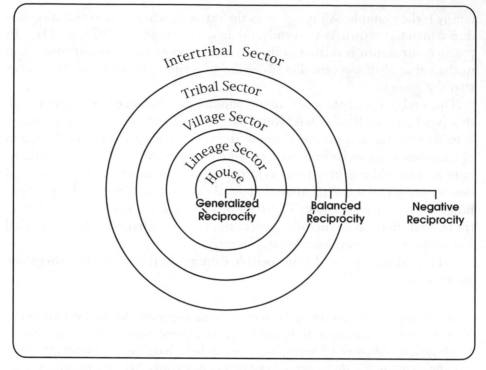

Source: This has been adapted from Marshall Sahlins, 'On the Sociology of Primitive Exchange', in Michael Banton (ed.), *The Relevance of Models in Social Anthropology* (1974), p. 152, by permission of Tavistock Publications.

Figure 3.1   Reciprocity and kinship residential sectors

   The basic principles outlined here are rather crude, and in any specific situation, the details would need to be modified, but they give a feel for the contribution an anthropological approach can make to areas which have become associated with economists. Sahlins suggests that 'trade' should be classified as balanced exchange, but in an actual trading situation social factors are hard to eliminate, and in the global community, rules will vary depending on the nature of the market concerned. The capitalist world is full of people trying to make something out of other people, and social distance is invariably a factor, which may have little to do with geographical distance. It will also be related to perceived relative wealth and status. Former school-mates, now trading between London and Auckland, New Zealand, for example, may well be kinder to one another than either will be to their Japanese business partners, but both could probably be persuaded to make concessions to a 'third world' economy.

Neither should 'barter' always be classified as 'negative reciprocity', just because it does not involve a third medium of exchange, such as money. It may be part of a highly moral system in various parts of the world, including housewifely baby-sitting circles in the English-speaking world, and it has also become a common form of business dealing in former Iron Curtain countries which have yet to establish a form of currency recognized by their capitalist partners. Furthermore, money may itself be valued in different ways in different parts of the world, and in the same parts of the world in different contexts (for further details see Parry and Bloch, 1989) – wrapping a bank note up in a special envelope, or placing a larger sum in a 'trust', may convert it into a gift, for example, and we are back to the various social and moral implications we considered above.

Objects Inalienable, Entangled and Wrapped

It is many years since the classic works referred to here were written, and their messages are clearly powerful, for they have probably inspired more reactions in the work of later scholars than any other related collection of ideas to be found in the subject. Some seek to refine the theoretical ideas put forward, others insist on a more thorough understanding of the ethnography, and, in between all this, the commentators comment on each other's reactions. It is particularly interesting to see whether the original peoples cited are still engaged in the forms of exchange described above, how they have been affected by outside influences, and whether subsequent studies have cast new interpretations on the material they collect.

One interesting study, which challenges the theories of both Mauss and Malinowski, is that carried out by Annette Weiner, who also travelled to the Trobriand Islands for her fieldwork, but who chose to spend more time with women than Malinowski did. She has published several books, examining various aspects of the lives of Trobriand women, but most relevant to this discussion is a book entitled *Inalienable Possessions: The Paradox of Keeping-While-Giving* (1992), which puts forward theory based on practices observed throughout Oceania. The Maori and Samoan ideas of *taonga* and *mana*, examined by Mauss, are considerably refined in this book, as are the notions of reciprocity advocated by both writers.

The basic principle she advocates is a distinction between objects which can be given away, or perhaps consumed, and those that remain what she calls 'inalienable', even though they may be passed to another person. In other words, the first person retains ownership of the object, and therefore a kind of domination over the person to whom it is passed. Inalienable objects

include mats, cloths and other materials made by women, each of which
retains a special quality of its own, and the continued possession while
passing around of these goods gives women a powerful political role
previously ignored by ethnographers. Thus, not only were women ignored
by a male bias in the early work of anthropologists, but, according to Weiner,

> the tenacious anthropological belief in the inherent nature of the norm of
> reciprocity . . . impedes the examination of the particular cultural conditions
> that empower the owners of inalienable possessions with hegemonic dom-
> inance over others. (1992, pp. 149–50)

Another recent study which attacks the notion of reciprocity is again
located in the Pacific, but Nick Thomas (1991) focuses on the different uses
Pacific Islanders and Europeans have made of each other's material artifacts.
Entitled *Entangled Objects: Exchange, Material Culture and Colonialism in the
Pacific*, this book examines the way material objects are allocated significance
in social life, but appropriated in different, but nevertheless entangled ways by
the various parties caught up in the colonial endeavour. Thus objects may
become something quite else from what they were made to be, depending on
the context in which they are found, and they may be interpreted in different
ways, depending on political factors inseparable from their acquisition or
appropriation.

To make clearer some of the ideas behind both of these studies, consider
the hypothetical case of a beautiful cloth which forms part of a museum
collection in a country which had colonized the island where it was made.
The object, transformed into a work of art, adds kudos to the museum, and
possibly also enhanced the reputation of the traveller who donated it. The
traveller might have perceived the acquisition of the cloth as a purchase, or a
straight exchange, whereas the producer expected continuing influence with
the apparently powerful outsider. In the long run, the producer, or her
descendants, may be right, as museums now find themselves negotiating
terms with indigenous people seeking to repatriate objects they describe as
their stolen heritage.

Situations of intercultural encounter are fertile areas for contemporary
anthropologists to examine, and they may provide an interesting zone of
contested understanding in the global market place. In Japan, all sorts of
social encounters are marked with gifts, and they are often presented in quite
beautiful and elaborate wrapping (see Photograph 3.2). This **wrapping**
conveys meaning way beyond the mere role of hiding the object inside,
indicating the degree of formality, and whether the occasion is a happy one of
celebration, or a sad one of condolence. This attention to presentation in

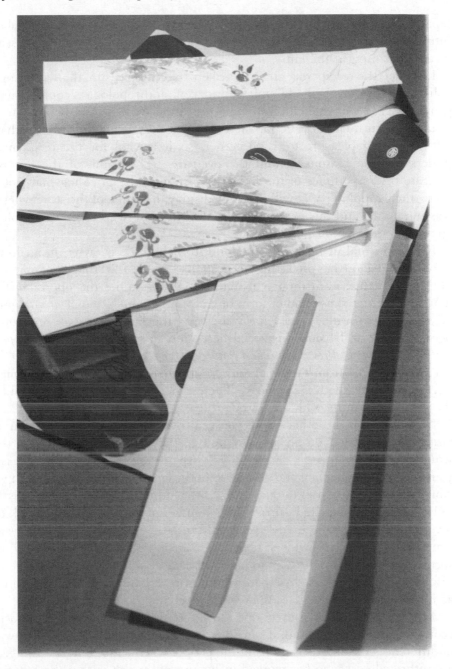

Photograph 3.2   Five pairs of disposable chopsticks, each wrapped in beautiful paper, packed in a box, and all wrapped again in paper marked with the Japanese department store where they were bought – quite a conundrum for the anthropologist to work out (photograph: Bob Pomfret)

Japan often delights the unsuspecting foreigner, but if they are serious about future relations with their Japanese partners, they should be aware of possible further meaning in the gift.

In Japan, the receipt of a gift is less likely to bring pleasure than a feeling of obligation, and this is the kind of information anthropologists could bring to people engaged in intercultural communication, who would be wise to be aware of such nuances. The Japanese donor is very likely to be aware that a gift will bring pleasure to a Westerner, so it is vital for the recipient to understand the reasons behind the overtures. The value of the gift will indicate the importance of the link, and although the price tag may not be there, the wrapping paper will probably display the name of the store where it was purchased and this is a clear indication to those who take the trouble to appreciate the significance of gifts.

It is also usual in Japan for the donor to belittle their own gift, as do the Trobriand Islanders, protesting in response to thanks that the object is nothing of value, even though it may actually be quite the opposite. This may be interpreted as another form of wrapping, namely the *social* wrapping of politeness formulae, and I have discussed the importance for anthropologists of looking beyond this social deception in a book entitled *Wrapping Culture: Politeness, Presentation and Power in Japan and Other Societies* (1993). Another example from the Japanese case is when you are invited to a meal, only to be greeted with the apology, 'There is nothing for you', whereas in fact the table is groaning with an abundant feast.

In Mexico, on the other hand, you are invited to make a house you are visiting your own: 'You are in your house', they assure you, although they would almost certainly be alarmed if you began to unpack your bags. 'It is at your service', they reply if you admire something, even a garment, though you would not usually expect to take up the offer. Little conventions like this are only gradually acquired during the course of field research, and the investigator may make many social gaffs in the early stages, but they are usually indulged, as outsiders, for at least an initial period. Eventually, the social deceptions may turn out to have rather deep and vital significance, as I discovered to be the case in Japan, where non-verbal communication can be as important, if not more so, than verbal exchanges.

As the world is increasingly open to intercultural encounters of a social, economic and political kind, it provides a tremendous advantage to be aware of differences in the expectations of the people with whom one is dealing. As an anthropologist who has worked in Japan, my hunch is that the Japanese abroad are much more aware of local expectations than foreigners visiting Japan tend to be. This is because they are aware of some of their own idiosyncrasies – indeed they have been accused of being obsessed by their 'uniqueness' – so they take the trouble to find out how things are done elsewhere.

My own compatriots tend to be less humble. British business people travelling abroad often do not even recognize a need to know much beyond the polite form of greeting in the countries they visit, and as for bothering to understand local systems of distribution, or notions of value which might influence their marketing strategies, they are liable to dismiss 'all that' as meaningless cultural relativism. This is an area where anthropological knowledge can have very practical advantages, however, and those who take the trouble to consult someone with a speciality in their area of interest would be likely to reap great benefits.

The polite form of greeting may have many different manifestations, as presents have many layers of wrapping, with a multitude of meanings. At the start of the chapter, I mentioned a small gift I was advised to take to my new neighbours in Japan – 'a towel or something'. The gift in this case could be quite small, indeed it *should* be quite small, for a larger one would incur unnecessary and possibly unwanted feelings of obligation (further discussed in Hendry, 1995). The purpose is to open relations, but to do it too forcibly could be counterproductive. I also mentioned that many people visiting Japan fail to carry out this small rite of presentation, and thus remain strangers to their neighbours. I rest my case.

References

Baumann, Gerd (1992) 'Ritual implicates others: rereading Durkheim in a plural society', in D. de Coppet, *Understanding Rituals* (London: Routledge).

Chagnon, Napoleon (1993) *Yanomamö: The Fierce People* (New York: Holt, Rinehart & Winston).

Hendry, Joy (1993) *Wrapping Culture: Politeness, Presentation and Power in Japan and Other Societies* (Oxford: Clarendon).

Malinowski, Bronislaw (1922) *Argonauts of the Western Pacific* (London: Routledge & Kegan Paul).

Mauss, Marcel (1970) *The Gift*, trans. I. Cunnison (London: Cohen & West).

Parry, Jonathan (1986) 'The gift, the Indian gift and "the Indian gift"',*Man*, **21**: 453–73.

Raheja, Gloria, G. (1988) *The Poison in the Gift* (Chicago: University of Chicago Press).

Sahlins, Marshall (1974) 'On the Sociology of Primitive Exchange', in Michael Banton (ed.),*The Relevance of Models in Social Anthropology* (London: Tavistock).

Thomas, Nicholas (1991) *Entangled Objects: Exchange, Material Culture, and Colonialism in the Pacific* (Cambridge, Mass.: Harvard University Press).

Veblen, Thorstein (1899) *The Theory of the Leisure Class* (New York: Macmillan).

Weiner, Annette, B. (1992) *Inalienable Possessions: The Paradox of Keeping-While-Giving* (Berkeley, Los Angeles and Oxford: University of California Press).

Further Reading

Hendry, Joy (1995) 'The Ritual of the Revolving Towel', in Jan van Bremen and D. P. Martinez (eds), *Ceremony and Ritual in Japan* (London: Routledge), pp. 210–26.

Parry, J. and M. Bloch (1989) *Money and the Morality of Exchange* (Cambridge University Press).

Riches, D. (1975) 'Cash, Credit and Gambling in a Modern Eskimo Economy: speculations on origins of spheres of economic exchange', *Man*, **10**: 21–33.

Films

The Feast (Timothy Asch and Napoleon Chagnon, 1970) is a classic 28-minute film, a combination of stills with explanation, and moving pictures without, about exchange of goods, feasts and warfare among the Yanomamö people of the Venezuelan–Brazilian borderlands.

The Kawelka: Ongka's Big Moka (Charlie Nairn and Andrew Strathern, 1974) is a Granada 'Disappearing World' documentary about assembling pigs and other goods for a feast which forms part of a long-term exchange system among the Kawelka of New Guinea.

Trobriand Cricket (Gary Kildea and Jerry Leach, 1975) is an amusing film about the introduction and adaptation of cricket to these same people.

The Trobriand Islanders (David Wasan, 1990), a 'Disappearing World' film, made with the help of anthropologist Annette Weiner, focuses on the female exchanges which complement the more famous *kula* practises. See *Off the Verandah* (p. 33 above) for more detail about the *kula*.

CHAPTER 4

The Ritual Round

Shoes and the Empty Ritual

Ritual is sometimes described as 'empty', or meaningless, and there are people who make conscious efforts to pare it away. They may decide to have a simple wedding, 'without any fuss', or a small family funeral, with 'no flowers please'. Some Christian churches make a virtue out of simplicity of design, cast away the ecclesiastical robes, and even abandon their notion of an order of service on some specially open occasions. In each case, there is an expression of rejection of the more complicated forms which may be regarded as wasteful of time and resources, or unnecessary adornment of the event. In a way, it's like leaving the wrapping off a gift in the interest of saving trees . . . but let us look at ritual a little more closely.

We talked in Chapter 1 about the importance of understanding systems of classification in order to understand the way in which people in different societies divide up the world into categories, and in Chapter 2, about notions of pollution and taboo which may be associated with the places which fall between those categories. The places and situations which fall between categories, the interstitial places as they may be called, are also often associated with danger in any society, and a common response to this kind of danger is to institute some sort of ritual. By looking at ritual, then, we can again learn a lot about the system of classification held by a particular people.

To illustrate this idea, we can return briefly to the example of Japanese shoes. It is an inviolable custom in Japan to remove your shoes before entering someone's house, as was discussed earlier. The place in which you remove your shoes is usually a porch which separates the inside of the house from the outside world, and this space may be described as an interstitial place between those two worlds. The act of removing shoes thus emphasizes the importance of the distinction between them, and it is an act so firmly prescribed by society that in the Japanese case it may be regarded as having the force of a ritual act. In fact we find that further rituals very often accompany the removal or donning of shoes in that space.

These include greetings, with fixed words, depending on whether one is coming in or going out, and there is a response, again fixed, from anyone who is inside the house. The announcement of an arrival literally means 'now', the response is something like 'welcome'. The call on departure means 'I go and come back'. A visitor to the house calls out 'I make disturbance' as they enter, and 'I make rudeness' as they leave. Mothers with small children will call out these greetings as they go in and come out whether there is anyone inside or not, because the rituals of crossing the threshold of the household are part of the training they feel they need to give to their child.

Further elements may be added to the ritual, such as the changing of clothes on returning home, and many mothers insist that their children also wash their hands and gargle. Husbands returning home from work may well head straight for the bath as a regular feature of their arrival, and some will change from their city suits into Japanese garments. The ritual for greeting guests includes bowing, and in the country where I did my first fieldwork, this was an elaborate performance involving kneeling on the ground and bringing one's head almost into contact with the floor. The guests would return the compliment, so this exchange would take place after the person had climbed up onto the matted floor.

Definitions of Ritual

It may be objected at this point that some form of greeting is carried out anywhere on entering or leaving a house, and people may also adjust their bodily attire. Why then should this be regarded as ritual? Let us turn first, then, to examine what exactly is meant by the term **ritual** in anthropology. In fact, there are several definitions of 'ritual', some of which restrict its use to describing behaviour of a religious nature (see, for example, Lewis, 1980, pp. 6–38; de Coppet, 1992) but most anthropologists these days prefer to adopt a broader one which can include secular activities such as greetings. For example,

● Ritual is behaviour prescribed by society in which individuals have little choice about their actions.

To test a form of behaviour to see whether it might qualify to be called ritual or not, one could try to change it, or omit it, and see how others would react. As mentioned in the previous chapter, refusing to reply to a greeting could be seen as most offensive. Omitting to greet someone on entering their house would seem churlish at the very least. In Japan, a visitor is expected to utter the appropriate phrases, and a child who failed to wash would soon be hustled into the bathroom, though the husband might get away with the odd lapse so that perhaps his practice would better be termed a routine, or custom. With this definition, rules about gift exchange can also be included, as can secular special occasions such as birthday parties.

After all, a birthday party, especially for a child, would hardly qualify to be such if it lacked certain elements: balloons, cards, presents, the cake, candles, the singing of a special song, and possibly the playing of games as well. In some areas, there are further expectations, perhaps about the provision of small gifts to take home, the wrapping up and distribution of pieces of cake, and a small ceremony when the birthday presents are opened, one by one, to a series of 'oohs' and 'ahs' from the assembled company. A parent who put on a party without the appropriate paraphernalia would run the severe risk of disapproval on the part of their own offspring, and possibly voluble complaints from the young guests.

A more restricted definition of ritual, which several anthropologists have used and which may therefore be referred to, is:

> prescribed formal behaviour for occasions not given over to technological routine, having reference to beliefs in mystical beings or powers. (Turner, 1967, p. 19)

Even in the case of religious ritual, the rites themselves must be examined separately from belief which may be associated with them, however, since people may participate for entirely social reasons. A funeral, for example, is attended by those who were close to, or who wish to express their respect for the deceased. Such participants will mourn, wear black or some other sombre colour, and if appropriate, they will attend a religious service. This says nothing about the individual beliefs of the participants with respect to God or gods and the service they are attending. It may not even say very much about their feelings for the dead. Perhaps they are attending to express sympathy for the bereaved.

Similarly, in the case of a marriage, or a christening, the participants may have very different views among themselves about the religious nature of the event. As the social anthropologist, Edmund Leach (1969), pointed out, a Church of England wedding tells us nothing of the bride or her beliefs, only about the social relations being established. In other words, we must separate personal beliefs from the social aspects of ritual behaviour. The latter is the domain of interest of the social anthropologist.

Rites of Passage

Much has been written on the subject of ritual, and there have been many theories about its interpretation, but there is one classic work which has stood the tests both of time and of further research. This is the study of Arnold van Gennep, first published in 1909, in French, and translated into English in a book called *Rites of Passage* (1960). Again, this writer refers to the people under discussion as 'primitive', and he talks mostly of people in small-scale society, but his theories have been shown to have applicability in any society in any part of the world. His notion of ritual is also closer to the second definition about religious behaviour, but it applies to ritual which fits the first in many cases as well.

These **rites of passage** are those which accompany the movement from what van Gennep describes as 'one cosmic or social world to another'. In the terms we have been using in this book, it involves a move from one social category to another, the passage of a person or persons in a society from one *class* to another. There are four main types of move:

(1)   the passage of people from one *status* to another, as on marriage or initiation to a new social or religious group:
(2)   passage from one *place* to another as in a change of address or territory;
(3)   passage from one *situation* to another, such as taking up a new job or school; and
(4)   the passage of *time* when the whole social group might move from one period to another, for example at New Year, or into the reign of a new king/queen or emperor.

If we think of occasions in our lives, and in those of people around us, when we might engage in some form of ritual, they are very often precisely the sort of passages which fit these descriptions. For example:

- Birth, marriage, death
- Christening, confirmation, a bar mitzvah
- A change of school, job or house
- Going away
- Coming back
- Birthdays, anniversaries, graduation
- Changes of the seasons, New Year

We ritualize these occasions in various ways, but some elements on which we draw are:

- Dressing up
- Sending cards
- Giving presents
- Holding parties
- Making and consuming special food
- Making resolutions
- Ordeals

By examining reports of rites of passage from various parts of the world, van Gennep noticed that certain characteristic patterns recurred in the order of the ceremonies even from places much too far apart to have influenced one another. First of all, there would be rites of separation from the old class or category, and these, he argued, are very often characterized by a symbolic death. There would also be rites of incorporation into the new class or category, and these would be characterized by a symbolic rebirth. Most striking, however, was the fact that these sets of rites would almost always be separated by a transition period when the participants would belong to neither one nor the other.

These rites he named as follows:

- Rites of Separation *or* Preliminal Rites
- Rites of Transition *or* Liminal Rites
- Rites of Incorporation *or* Postliminal Rites

Not all of these rites would be equally developed in each ceremony, since they would be of differing importance depending on the nature of the ceremony – for example, one might expect funerals to have more developed rites of separation – but van Gennep argued that this general structure is characteristic of rites of passage everywhere. Moreover, if the liminal or transition period is a particularly long one, for example during betrothal or pregnancy, there might be a set of each of the three types of rite at each end of it. He also noted that other kinds of rites – perhaps for fertility at marriage, or protection at birth – may be superimposed on the rites of passage. Let us examine some examples of the types of rite of passage he proposes.

Territorial Rites of Passage

Van Gennep's book is full of examples of rites of passage of different types, but most of these are set in small-scale societies which he argues imbue all such movements with ideas of a magico-religious variety. Since his book is still available and in print, let us turn here to examining some examples of secular rites of passage which may be familiar to a wider range of readers. The prototype for rites of passage is, according to van Gennep, a territorial passage from one social space to another, a passage which he argues often involves passing through a transitional area which belongs to neither side, a kind of no-man's land in the middle.

Van Gennep discussed passages from one tribal area to another, or between different inhabited regions, but his ideas also work in a consideration of the bureaucratic rituals associated with making a passage from one nation to another. First of all it is necessary to acquire a passport, sometimes quite a complicated and time-consuming process. In the case of many countries, it is also necessary to acquire a visa for entry. If the journey is to be of a considerable duration, friends and relatives may hold a farewell party and offer gifts and cards of well-wishes. The moment of parting, at the airport, dock or station, will be marked with kisses, embraces and/or handshakes, and the passenger will be exhorted to telephone on arrival.

In an airport, one is then forced to pass through a series of physical barriers involving the showing of passports and visas, the checking of luggage through security screens, and, until arrival at the point of destination, one is quite literally in a zone of transition. If friends or relatives are waiting, the rituals of departure are repeated in reverse on arrival, and despite the high probability of immense fatigue and over-indulgence in food and drink, it would be regarded as most unfriendly to refuse the welcoming rituals of hospitality. The phone-call of arrival is a reassurance for those left behind that the zone of transition is safely crossed, that the traveller has entered another social world. It may be a world relatively dangerous and unknown, but at least it is a world!

Van Gennep also discusses rites for crossing thresholds, and the Japanese example given above would fit his theories perfectly. The zone of transition is most clear at the entrance to a Japanese house, and it is often filled with shoes, but there are parallel rites for entering a Jewish house, where the Mezuzah must be touched, and churches and temples have some form of ritual act as one moves from the profane to the sacred. This may involve the removal of pollution, with a touch of holy water, it may involve a bow, a sign of the cross, the removal or donning of shoes or headgear, or simply a lowering of the voice. Again, the crossing of the threshold involves a passage from one cosmic world to another.

These rites also represent a form of security for the world which is being entered. In the case of countries, the checking of the passport is a way of controlling immigration; in the case of the church, there is an opportunity to remove the pollution of the mundane outside world. In any house or community a stranger may represent a threat, and ritual is a way of neutralizing the potential danger. Van Gennep describes society as 'similar to a house divided into rooms and corridors' (1960, p. 26) and territorial rites of passage associated with entering and moving about in a house may thus be seen as a model in spatial form of the rites which accompany moves from one section of society to another.

Pregnancy and Childbirth

The arrival of a completely new member of society is an occasion for ritual observance anywhere, and it also provides a threat to the mother who will give birth. In some societies women are regarded as polluting throughout their pregnancy and they must live in a special hut removed from the public sphere. They are thus removed physically from their normal lives to live in a 'liminal' part of their social world. They participate in rites of separation before they go, rites of transition while they are there, and only become incorporated back into society after the baby has been born. The baby, too, must be welcomed into society through rites of separation from the mother and rites of incorporation into the new social world it has joined.

Although there are few formal periods of separation for pregnant mothers in the cosmopolitan world, the English language does still contain the tell-tale word 'confinement' which refers back to a period when it was considered inappropriate for heavily pregnant women to be out in the world at large. Moreover, pregnant women in almost all societies do observe various restrictions on their usual behaviour, perhaps in variations to their culinary practices, as we saw in Chapter 2, or the avoidance of alcohol and smoking, as well as the careful control of drugs and remedies. Others who are aware of their condition will carry heavy objects for them, seek out titbits for them to consume, and generally offer special care during this transitory period. Women who suffer high blood pressure and other serious complications may be literally removed from society to hospital for the waiting period.

In Japan, many women bind themselves up in a special corset during pregnancy, and the first donning of this garment may be accompanied by a party which makes official the announcement of the impending arrival. The celebration is held on a day of the dog, according to the Chinese calendar, because dogs are said to give birth relatively easily and it is hoped that this birth will be likewise. Women also often return to the homes of their own parents in order to give birth and they may stay away from their marital home for up to a month afterwards. Their return is celebrated with a visit to the local shrine to present the baby to the local protective deity, and a party will also be held to incorporate mother and child back into the community.

In most societies there is some form of celebration following a birth. Among Christians, the christening is a formal naming ceremony in the church as well as a presentation of the child to God, and the Church of England used to have a ceremony for mothers known as 'churching' which incorporated them back into normal life. During the christening service the baby is taken from its mother by the minister, who holds it throughout the most crucial part of the ceremony, and it may be handed back to a godparent as well. Elsewhere, there is a rite of separation of the baby from its mother associated with the cutting of the cord, and the cord itself may be buried in a special place with some significance for the future.

In some societies in South America, the father of a baby goes through a series of rites parallel to those undergone by the mother as a way of expressing and confirming his paternity. This practice, known as **couvade**, may involve a simulated pattern of suffering as well as a period of seclusion. This practice could be compared to the way fathers in the UK, as elsewhere, attend and participate in ante-natal classes with their pregnant partners so that they may assist at the birth of their children. These classes sometimes demand quite serious commitment on the part of the fathers, who must carry out the breathing and relaxation exercises along with the mothers. The provision of paternity leave in some countries recognizes the important role fathers are recently expected to take in the birth of their children, and the ritualization of this practice may be seen in Britain now in the way a mother whose husband cannot be present is encouraged to take in a 'birthing partner' instead.

A role has been created here which has little to do with the 'safe' delivery of the baby in a purely medical sense. Rather it was created to provide psychological support for the mother in a highly intimate situation which had become almost entirely impersonal. Before hospitals were deemed the appropriate place for childbirth, other women would usually surround and help a woman giving birth, and although a specialist might have been called in, it was for close kin to provide more familiar backup. The recently created role for the father reflects the importance and isolation of the nuclear family unit as well as a breakdown in the sexual division of labour which separated men from the care of their young.

Initiation Rites

During childhood, rites may be held in different societies to mark various stages of development which are regarded as important. These may include regular events such as birthdays, or accomplishments such as the first outing, first food, first haircut, first teeth (or loss of same), first day at school, and so forth. In some societies physical changes are made such as circumcision or ear-piercing. The periods which are marked reflect the local system of classification of life into stages and some societies are divided into age sets where groups of children born within a particular period move through the stages together. Others move through on an individual basis. In either case, there will be rituals to mark the passages from one stage to another.

Social recognition of the physical changes of puberty provide widespread examples of clearly defined rites of passage which ritually turn children into adults, and these again involve a substantial period of separation and/or special treatment. Among African tribes such as the Masai of the Kenya–Tanzania borders, and the Ndembu of Zambia, for example, young men are turned out to fend for themselves in 'the bush', and they may be regarded as dead for the duration. Special rites precede and follow their absence, and their physical appearance will reflect their stage in the process. The Masai allow their hair to grow long and unkempt in the bush, but shave completely on their return, painting their bare heads with shining ochre to mark their rebirth into society. The Ndembu have female puberty rituals which take place when a girl's breasts begin to form. They are confined to the village, but the girl is wrapped up in a blanket and lain under a tree where she must remain motionless for the whole of a very often hot and clammy day while others perform ritual activities around her (see Chapter 5 for further detail).

This kind of ordeal is characteristic of many initiation rituals, which may again involve mutilations of the body of one sort or another. The proximity of these events to the flowering of sexual maturity may focus attention on the genitals in the practice of circumcision again, or even clitoridectomy. In some societies, incisions in the face will leave permanent scarring indicating membership of a particular tribe or lineage. Undergoing the ordeal associated with these practises is supposed to demonstrate the readiness of the child for adulthood, and the permanent markings left behind will illustrate their new status once and for all.

Education of some sort is also often involved, and youths may be taken for the first time into the men's hut to be shown ritual objects, or taught tribal lore to be kept secret from the women and children. Likewise, girls may be taught certain esoteric elements of female life. In many societies, these young initiates are regarded as immune to social sanctions for the period of transition, and they may engage in all sorts of outrageous anti-social behaviour. Even if they are not in the bush, they may live for a period in a special house where they can experiment with adult activities and practice various social aberrations while they are in the intermediate stage between two categories.

Something of the same tolerance is accorded to university students in many societies, in Britain especially during the institution known as 'rag week'. In the last few years in Britain, there has also been an extraordinary amount of apparent tolerance for a practice known as 'joy-riding', during which youths sometimes as young as 12 years of age steal expensive cars and drive them wildly around the countryside before abandoning them. The owner reports the theft to the police, who usually locate the vehicle within a few days, but even if the culprits are caught they are often let off with little more than a warning. They are too young to charge, and have few resources to pay for the damage they cause, so society seems to tolerate the practice.

Whether this represents a stage of transition between childhood and adulthood is a matter open to debate, but if the youths are not seen as responsible for their own behaviour, and their parents are not held responsible for them, then it seems that they must fall between these categories of childhood and adulthood in the legal system at least. In the more acceptable version of education, these youths may not be doing particularly well, and they may be living at home, but they are gaining the skills of theft and manipulation of powerful motor cars at an extremely early age, and they are exposing themselves to the risks and ordeals that other societies institutionalize for their youngsters.

The recent popularity of voluntarily piercing various parts of the body in countries such as Britain, Australia and the United States, is interesting in that these societies now have few clear ritual occasions to mark the transition from childhood to adulthood. The bar mitzvah is an exception to this general rule, and it is taken seriously, but the former twenty-first birthday, or 'coming of age', is practised rather sporadically, now confused in Britain, at least, with the eighteenth birthday since legal changes brought more rights, and neither has clear rules of procedure. There is a sense of special occasion, and woe betide the parent who fails to do anything unusual on both occasions, but they are difficult ages at which to please. It may be that the people engaging in 'piercing' or possibly tattooing themselves are actually trying to express their independence from the parental fold by inventing a small ordeal.

Other forms of initiation to secret societies or esoteric bodies such as priesthood, as well as the enthronement ceremonies for a king or emperor, follow the same principles as initiation to adulthood. There are rites of separation of the principals from their previous lives, periods of transition involving education and training, and rites of incorporation representing a rebirth into their new roles. In some societies the period of interregnum between one ruler and his or her successor allows anti-social behaviour for the whole people, and steps are sometimes taken to keep the death of a king secret until the arrangements are ready for a quick succession to cut down on the disorder.

Marriage Rites

Marriage is a most important transition in most societies and it may coincide with the attainment of adulthood so that the rites associated with the wedding come at the end of the period of separation associated with the initiation into adulthood. In other societies there will be a long period of betrothal which may be regarded as a period of transition with rites at the beginning and end. In any case, in most societies this is a passage well marked with rites of separation, transition and incorporation, although the details may differ.

In Mexico, for example, a party held for girls who have become engaged is called the *despedida de soltera*, or seeing off the state of being single. Friends of approximately the same age gather to drink and eat together, and they dress up and act out some of the events which will follow for the bride, an occasion usually of considerable laughter and frivolity. The 'shower' for girls in the USA serves a similar role. These rites separate the bride from her previous life in preparation for the new state to come. The version for the bridegroom is also commonly an all male occasion known as a stag party, where serious drinking seems to be the order of the day.

In the country in Japan, where I did my own fieldwork, there were several rites of separation before the bride left her village to marry into a house elsewhere. A party would be held for her age-mates, both boys and girls this time, and there would be a display of the betrothal gifts she had received and the clothes and furniture she would take with her. Friends and neighbours would call round to see them, bringing gifts of money to send her on her way. On the morning of the wedding, there would be a farewell breakfast with the closest relatives, who would then travel together to the ceremony, and the bride would say a formal prayer of departure to the ancestors in the household Buddhist altar. After she had left, her rice bowl would be broken, just as if she had died to the house.

The bride in Japan wears a white garment under her colourful wedding kimono and this is said to represent a clean slate for her new life. In this way she resembles a corpse, as she dies to her old house, and a baby, to be born again into the new one. After the ceremony itself, the bride goes through a series of rites of incorporation into the new house and community, greeting her new ancestors, visiting the new local shrine, and being introduced to the new neighbours. According to Walter Edwards, in a book about modern Japanese weddings, the bride and groom are ritually separated from the rest of the party for the sharing of cups of *sake*, the crux of the marriage itself:

> In ethnographic accounts of prewar and early postwar home weddings   the exchange is described variously as taking place in a separate room; as occurring

behind a screen; and as being attended only by the *nakôdo* [go-between] or someone to pour the *sake*. In the contemporary Shinto ceremony the physical isolation is less extreme, but it is there nonetheless. Together with the *nakôdo*, the bride and groom sit in the center of the shrine room, apart from the rest of the group. (1989, pp. 107–8)

In many parts of the world it is customary for the bride and groom to go away for a honeymoon after their wedding and this practice can be seen as a rite of transition for the couple as a new unit. This time they will be formally separated from the crowd of family and friends who have come to wish them well, and various rites may be practised as they leave. Throwing of confetti is one example, tying boots to their car another. Some people go much further, and my own brother was kidnapped by his old friends, who tied his hands and feet together and hailed a passing van to drive him away around the streets of Glasgow. Again, this is a period of liminality when few rules apply. Later the couple will be properly married, and treated as such. In the meantime, there would seem to be no end of fun to be had.

In recent years, there has been a noticeable breakdown in the institution of marriage in several countries. Many couples live together now without undergoing any formalities at all, and may split up just as easily if things do not work out. Even those who do marry seem to find themselves as likely to be divorced after a few years as to be still married, so the whole exercise seems rather hollow. Marriage is by no means disappearing, however, and people seem still to be happy to spend vast sums of money on their weddings. According to one of my students, a 'hand-binding ceremony' has also recently been instituted for a short-term union, and various rites of divorce are discussed from time to time in the media.

Funerals

Rites of separation are highly developed at a funeral, but there is again a period of transition, both for the deceased on his or her way to the afterlife, and for those who remain behind to come to terms with their loss. At Christian funerals, the custom of throwing a little earth into the grave is a way of saying farewell, as is the practice in Japan of adding a pinch of incense to the burning pile. In Roman Catholic and Afro-Caribbean communities, the custom of holding a wake allows a more elaborate venue for the final farewells, and elsewhere there is open house for the bereaved to receive the condolences of their friends and relatives.

During the period of mourning people may alter their lifestyles a little, refraining from celebrations and jollification perhaps, and making regular visits to the grave of the loved one. In Japan, a notice is pasted to the door which not only identifies the house as one in mourning but also makes explicit the idea of pollution associated with the period in question. During this time, no meat is to be eaten, and there is a special diet for the bereaved. Various rites are held to mark stages in the progress of the soul, and these coincide with gatherings to thank those who helped at the funeral, and generally to redefine the social relations of the members of the family left behind. In some countries, a widow will continue to wear black for the rest of her life, but in most cases there is a means of incorporating the living back into normal life.

Festivals and the Passage of Time

Finally, there are in most societies rituals regularly to mark the passage of time. These reflect the classification of time in the way that the rituals associated with territorial passage reflect the classification of space into homes, villages, countries and so forth. As with the rites of passage through life, these events regularize in a social form natural cycles, though this time of the earth and moon, rather than the human body. Thus, the year is divided in various ways depending on the local climate, though provision is usually made for a festival to mark the harvest, at least in agricultural communities, and in countries with a severe winter there might be a rite to herald the arrival of spring.

In the summer, in Europe, the year is clearly broken with holidays, and this ritual break in the normal routines of life is especially marked in countries such as France and Italy where there is a long and serious period of play which is virtually compulsory in its effective interruption of the ordinary. In France, the motorways are cleared of lorries and roadworks, and it seems as though the entire population heads south to the sea and the sunshine. Certainly it is difficult to get anything done in government buildings, or, indeed, any number of other city offices.

The pattern of breaking work with play is of course repeated weekly in many parts of the world, but this is a system of classification originally based on the Biblical story of the creation of the world. Elsewhere the breaks will come at different times. The lunar month is a more universal segment, and, especially before the advent of electricity, many people would organize events to coincide with the light of the full moon. Approaching the equator there is little difference in the climate between winter and summer, and seasons and their markings may be organized instead around wet and dry periods, or some other local climatic variable.

In Britain the year is broken clearly during the season of Christmas and New Year when all usual activities are suspended for a period of some two weeks, preceded by preparations which may last for another couple of months. This 'festival' is, strictly speaking, a celebration of the birth of Jesus Christ, but it takes place at a time chosen by early Christians to coincide with winter solstice celebrations in northern Europe, and it is characterized as much by feasting and resting from usual routines for many of its participants as for any religious rites. Moreover, in Britain, followers of other faiths observe their own rituals, such as the Jewish Hanukah and Hindu Diwali, close to the winter break from routine which we are almost forced to share.

These local differences are not actually as new as they may seem, for the Scots have long distinguished their winter celebrations from those of the English by placing greater emphasis on Hogmanay, celebrated on New Year's Eve, than on Christmas, whether they are Christians or not. Brought up as an ex-pat Scot in England, myself, I was made aware of this distinction from an early age, and our annual Hogmanay party encapsulated very clearly the elements of van Gennep's scheme: the old year seen off with a rendering of Auld Lang Syne, a liminal period passed listening to the chiming of Big Ben, and then greetings, accompanied by handshakes, hugs and kisses signalling a communal incorporation into the New Year which had opened.

At our parties, we would follow all this with a wild Eightsome Reel, as fellow Scots kicked their heels in an expression of togetherness as Scots, as well as to their specific friends and relatives, but although some English people I know have chosen to celebrate the New Year in this traditional Scottish celebration, and they dress themselves in kilts and other 'Scottish' garments, they draw the line at a dance so common and apparently unrefined. These groups practice weekly all manner of complicated Scottish dancing, and although they incorporate a rite of 'first-footing' into their Hogmanay celebrations, another Scottish practice which echoes the theories of van Gennep, their togetherness is based precisely on excluding dances that any outsider can do, just because they are Scottish (see Photograph 4.1).

The element of abandonment which the Eightsome Reel signified for me, growing up, and which is expressed by the only element of Hogmanay which all Scots agree about – namely, that one must get very drunk – is a characteristic of the liminal period of many festivals for the people concerned, as were initiation rites for youths passing into a transition state before becoming adults. This is well illustrated by carnivals such as Mardi Gras, another Christian feast which has taken on wider appeal, but which is actually the beginning the period of fasting called Lent, and another example of a rite of passage marking a longer period of transition, culminating in Easter in the Christian calendar.

Photograph 4.1   Scottish dancing in England to celebrate Hogmanay (photograph: Joy Hendry)

Edmund Leach (1961) has written an interesting little article entitled 'Time and False Noses' in which he examines the way people dress up, sometimes smartly and sometimes in quite bizarre ways, during ceremonies and festivals which mark the passage of time. He notes also that people sometimes even perform roles quite the opposite of their usual ones on these occasions – men dressing and women, kings as beggars, and vice versa. His thesis is that where rites of passage are marked by these examples of *formality* and *masquerade*, they form a pair of contrasted opposites to stand at either end of ritualized breaks in the passage of time. *Role reversal*, on the other hand, marks the middle period when normal time has stopped – another example of the period of liminality.

The British custom of performing plays known as pantomimes during the Christmas period is a good illustration of this phenomenon, for there is always a 'Dame', a buxom female role played by a man, and the main male role – who may be a prince in disguise as a pauper, for example – is very often played by a young woman. There is usually a 'princess', or some other female role played by a girl, too, so that the love scenes between her and the lead 'male' may seem physically homosexual, though the symbolism is clearly heterosexual. The general entertainment value of pantomime, carnival, holidays and the more original holy days is commented upon in studies made around the world, and ritual, however solemn, usually has its fun side too, as Leach suggests.

Not surprisingly, then, an interest among anthropologists in the study of theatre, media and other types of performance is related to ritual (see, for further reading, Hughes-Freeland, 1998). This, too, marks, for the audience, if not for the players, a break from the routines of working life. Like ritual, performances of one sort or another provide a place and period of separation from 'real life', a break in the relentless passage of time. For the players, theatre and media allows a period of (artistic) licence to behave quite outside the regular norms of social life, and in both ritual and theatre, people take on the task of performance of one sort or another.

My own recent research on theme parks is precisely about places which allow everyone to participate in a world of fantasy whenever they feel inclined – or, at least, when they have the funds available to take a holiday. Here too individuals may choose their own breaks in routine, but still with the possibility of reversing usual roles, and removing themselves from the exigencies of 'real life'. Some of the parks in Japan that I studied recreate the experience of visiting a foreign country, inviting their customers to spend a day or more imagining themselves to be in Canada or Spain, Germany or Holland, even dressing up to play the part of a native.

The apparent allure of cultural themes is found in many other countries, local culture being displayed for visitors in Taman Mini Indonesia Indah, just outside Jakarta, and parks in Taiwan, Singapore and China, although Shenzhen has a funfair of global culture in a park called Windows of the World. In Hawaii, there is a popular Polynesian Cultural Centre, and theme parks in other places offer a trip back in history, sometimes preserving buildings in the process. Colonial Williamsburg and Upper Canada Village in North America, Sovereign Hill in Australia, and Skansen in Sweden, are all early examples of places which encourage visitors to remove themselves, temporarily, to a former period in time. Julian Barnes's novel, *England, England*, depicts a futuristic view of the phenomenon.

Rituals, wherever they are found, mark out the social categories for the people in question. They may be more or less related to the natural cycles of the seasons, the moon and the human body, but they will always be ordered in a cultural way related to ideas about the social world in which they are found. The range of possibilities offers an element of choice which might seem to contradict our initial definition of ritual, but the appearance of fixed elements of culture in a slippery flexible world may be the attraction to people seeking an identity to espouse – especially if they feel that more traditional rituals have become empty.

References

Coppet, D. de (1992) *Understanding Rituals* (London: Routledge).
Edwards, Walter (1989) *Modern Japan Through Its Weddings* (Stanford: Stanford University Press).
Gennep, Arnold van (1960) *Rites of Passage* (London: Routledge & Kegan Paul).
Leach, Edmund (1969) 'Virgin Birth', in *Genesis as Myth and other Essays* (London: Cape).
Leach, E. R. (1961) 'Two Essays Concerning the Symbolic Representation of Time: (ii) Time and False Noses', in *Rethinking Anthropology* (London: Athlone Press).
Lewis, Gilbert (1980) *Day of Shining Red: An Essay on Understanding Ritual* (Cambridge University Press).
Turner, Victor (1967) *The Forest of Symbols: Aspects of Ndembu Ritual* (Cornell University Press).

Further Reading

Cannadine, David and Simon Price (1987) *Rituals of Royalty: Power and Ceremonial in Traditional Societies* (Cambridge University Press).
Hendry, Joy (1986) *Marriage in Changing Japan* (Tokyo: Tuttle).
Hughes-Freeland, Felicia (1998) *Ritual, Performance and Media* (London: Routledge).
Huntington, Richard and Peter Metcalf (1979) *Celebrations of Death* (Cambridge University Press).
La Fontaine, Jean (1985) *Initiation* (Harmondsworth: Penguin).
Turner, Victor (1969) *The Ritual Process* (London: Routledge & Kegan Paul).

Novel

Barnes, Julian (1998) *England, England* (London: Jonathan Cape).

Films

Masai Manhood (Chris Curling and Melissa Llewelyn-Davies, 1975), another classic 'Disappearing World' film about initiation among these pastoral people of East Africa, also demonstrates cattle values, male–female relations and the power and influence of the elders. There is a companion film called *Masai Women*, made by the same team.
Osôshiki ('Funeral, Japanese-style'), an Itani Junichiro feature film, is an irreverent but interesting depiction of events surrounding death in modern Japan.

CHAPTER 5

Society: A Set of Symbols

What is a Symbol?

In the last chapter we talked of examining ritual to help our understanding of systems of classification. We referred to the scheme identified by Arnold van Gennep which seems to recur throughout the world in rites of passage, and we discussed various examples which would appear to illustrate it. This scheme makes sense of a wide variety of behaviour in an overall way, but let us turn now to see how we interpret these rituals in practice. What we can most easily look at when examining ritual behaviour are the material objects involved, the fixed elements of human behaviour, and the way the humans dress themselves. We divide the whole performance into small units – the clothes, the cards, the gifts, the food – all of which may be seen and interpreted as **symbols**. Symbols may be regarded as the smallest units of ritual and we can learn a lot by examining them in their own right.

Symbolism is of course a huge subject which crops up in almost every sphere – in literature, art, religion and psychology, as well as in anthropology. There are certain differences in the way we interpret symbols in these different subjects, and there are various sorts of symbols to be interpreted. For example, there are private or sensory symbols which refer to emotional aspects of human behaviour and fall more into the domain of psychology or psychiatry. The symbols which interest social anthropologists are *public symbols*, shared by members of a particular social group. They express aspects of the ideology of the group, understood within a specific social and moral system, and the same symbols may mean something quite different to members of another social group.

Symbolism pervades human behaviour, at even the most mundane levels, and the ability to use symbols, including speech, is one of the ways in which the behaviour of humans is said to be distinguished from the behaviour of other animals. We have already seen examples of symbolism in the use of greetings and gift exchange, where we noted that social relationships would be invisible without some clearly defined way of expressing them. In anthropology we are particularly concerned with the variety of ways in which symbols may be interpreted in different societies, and between different groups in the same wider society. A large part of our work is to make sense of these units of communication in social life.

The definition of a symbol given in the *Concise Oxford Dictionary* is:

- a thing regarded by general consent as naturally typifying or representing or recalling something by possession of analogous qualities or by association in fact or in thought.

These associations are specific to a particular society, though the analogous qualities could be clear to an outsider, and the 'general consent' is of course only general within a particular social or linguistic group. It is interesting that the definition uses the word 'naturally' because it is often the case that people within one society remain blissfully unaware of the relativity of their symbols. A connection which seems natural to one people may be quite contrived to another.

A **sign** is rather similar to a symbol, but it is a much more straightforward representation of something which is easy to describe in other ways. A symbol, on the other hand, is more open to different interpretations. It generally has more semantic content, more meaning, than a sign. As Jung put it, although he was referring to the analysis of dreams,

> The sign is always less than the concept it represents, while a symbol always stands for something more than its obvious and immediate meaning. (1964, p. 55)

A traffic light is a sign – red means stop, green means go – now quite universally, though hardly natural. The wearing of red and green may be open to much more complicated interpretation – it may be nothing more than a fashion statement, or it may be associated with Christmas, or with the colours of a European flag. It could also be criticized, for there is a saying in the English language which goes 'red and green should never be seen except on an Irish Queen' – an Irish Queen?

Because public symbols are shared by members of a particular society, it is essential that an anthropologist studying that society learn to use them too. They are the visible features of invisible aspects of social organization, as was demonstrated in the case of gifts. They provide objects of study, and of discussion, which lead to an understanding of that society. Symbols in any society must be used in a systematic way, or the members would be lost, just as the outsider feels lost on first exposure to the society. In fact, it would not be going too far to describe the whole concept of society as a set of shared symbols. Let us examine some examples.

Bodily Symbols

Individuals in Western societies like to think of themselves as unique. They choose clothes and accessories to express their personalities, and they wear their hair in a style which they feel suits them personally. They are expressing themselves through the symbols of the society in which they live, however, and their range of choice for dress and adornment is limited to what is acceptable in that society. Even the most outrageous outfits must cover certain areas of the body, and a person who painted themselves and appeared on the streets with no further apparel would in Britain be arrested unless the painting looked like very convincing clothes. Elsewhere paint may be the appropriate attire for the most formal occasion.

Bodily attire provides a huge range of possibilities for symbolic communication, some relatively permanent, some entirely temporary, and the messages which are expressed may be interpreted at different levels by different groups of people within the same wider society. In societies less concerned with individualism as an ideology people are happy to dress much as their neighbours do, and they will express allegiances to certain groups in their appearance, or perhaps be more concerned to demonstrate the nature of an occasion in the way they present themselves. They may also indicate their level of status within their own society in the way they appear.

In markets in rural Mexico, for example, groups of indigenous people may easily be identified because of the costumes they wear. Those groups who still live in relatively isolated communities continue to wear colours and styles which identify their groups rather than their personalities, and they may be picked out easily in a mixed crowd. Mexicans who have become part of the wider community have adopted more universal clothing which may be judged according to taste and quality, but they would not necessarily be picked out in a cosmopolitan city as Mexicans unless they chose to wear the sombrero, which has become a symbol of the Mexican people.

In some cities, people from different religious groups are easily identifiable by the clothes and hairstyles they choose to wear. In Jerusalem, for example, orthodox Jews may be picked out by the hats and black garments which symbolize their allegiance to the faith, and priests of the Armenian church wear tall hats which distinguish them from other Christian groups who reside there. Visitors from religious orders may also choose to wear the habits which express their particular allegiance in this holy city. In each case, the individuals express their membership of a religious order over any other allegiance. Here, too, however, the street vendors become adept at assessing the nationality of the tourists from their apparel so that they know what language to use in their sales patter.

These distinctions are more subtle, because the individuals concerned probably did not get up in the morning intending to dress in their national costume. They may be wearing clothes to express their individuality, but their choices will reflect to an outsider something about their social group, national and regional. Many of them will be wearing jeans, a kind of universal unisex garment, apparently, but sometimes worn with sandals, sometimes with high-heeled shoes, sometimes with Dr Martens, and sometimes with trainers. Some jeans are shrunk, some are purposely faded, some are chosen for their designer label, and some are worn with colourful patches or indecently open holes in them. They may be worn with smart shirts and jewellery, or with a nondescript baggy T-shirt.

Some of these differences indicate information about the wearers which they may not consciously have thought about, although people are usually influenced by the way they think others will perceive them. Another almost universal garment is the two-piece (or three-piece) suit, yet almost no one would be willing to go to work in any garment just because it fell into that category. The tie is a particularly useful piece of apparel to be used symbolically, especially in Britain, where men express their allegiances to clubs, schools and colleges in the more traditional examples of the genre; assess one another's taste and judgement in the more decorative versions; and reject the whole system by leaving them off altogether. On special occasions the long variety is replaced by a bow, of course, and in some parts of America, the usual version is an object which would be used to lace shoes in the British Isles.

Within particular groups, different messages are communicated from those picked up by outsiders. Consider the case of headgear: although both may be Scottish, a deer-stalker tells quite a different story from a tartan cap with a peak at the front, just as in England a top hat will convey different information from a bowler. A Jewish skull cap to a non-Jew will tell only that the wearer is almost certainly a Jew, probably orthodox. Within a particular Jewish community, however, these small items, where possible carefully crocheted in the home, allow women great scope to transmit messages, both to their menfolk for whom they make them, and to the wider world about their menfolk's caretakers and loved ones. As a corollary of this, women are apparently also quite prone to judge one another on the basis of the skill they witness in these rather neat exhibitions of their handiwork (Baizerman, 1991).

Jewellery and other types of adornment are highly symbolic too. There is a kind of thick, gold jewellery abundantly available in airport shops which is a clear, international expression of wealth, just as designer scarves and handbags are. Among the nomadic Fulani people of West Africa, women wear coins in their hair to express the same meaning, and the Bella, their former slaves, decorate their hair with buttons to follow the style but without the same resources. The Rendille women of Kenya wear arm bands to show that they are married, just as men and women elsewhere wear rings on their fingers, but the Rendille add further bands to demonstrate the stage of life their sons have reached. They also wear their hair in an enormous coxcomb from the birth of their first son.

In the highlands of New Guinea, among the Wahgi people, men wear beautiful headdresses made of the feathers of local birds, and adorn their skin with the shiny fat of the pigs they value so highly. These forms of display (see Photograph 5.1), worn on certain special occasions, symbolize political and military might as well as status in the community. Michael O'Hanlon devotes a whole book, *Reading the Skin: Adornment, Display and Society among the Wahgi*, to the subject, but a few of his words gives a feeling for the communicative possibilities:

> in a turbulent social landscape of shifting alliances and insistent rivalries, impressive displays are felt to intimidate rival clans, and to deter enemies from attacking . . . the appearance of those displaying is thought of as an external reflection of their inner moral condition . . . evaluations of adornment and display emerge as a dynamic idiom in terms of which moral issues are discussed . . . in the rivalrous Wahgi social environment, displays are credited with exerting a direct influence over the military policies of spectator clans. (1989, pp. 124–5)

In Polynesia, people tattoo themselves to make a more permanent statement about their role and place in society (see, for example, Gell, 1993). In Japan, too, some gangsters wear beautiful tattoos which cover a large part of their bodies, and depict scenes from the country's abundant religious and mythological artistic repertoire, but they keep them hidden under their clothes most of the time because the wider society finds them offensive and disgusting. To have one done – a painful process of more than a year – therefore symbolizes an irreversible commitment to the life of the underworld, and even only part of them, revealed at a strategic moment, makes a powerful statement about such an allegiance.

Hair on the head is an excellent medium for making symbolic statements of a striking if only semi-permanent nature. In several parts of the world shaving the head is a custom associated with initiation, for example, as was seen with the Masai in the last chapter, where leaving the hair to grow in an unruly fashion was also part of the process. Where there is a prevailing

Photograph 5.1 A Wahgi man from the Highlands of New Guinea, in full festive adornment (photograph courtesy of Michael O'Hanlon, Pitt Rivers Museum, Oxford)

custom about hairstyle, such as the short-back-and-sides arrangement for men, some people can express a rejection of the mainstream by allowing their hair to grow long. When this practice was first coming into its own in Britain, Raymond Firth (1973, p. 272), who had been working in Tikopia, an island in Polynesia, noticed that there had been a curious reversal of custom between the two places. When he left for fieldwork, men in Britain had worn their hair short, and women very often long, whereas in Tikopia he found this convention reversed. During his stay, the Tikopians began to follow outside influence and cut their hair to coincide with the Western way of doing things. Firth was surprised on his return to Britain to find that the situation seemed to have reversed there too, at least among some of his students.

Young people in Britain have been through various stages since that time, often choosing a style which contrasts sharply with the previous generation of youth. The long-haired beatniks which Firth encountered were a complete change from the 'teddy' boys and girls who preceded them, with their neat quiffs and hair grease. These in their turn were rejected and opposed by the short-haired 'mods' who came afterwards, themselves contrasted with the unkempt 'rockers' of the same generation. Skin-heads and 'bovver-boys' wear their hair short to look threatening, as do the more lavishly turned-out punks, clearly expressing something animal or 'primitive' in their elaborate cox-combs, both rejecting the society of their parents and other elders.

One of my students recounted during a lecture on this very subject how he had chosen a punk hairstyle in order to be 'different' from everyone else. He was disappointed, however, for when visiting a night club he found the whole floor to be seething with variants of himself. As he put it, 'it seemed I had joined a convention of parrots'. He then decided to try another tack in his quest for individuality, and attended the same venue wearing a short haircut and a three-piece suit. He certainly looked different then – so different that he was beaten up.

In nineteenth-century Japan, people wore particular hairstyles to show their social status, and children in that world celebrated stages of life by altering their hair, the first hair-cut being a sort of initiation into childhood. Members of the *samurai* class had a topknot which was not allowed to lesser mortals, and although unmarried women could wear their hair loose, once married they were obliged to keep it in a kind of bun. In the film *Shinju* a couple who ran away to commit suicide together, because they had developed a socially impossible relationship, let their hair down and cut it off to symbolize their rejection of society before they carried out the desperate act.

This relationship between hair, power and sexuality has been reported widely. For example,

In pre-Christian Polynesia, the head was *mana* . . . The Samoan word for head (*ulu*) can mean 'head' or 'hair'. Not surprisingly, hair was treated as if it too were *mana*. The hair of Samoan chiefs, for example, was cut by special attendants . . . *Mana* was associated with the vital energies of the natural world and was synonymous with fecundity . . . In pre-contact Samoa, women grew their hair long only during pregnancy . . . The implication is that long hair alluded to the pregnant or fecund state. (Mageo, 1994, p. 410)

Several anthropologists have put forward theories about the way hair is used symbolically, some suggesting universal ideas, and Mageo's (1994) article examines these in the light of Samoan material she gathered over a period of eight years' residence there. This is particularly interesting because, like the Tikopian case mentioned above, the way hair is worn in Samoa has changed greatly over the period of colonial influence, and Christian morals have come to play an important part, so that the positive role of fecundity has become tarred with a negative attitude towards excessive sexuality. Mageo also addresses the question of overlap between public and private symbols.

Symbolizing Relationships

We have pointed out already that relationships are expressed in various symbolic forms, notably in Chapter 3 where we discussed gift exchange. Here we discussed the way gifts are given on particular occasions, perhaps wrapped in an appropriate fashion, so that the object and its presentation make statements about the relationship between donor and recipient. We discussed the importance of reciprocity in the exchange of gifts, and other modes of communication, if a relationship is to proceed smoothly, and we considered the problems which may arise when people from different cultural backgrounds misinterpret the significance of presents they may receive.

Again, the symbols are part of shared meaning peculiar to a particular society, and it is another role of the anthropologist to examine the local significance of such exchanges. Japanese people are well known for their generous and beautiful gifts by foreigners who have even the most tenuous of social relationships with them, but, as we mentioned, few foreigners are aware of the importance attached to the practice of gift-giving in Japan. Those who simply try to keep up with or outdo the cost of gifts they have received, and neglect factors such as relative status and non-material favours, when they make their returns, could find themselves in a rapidly escalating and quite inappropriate contest of affluence.

Relationships may also be modified in a subtle manipulation of the local practice of gift exchange. An unexpected gift could of course signal a desire to intensify a relationship, but it could also mark the end of a series of exchanges, or a way of expressing empathy for a situation difficult to discuss. Gifts of perishable food received may provide a good excuse to express friendship by inviting round a neighbour or colleague on the pretext of avoiding waste, but also purposely to further the acquaintance. A usual gift withheld, or noticeably cheaper than expected, can create distance when a relationship is becoming too close, or symbolize a rejection of an unwanted approach. A gift returned may seem like a clear symbol, but it must be interpreted within the range of possibilities of a particular social system.

Greetings are another important way of expressing relationships, and again these can be manipulated for more subtle communication within a particular society. The handshake has become an international symbol of agreement and accord, so that important treaties may be sealed in such a way, and photographs of handshakes frequently embellish the cosmopolitan press. Within Europe, customs vary, but generally handshakes express goodwill. In some countries they are practised daily within the family, in others they are reserved for first meetings and special occasions such as the conferment of a degree or a prize. People use them to seal a new arrangement, or to express the resumption of good relations after a quarrel.

In some situations a handshake would be too cool a greeting, however, and various forms of kisses are practised within the same continent of Europe. The lips are usually involved, though they may merely be pursed in the air as cheeks brush gently together, especially when women kiss one another in public. In some social circles, it is imperative to kiss on either cheek, a practice found more on the continent than in Britain, except among staunch Francophiles and the like. In Poland, it is usual to kiss three times. The significance of a kiss in more intimate relationships is also culturally variable, which may come as a surprise to some readers. In pre-modern Japan it was not even thought to be particularly erotic.

Kissing and hugging are rather intimate symbols in Western society, and they are not often practised between men, as was discussed in Chapter 2, but in parts of the Middle East, they may be more usual than a handshake, even in public situations. Before the historic meeting in 1993 between the Israeli prime minister, Yitzhak Rabin, and the leader of the Palestinian Liberation Organization, Yasser Arafat, speculation was rife about how their greeting would be expressed. Many hoped for a hug, but this was not forthcoming. Their handshake was celebrated all over the world, but for local people it may have seemed rather cool.

In Japan, the usual form of greeting is a bow, and this has many variations. From a standing position the depth of a bow indicates a degree of deference, and two people bowing to one another will indicate their relative status in the angle of their acknowledgement. It is also expected that the lower ranking person will allow the superior to rise first, so the situation can become quite comical if both parties are trying to defer to the other. In a *tatami*-matted room, where people habitually sit on the floor, there are various types of formal bows which may be carried out, and these involve bringing the head almost in contact with the floor. It is said that men in *samurai* times were taught to keep their eyes on their greeting partners, however, in case they proved to be enemies who would take advantage of the defenceless position.

Symbols are of course also used to express enmity and ferocity, and the *samurai* would wear a pair of swords to demonstrate his invulnerability in this respect. The sword would also demonstrate his status in society, but in pre-modern Japan it could be used with impunity to decapitate a disobedient subject. In the United States, it is more acceptable to carry a gun than in some other countries, although the gentlemen's duel at dawn was for long a highly ritualized and therefore symbolic way of solving a dispute in European countries. Suits of armour, now thankfully usually only on display in museums and castles, are also a repository of symbolic ferocity, and helmets or breastpieces very often sport a mark of allegiance as well.

Group Symbols and their Interpretation

In battles and warfare, symbols such as these abound, representing the whole social group involved. Flags represent the nation or the particular people concerned, and the human beings are decked out in clothes which make their adversarial activity their prime purpose. Battle dress comes in a variety of forms, and uniform, or previously armour, is a powerful symbolic tool in rallying people to a cause. It clearly subordinates the individual to a greater social entity, in which personal qualms must be set aside for the wider common good. In such a guise human beings can carry out acts of violence which would abhor them in normal life and which would probably bring about their arrest and imprisonment.

National anthems and marching songs are designed to invoke a pride of participation in those who listen to them, as are words of rhetoric turned out to whip up enthusiasm for a cause, whether it be bellicose or peaceful. The ban-the-bomb symbol has been one of the best known and most powerful in recent years, though it has various origins and interpretations in different parts of the world. Anthropologists analyse the language and paraphernalia of the social groups they study in order to identify symbols which are important to the people concerned. These can in turn lead to an understanding of the ideology or ideologies they live by, and may be related to other aspects of social life.

A useful book, set in Britain and compiled and edited by Anthony Cohen, is entitled *Symbolising Boundaries*. It considers the symbolism used to express and identify differences within communities, between the worlds of men and women in Devon, between households in Yorkshire and Battersea, between neighbouring settlements in Lewis, and between Catholics and Protestants in Northern Ireland. The articles examine and illustrate the complexities and ambiguities of these distinctions. The second part of the book moves into the mechanisms used by certain groups to express their distinctions within the wider society, for example by adolescents in an adult world, by suburban occupants of a northern city, and by Glaswegians in reference to the image they portray abroad.

Cohen introduces the interesting idea of the malleability of symbols in a complex community:

> The efficacy of symbols which we recognise here is their capacity to express in ways which allows their common forms to be retained among the members of a group, and among different groups, whilst not imposing upon these people the yoke of uniform meaning. Symbols, being malleable in this way, can be made to 'fit' circumstances. They thus provide media through which individuals and groups can experience and express their attachment to a society without compromising their individuality. (1986, p. 9)

Anthropological Interpretation of Symbolism

Much has been written on the subject of **symbolism**, and there has been some dispute among anthropologists about how far an outsider should go in the interpretation of the symbolism of another people. As Cohen puts it:

> The ethnographic difficulty for us, therefore, is that not only is symbolism a matter of interpretation (as it is everywhere); but the interpretation of behaviour as symbolic in character is itself a matter of conjecture and judgement which is only demonstrable through notions of plausibility or of theoretical 'fit' . . . The danger is, of course, that rather than using my imagination as an interpretive *resource*, I risk allowing it to constitute the data themselves . . . I have written about the croft, the spree, the burial as symbolically significant . . . But significant for whom? The people we are supposedly describing. Or ourselves? (1986, p. 7)

Victor Turner is one of the anthropologists who has made a great contribution in this field. In his book *The Forest of Symbols*, he suggested that the structure and properties of ritual symbols could be inferred from three classes of data:

(1) external form and observable characteristics;
(2) interpretations offered by specialists and by laymen;
(3) significant contexts largely worked out by the anthropologist. (1967, p. 20)

It is this last category which is most contentious, because it goes beyond the second, and sometimes even contradicts it. Different anthropologists also disagree at this level, although this is not unusual in this subject, as was pointed out at the beginning of this book. Turner stresses the importance of putting sets of symbols in the total context of the ritual in which they appear, other rituals and their performance, and the wider society of which they form a part, including notions of class, lineage, generations and so forth. This, he argues, is easier for an outsider than for a subjectively involved participant, as the latter regards as axiomatic the ideals, values and norms expressed or symbolized.

Turner gives as an example the case of the Ndembu girls' puberty ritual, which was mentioned in the previous chapter, where a girl is lain under a tree for a whole day. The tree, which is called a *mudyi* tree, exudes milky beads when the bark is scratched, and this, for the Ndembu, is its most important 'observable characteristic'. Women explain that this liquid stands for breast milk, and indeed, for the breasts which supply it. They further explain that the tree represents the relationship between mother and child, and the continuing line from woman to woman which stands for the tribe itself, including the men. When observing the ritual, however, Turner noticed that it actually serves to symbolize the separation of mother and daughter, as the latter reaches puberty, to separate women from men, and even to separate some groups of women from others.

This was clear to him in the following ways. First, the mother of the initiate is excluded from the group of women who dance around the motionless girl under the tree. She is not allowed to participate in this important part of her daughter's puberty rite. Secondly, men are excluded from the ritual altogether, and the matter is handled entirely by women. Thirdly, when the mother brings out food for the participants, there is a kind of competition to be the first to take some, for that person's origin is said to indicate where the girl will marry. The Ndembu informants were unable to recognize these apparent contradictions, and Turner argues that it is only possible to infer them with a wider knowledge of the society, which is also made as a relatively objective outsider.

In British society, which has a large number of Christians, a parallel may be made when anthropologists take a look at Christianity. Edmund Leach (1969) upset a lot of people in England when he discussed Christian practises in anthropological terms, writing essays entitled 'Genesis as Myth' and 'Virgin Birth', which will be considered in Chapter 7 of this book. His intentions were seriously academic ones, but putting Christian rituals in the context of those held in societies regarded as 'pagan' by Christian believers, undoubtedly offended against their systems of classification, and struck a chord of taboo. Those people who are committed to one form of religious worship may find it difficult to stand back and view their practices in the context of other forms.

Nor may they necessarily understand all the elements of their activities. As John Beattie pointed out long ago in an excellent article about ritual, the fact that a Christian communicant may not understand the doctrine and full meaning of the Eucharist (or Holy Communion), does not mean that it does not have such a meaning (1966, p. 67). Even specialists may disagree in explaining ritual events, and the Eucharist is a good example again, for while a Protestant minister will explain that the bread and wine represent (or symbolize) the body and blood of Jesus Christ, a Roman Catholic priest will say that the bread and wine *become* the body and blood of Jesus Christ. There is a fundamental difference of views here, which makes it difficult for believers and participants alike to make an objective analysis.

In Japan a similar problem may be observed. After the Second World War, the indigenous religion, Shinto, was officially denigrated as associated with the notion of a divine emperor and the whole disastrous war effort. Buddhism, on the other hand, was unaffected in this way, and for many years people would talk only of Buddhism as religion, tending to describe Shinto activities, which did continue, as 'superstition'. It was thus rather easier to investigate Shinto practices than Buddhist ones, for the former had been stripped to some extent of their mystical elements. The mysticism attaches an awe to elements of religious faith which may make it difficult for people to discuss them without offending their own system of classification. They have been affected by the kind of taboos we discussed in Chapter 2.

Not so sacrosanct are secular elements of rituals, and people are quite happy to speculate about things such as cakes and costumes which mark rites of passage in Britain. An anthropological study carried out by Simon Charsley in Glasgow examined the meaning and purpose of the wedding cake in Scottish weddings. In fact he was disappointed by the lack of ready interpretation of this apparently essential feature of the great day, but some ideas of his own were quite fruitful, if only in a negative way. He was impressed by the idea that the white wedding cake might stand for the white-clad bride, and 'cutting the cake', actually 'plunging the knife' into the centre of the cake, would then clearly represent a breaking of the 'virginal white outer-shell' (1987, p. 106).

Much of Charsley's article is a discussion about the degree to which an anthropologist is legitimately entitled to interpret beyond the explanations of the participants, just as Turner suggested, and an interesting twist to his investigation occurred when a couple actually came up with this meaning for the cake. They had heard it from someone else, but they were so horrified by the inequality they felt it expressed between bride and groom that they decided to do away with a cake altogether. Charsley then examines the interesting question of whether a rite can only be practised if a possible meaning for its symbolism has not been noticed. He rejects this idea, however, pointing out that it was not the idea of virginity and its loss which upset this particular couple, but the idea of inequality which they themselves felt it represented.

Interestingly, many people are more concerned in the arrangements of their own weddings, and even more so with those of their children, that things should be done 'properly'. They seek the 'right' way to do things, rather than examining the meanings in order to impose their own inter-pretations. A veritable barrage of wedding magazines stand ready at book-shops and newsagents to provide instant advice, and most people are quite happy to be informed of the appropriate etiquette. Rather than do away with a wedding cake, then, people may use it to express something personal about their relationship, according to Charsley's research, and he reported one couple that chose the icing decoration of a sofa depicting themselves and their children by previous marriages. British friends of mine who had worked in Japan chose to cut their cake with a *samurai* sword.

Ideas for symbolism may be discussed, then, and alternatives considered, but in any society there will be a set of underlying notions which form the basis of these deliberations. It is fine to be outrageous, if that is understood, and some may express messages selectively to a close group of friends or relatives, but it would be pointless in terms of communication to do something so unusual and different that nobody could discern the meaning at all. These basic tools of communication are the **collective representations** we discussed in Chapter 1, following Durkheim's terminology. They include the 'set of symbols' after which we named this chapter, and they form some of the most basic subject matter of social anthropology.

References

Baizerman, Suzanne (1991) 'The *Kippa Sruga* and the Social Construction of Gender', in Ruth Barnes and Joanne B. Eicher, *Dress and Gender: Making and Meaning* (Oxford: Berg).

Beattie, John (1966) 'Ritual and Social Change',*Man*, **1**: 60–74.

Charsley, Simon (1987) 'Interpretation and Custom: The Case of the Wedding Cake',*Man*, **22**: 93–110.

Cohen, Anthony (1986) *Symbolising Boundaries: Identity and Diversity in British Cultures* (Manchester University Press).

Firth, Raymond (1973) *Symbols, Public and Private* (London: Allen & Unwin).

Gell, Alfred (1993) *Wrapping in Images* (Oxford: Clarendon Press).

Jung, Carl G. (ed.) (1964) *Man and his Symbols* (London: Aldus).

Leach, Edmund (1969) *Genesis as Myth and other Essays* (London: Cape).

Mageo, Jeanette Marie (1994) 'Hairdos and don'ts: hair symbolism and sexual history in Samoa', *Man*, **29**: 407–432.

O'Hanlon, Michael (1989) *Reading the Skin: Adornment, Display and Society among the Wahgi* (London: British Museum Publications).

Turner, Victor (1967) *The Forest of Symbols: Aspects of Ndembu Ritual* (Cornell University Press).

Further Reading

Douglas, Mary (1975) *Implicit Meanings* (London: Routledge & Kegan Paul).

Eicher, Joanne B. (ed.) (1995) *Dress and Ethnicity* (Oxford: Berg).

Firth, Raymond (1937) *We, the Tikopia* (London: Allen & Unwin).

Needham, Rodney (1979) *Symbolic Classification* (Santa Monica, Calif: Goodyear).

CHAPTER 6

Beauty and Bounty: Treasure and Trophies

Seeing and Value

An interesting aspect of the interpretation of objects and symbols in a particular society is the aesthetic one, and the anthropology of art and aesthetics has recently become a particularly lively branch of the subject. There are various reasons for this, but one of the most important is reflected in the title of this chapter. One person's art is for another a **commodity** to be exploited, and the world of 'art' has truly become a **global** concern. At the beginning of Chapter 1 we talked of souvenirs and different ways of 'seeing the world', and then we went on to examine various ways of understanding these different worlds. In this chapter we return to 'seeing', but add the subject of value, notably but not exclusively aesthetic value.

In the cosmopolitan world, there are people who make a very tidy living by being acquainted with the value of *objets d'art*, while others feel excluded and possibly diminished by being uninformed on this subject. The value of art objects is, however, entirely relative to the place they are assigned in this exclusive world, and some people are able to take advantage of others in manipulating the system which appears to come into existence. Indigenous (or, earlier, 'primitive') art has been increasingly valued in this cosmopolitan world, but in recent years the indigenous artists have begun to join the fray, with interesting effects.

The value of objects for gaining access to an understanding of people and their views is still of prime concern, but it is also important to realize that interpretations may be seen in a particular light. Some people may feel aggrieved, or misrepresented, by the way in which their objects are used, and they may disagree with the interpretations assigned to them, whether by anthropologist or art historian. When people become aware of the value assigned elsewhere to their work, they may be influenced to respond to an apparent need, especially if it is economically or politically beneficial to them to do so. The outsiders, in their turn, may feel aggrieved that the 'pure' art forms of the people concerned have been corrupted. A good example of this phenomenon forms the subject matter of an ethnography of Japanese potters whose work gradually changed when it was chosen as the epitome of Japan's 'folk art' (Moeran, 1984).

The relationship between art and the spiritual or transcendental is another source of intrigue and fascination to anthropologists, and this chapter will try to show how difficult it may be to separate works of art from their cosmological context. In practice, some objects have acquired different levels of interpretation in different situations, and the art of the Australian Aboriginal people is a case in point. Spiritual meaning is apparently preserved for the artist and those of his or her own society while explanations provided for the tourist are much more limited, which would seem to be quite appropriate in a society which attaches value to secrecy, as is the case in many Aboriginal communities.

It is possible that there is also a certain attraction for the consumer in knowing that their purchase may carry some esoteric value, and although the layers of meaning may not be appreciated by indigenous artists, it is likely that their advocates are aware that those who wish to acquire it may be seeking more than just an attractive souvenir. Early Western paintings of the native inhabitants of the various idyllic isles discovered by Captain Cook and his sailors depicted people in a situation resembling the Garden of Eden, a fictional paradise quite in keeping with the Rousseauan ideas of the noble savage current at the time. Indigenous art may still carry a tinge of spiritual healing, which appeals to those seeking solace from the fast city life of the high-tech world.

Living Art

The anthropology of art is not confined to the study of marketable objects, however. In many societies people assign aesthetic qualities to the decoration of their own bodies, sometimes spending days in the preparation of a particular display. Some cases of bodily decoration, and its symbolic associations, were raised in the previous chapter, but a particularly striking example of the aesthetic appreciation of bodily decoration is to be found among the Nuba people of Southern Sudan. Here young men and women spend time every day making themselves up and rubbing oil into their whole bodies to make them shine, some of the most attractive designs being found among pubescent boys between the approximate ages of 15 and 20.

According to the anthropologist, J. C. Faris (1971), this activity is purely aesthetic, to express the beauty of healthy nubile bodies, which are idealized in this society. To attach aesthetic value to an idealized form of the human body is of course found in many societies, possibly universally, and examples probably overlooked by art historians abound in film series such as *Bay Watch*, where the story line would seem much less important than the health and youthful vigour of the characters on display. The technical term for displaying and admiring nubile bodies in their physical and sexual prime is **ephebism**, although how the ideal body is conceptualized will vary from culture to culture.

Tattoos are a permanent type of bodily adornment requiring considerable investment of time and resources which may also bestow a long-term political advantage, as we discussed in the previous chapter. In some societies they express a man's place in a hierarchical scheme, in others they are chosen to demonstrate a kind of *macho* ability to endure pain, but people also choose them for their aesthetic appeal. The 'disgusting' Japanese tattoos we mentioned draw on the same fund of mythological inspiration as do woodblock prints, exported as examples of Japanese cultural achievement, and tattoo artists around the world have chosen elements of them to offer to their clients, along with a range of examples from other cultural sources.

It has also been argued that aesthetic appreciation is expressed in mundane aspects of everyday life, and Jeremy Coote (in Coote and Shelton, 1992) has demonstrated that the artistic focus of attention to colour, shading, shapes and patterns for Nilotic herding people such as the Nuer and the Dinka, is the cattle which form the basis of their livelihood (see Photograph 6.1). The languages of these people have extensive vocabulary with which to discuss and express the finer variations of the animals' markings, and a conversation about them is said more to resemble one of antique dealers or wine connoisseurs than what might be expected elsewhere from stockbreeders. In the Nuer and Dinka languages, words which might be translated as 'piebald' and 'guernsey' take on a whole new set of values.

Another interesting area of living art brings us back to a most conventional form in European terms, namely the area of gardens and landscape. The history of decorative gardens is a history of cultural influence, appropriation and creativity, and signs of the Far Eastern garden in Britain provide an excellent example of the process. Indeed, most of the flowers we value for cultivation have their origins in China, as do features of the Japanese garden to which we attribute many favoured varieties of trees and shrubs. Japanese gardens were created by several wealthy families in Europe and elsewhere in the nineteenth century, and finding and restoring these has become an aim of a Japanese Garden Society created in Britain in 1993.

The appeal of these Japanese gardens does not often derive from a wider interest in Japanese culture, but their intrinsic aesthetic qualities seem to offer something intangible to their aficionados, sometimes described as 'haunting' or 'spiritual'. They provide a way of creating a 'scene' or a possibly miniature

Photograph 6.1   An example of Dinka cattle, whose aesthetic qualities are discussed in this chapter (photograph courtesy of Jeremy Coote)

'landscape' which has been a European endeavour for centuries. Whether in practice in a tiny space or a country estate, or in two-dimensional form in a painting, creating a landscape has been an important part of the artistic worlds in the East, too, and this has been an area of the deepest cultural reciprocity. It is not necessarily the way in which the world is depicted or perceived in all societies, however.

In several of the major galleries of Australia (and undoubtedly other countries with a parallel history) it is possible to observe a selection of depictions of the local landscapes made through the period of colonization and beyond by artists who variously came from Europe, were born in Australia, and those whose origins are largely Aboriginal. Since many of the galleries also boast a collection of European art, it is quite easy to discern the same periods and styles in the early European paintings of Australia, and distinguish these from the later Australian schools which developed as people born and brought up in the Australian landscape perceived their surroundings in a way less dominated by European traditions.

The stark contrast with Aboriginal depictions of some of the same scenery, which forms much of the subject matter of Howard Morphy's book,*Ancestral Connections* (1994), immediately opens up questions about the systems of classification which underlie the whole endeavour of two-dimensional representation of an environmental landscape. Landscape paintings, like maps, illustrate a culturally specific form, dating back to classical antiquity in the West, where it was rediscovered in the Renaissance, but even the idea of a landscape is not as universal as might be imagined. A collection of papers on *The Anthropology of Landscape* (Hirsch and O'Hanlon, 1995) provides some excellent examples of alternative ways in which this notion, which the editors see as a relationship between ideas of 'place' and the here-and-now of foreground actuality, and 'space' of background potentiality, may be understood.

> The model of landscape developed . . . is one predicated on the idea of landscape as process . . . this process is one which relates a 'foreground' everyday social life ('us the way we are') to a 'background' potential social existence ('us the way we might be'). It is a process that attains a form of timelessness and fixity in certain idealized and transcendent situations, such as painted landscape representation, but which can be achieved only momentarily, if ever, in the human world of social relationships. (Hirsch and O'Hanlon, 1995, p. 22)

One paper, which discusses the Piro people of Amazonian Peru, makes the point that in the rain forest the horizon does not recede away from the point of observation. The vegetation pattern which surrounds villages is 'seen' in terms of kinship and past activities associated with it:

> It is hard to see Amazonia as a landscape . . . The land does not recede away from a point of observation to the distant horizon, for everywhere vegetation occludes the view. (Gow, 1995, p. 43)

> For the native people of Bajo Urubamba, the local environment is a lived space. It is known by means of movement through it, seeing the traces of other people's movements and agency, and through the narratives of yet other people's agency. (Ibid., p. 59)

In Australian examples, too, notions of kinship are intimately bound up with ideas of place and space, through the ancestral connections with which they are attributed, and these are also bound up with notions of time and the passage through life and death. In another paper about a dense forest people, this time of Papua New Guinea, we are told about the importance of sounds to an understanding of the landscape. Here 'hiddenness' is perceived as inaudibility, rather than invisibility, and the landscape is one of 'articulation'.

Art for Gaining Access to 'Seeing the World'

As an anthropologist embarks upon a study, however, material objects in any society provide a useful focus for attention, a concrete set of phenomena for investigation and discussion with informants, and a fertile source of information about the people who make and use them. Local interpretations and evaluations of objects offer an excellent way to gain access to indigenous systems of classification which underpin the modes of thought and expression of the people under study. As Coote and Shelton point out in the introduction to their book on the anthropology of art and aesthetics, 'the art of a society can provide a fruitful starting-point for the analyst's explication of its world-view' (1992, p. 5).

A good explicit example of this is to be found in the paper by Ross Bowden in the same book, on the art and architecture of the Kwoma people of the Sepik River region of Papua New Guinea. Bowden has also written a fascinating book (1983) about the sculpture found among these same people. In all cases, art, architecture and sculpture, intricately carved and painted material objects strike the visitor as the epitome of what we have come to call primitive or tribal art, and examples are to be found on display in the most famous museums of the Western world. For the Kwoma, themselves, these objects are assigned quite different value: political, spiritual and symbolic, and they thus offer a particularly enlightening window to understanding the way they 'see the world', or their **collective representations**.

Bowden argues, for example, that the lavishly decorated ceremonial houses form visual counterparts for the roles men, in contrast to women, play in the structure of Kwoma social groups. These houses, where male members of a community meet for informal social interaction and to perform ceremonies, are located in the centre of villages, a geographical location which corresponds to the structurally central position men have in clan organization. Villages are made up of a group of related men, who remain together throughout their lives, and women move in and out of the village on marriage, which, in a society where divorce is common, may be quite a frequent occurrence.

Reflecting this, domestic homes, where individual men live with their wives and children, are scattered adjacent to the forest on the margins of the village. Unlike men, women do not form groups except in relation to those of their husbands, and they are excluded from the ceremonial house. Bowden argues that women's peripheral geographical position within a village expresses their 'peripheral' position structurally: that is the way they, as wives, form the links between groups rather than constituting their residential and social cores. Interestingly, Kwoma women display the art with which they are associated in the form of elaborate decorative scars on their own bodies (Williamson, 1979), art works which are of course carried with them when they move.

The construction of the ceremonial house, on the other hand, expresses male attributes sought and admired in Kwoma society. Men aspire to be killers in warfare, and to produce many children and great gardens, and these same qualities of homicidal aggression and human and horticultural fertility are attributed to ceremonial houses as well. This is explicitly expressed in the choice of timbers used to construct the elaborately carved and painted ridge pole and the longitudinal side beams, customarily made from the wood of a tree which in myth is ascribed superabundant masculine sexual potency. In the story this tree stands beside a forest track and whenever a woman, or girl, steps over one of its roots she immediately becomes pregnant, but girls who are not yet sexually mature are condemned to die in childbirth.

The splendid figures found in the carvings on the posts and beams in these buildings (see Photograph 6.2) also depict culture heroes which feature in Kwoma myths about the creation of fundamental features of Kwoma culture, such as the types of plants on which Kwoma rely for food, sago plants which yield the highest quantities of edible starch, and the central role played by exchange in the structure of Kwoma society. The literally hundreds of bark paintings on the ceilings illustrate the species of plants and animals that belong to the different clans, and Kwoma people say that any knowledgeable person that walks into these buildings can immediately determine the clan composition of the community from the paintings on display.

Art and Status: the Status of Art

An important aspect of the way in which objects may be interpreted in an ethnographic context is to see how they express and relate to systems of hierarchy and power. Among the Kwoma, described above, the Yena sculptures represent the spirit world which guarantees the continued fertility of the gardens and people, and underpins their system of morality and law. In the men's house they look down on discussions of social concern, and protect the human protagonists, who may not strike one another in the presence of the spirits. They stand for the authority and continuity of the wider community, and the skills men display when carving and painting these objects are thought to come directly from the supernatural world.

Photograph 6.2   Detail of the sculptures and bark paintings that decorate the ceiling of the Kwoma ceremonial men's house named *Wayipanal* in Bangwiss village, 1973. The sculpture depicts a clan spirit and the paintings are clan totems (photograph courtesy of Ross Bowden)

Elsewhere, notably in Africa, masks are used to disguise individuals handing down the judgements of the ancestors or spirits, and to separate the authoritative role being played from the person who is called upon to play it. The voice used during judgement will also very often be changed. Some art objects are shown only to people in certain positions in society. In several parts of the world it is an important feature of adult initiation rites to reveal ritual objects, which are often so beautifully carved that they are also easily classified as works of art. Anthony Forge (1970) wrote of the Abelam people, in Papua New Guinea, that showing the ritual objects for the first time towards the end of a traumatic initiation procedure heightens their apparent power, as well as increasing the significance of the whole ritual. A knowledge of how to perform such rituals, and even more of the creation of the art objects, demonstrates a special relationship with the supernatural world and a sure way to success in the local system of politics.

We shall return in the next section to examine further the meaning of art objects in a particular context, but it is interesting that an association with secular art is also capable of bestowing status. It was mentioned in the introduction that in cosmopolitan societies people accrue considerable status, and potentially wealth, through a knowledge of the value and authenticity of *objets d'art*. Furthermore, those in the most powerful positions influence the extent to which a work will be assigned a high value in artistic terms, or even whether it will be classified as art at all. In an exhibition at the Victoria and Albert Museum in London in 1995 one of the most appealing exhibits was an arrangement of garden gloves. For a collection of garden gloves to be deemed a work of art requires not only the declaration of the artist, but the agreement of a number of other agents along the way. In this case, members of the viewing public seemed to acquiesce with the decision, but they are sometimes left bewildered as to why mundane objects are attributed with such status.

In practice, it is not even necessary for people to understand why art is assigned a high value in order to acquire status through its ownership or display. Collections of art are commonplace in European country houses, which thereby express their heritage, if not necessarily any longer wealth, but in recent years it has become fashionable for companies to buy and display paintings in their foyers and executive rooms as an expression of their sophistication and economic power. The ownership of these paintings says little about the understanding of the company employees of the aesthetics and meaning of the object, rather the aim is to demonstrate corporate access to the elite world of high art with which it gains kudos by association.

We should not therefore be surprised to discover that some indigenous people also sport apparently meaningful objects largely for the kudos they acquire, rather than for any deep significance they display. An example of this is to be found in the elaborate **totem** poles owned by north-west American Indian peoples such as the Kwakiutl, Tlingit and Haida (whom we met in Chapter 3), which depict animals and, possibly, characters from their folk tales (see Photograph 6.3). These features are sometimes quite stylized, and they are open to symbolic interpretation, but their owners are usually much more concerned with the status they represent than with any stories they might depict:

> A piece carries with it a message that bears no palpable resemblance to the image itself: It is a 'status symbol.' The totem poles, houseposts, and most of the masks were signs of the high social standing of their owners. Even if a native viewer did not accurately decipher the iconic message of a given art work, he or she undoubtedly appreciated the social significance of the piece. The quantity and elaborateness of the works of art possessed by a person were public statements of the individual's relative position in the social hierarchy. As we know, members of Northwest Coast societies were vitally concerned with their relative social standing, so to them the symbolic messages transmitted via their art were far from trivial. (Anderson, 1989)

In neither case, corporate art or **totem** poles, is the iconography particularly significant, for it is the possession of the objects which is the crucial factor.

In an international context, people allocate one another status in a preconceived view of aesthetic value, and evidence of a highly developed aesthetic sense may be cited as an index of civilization. The reciprocal influences which have run between East and West since time immemorial are an illustration of this process, and in Europe the value placed on the acquisition of Chinese ceramics and Turkish carpets are just two examples where status has been assigned in one society to an art form developed in another. This is an area open to considerable negotiation, of course, and Japan now sports as characteristically Japanese many art forms originally developed in China.

Indeed, some Japanese writers claim that their country is superior to all others because their artistic accomplishments are developed in such subtle and deceptively simple ways. A single leaf, or a simple twist of paper, may be regarded as aesthetic achievements of the highest quality, and attention accorded to the wrapping and presentation of objects and ideas, as already discussed, is said to be greater than in any other civilization. Even objects wrapped for the most mundane reasons will receive a meticulous care which has brought Japan into the forefront of microchip technology, but it is the appreciation of aesthetic qualities which raises the level of civilization in a Japanese view.

Photograph 6.3 This Haida totem pole, originally from Queen Charlotte Islands, British Columbia, was acquired by Edward B. Tylor, and is now on display in the Pitt Rivers Museum, in Oxford (photograph: Joy Hendry, with permission of the Pitt Rivers Museum)

One Japanese author who has written on the subject of wrapping is Nukada Iwao, who argues that wrapping was first used everywhere for practical reasons, to carry food safely from the fields to the home, to keep the body warm in winter, and to protect from the elements. With the development of spiritual and religious ideas, this material form acquired all kinds of new significance in the realm of the sacred, he argues, and he cites examples from different parts of the world. The third and fourth stages of development, in his view, are those of art and courtesy. The wrapping forms took on an aesthetic quality, and provided a medium for the elaboration of beauty, but they also enabled their creators to communicate deeper expressions of concern and appreciation. They offered a way to communicate the status which an appreciation of beauty implied, both on the part of the donor and in recognition that the efforts would be appreciated by the recipient.

This kind of subtlety of communication is highly regarded in a Japanese view, and it is by no means limited to material culture. The choice of words and language is also tinged with an aesthetic quality, even in everyday discourse, as is the choice of clothes and interior design. These concerns are not, of course, unique to Japan, but the areas of overlap in artistic achievement recognizable in a Western context bring Japan into a universe of discourse more readily shared in the cosmopolitan world than are some of those found in societies technologically less developed. This is deceptive, however, because some of the deeply engrained differences may be overlooked.

Art and Meaning

In Chapter 3 I gave some examples of the kinds of meaning which may be transmitted in the wrapping of a gift, but it is important to remember that the whole notion of gift wrapping may carry different meaning in a Japanese view from that expected in many Western countries. In formal presentations, the wrapping may even be more important than the gift inside, and I know several Japanese people who have put the gifts they have received away without even opening them, perhaps to use again when they need to make a presentation. The wrapping is not 'mere decoration' to be ripped off and thrown away. It is itself, in all its glory, the medium of the message of the gift.

This quality of what outsiders may see as 'mere decoration' to carry deep and meaningful messages was raised in the last chapter when we considered the work of Michael O'Hanlon (1989) in his book about the Wahgi people of the Highlands of Papua New Guinea. Like Japanese wrapping, the adornment provides the medium which carries the message, the beautiful headdresses exhibiting directly the political clout of their wearers, and the use of the special shining qualities of pig's fat to embellish the skin is a direct demonstration of the health and fertility of the most important medium of wealth and exchange in this society. O'Hanlon elsewhere examines the implications of this lack of exegesis about artistic accomplishments among the peoples of Papua New Guinea (1992).

Also talking of Papua New Guinea, other writers have emphasized the competitive element of the ritual bodily attire. Just as gifts from one group to another are lined up in an ostentatious display of wealth, one of the aims of the headdress is to impress and overawe the spectators who attend. The body is decorated to an enhanced, idealized form which in this case is a general representation of the collective health and prosperity of the wider group. In the Trobriand Islands, it is the canoe boards which play this role:

> The function of the Trobriand canoe-boards is to dazzle their owners' Kula trade partners, making them take leave of their senses and trade more of their valuables than they otherwise would have done. The designs on the canoe-boards identify the boat with the original flying canoe of Trobriand mythology, and symbolise slipperiness, flowing water, and wisdom, all of which help to attract the luxury goods the expedition hopes for. In this example, the form and content of the art work together to produce magical, aesthetic effects (Coote and Shelton, 1992, p. 9)

This is essentially the same competitive element mentioned above in reference to corporate art, and bodily and other art is also found in complex societies as an index or reflection of structural divisions within that society. The hairstyles discussed in the previous chapter provide an excellent example, as do other forms of bodily attire. People in complex societies do not necessarily share taste and the fact that punk bodily art differs from more acceptable tastes expresses their rejection of wider society. Similarly, if one section of society expresses a preference for art forms of a certain kind, another section may well define their own boundaries with that section by belittling it. Popular music is a particularly apt example.

The notion of 'taste' underlies this phenomenon, as social groups express their shared ideas in terms of what they admire and seek to acquire. 'Taste' becomes a way of expressing values which are clearly 'contested' by different social groups, and this notion of contested value is an area of recent interest for anthropologists. In small scale societies, in contrast, taste tends to be shared by members of different generations, genders, economic groups and so forth. In complex societies these are the lines along which divisions of opinion may occur, as well as along lines of education and social class. Interestingly, however, artistic taste would seem to be one area where there is little difference based on gender.

Aesthetics

These aspects of the communicative properties of art and decoration are again difficult to describe in detail. Why one object should be regarded as tasteful by one social group and distasteful by another is beyond easy explanation. Indeed, the explanation may be couched in terms of upbringing and education. One learns how to recognize a valuable object by being around objects assigned value in a similar value system. One acquires a gut reaction which will coincide with those whom one respects and admires, or, in the case of punk and other revolutionary art, one specifically sets out to flout those accepted values and produce something which will shock. In all these cases, there is meaning which lies embedded in the art itself, and one area of meaning is concerned with the quality we call *aesthetic*. This is an area about which anthropologists themselves disagree.

On the one hand, there is the view that the whole idea of aesthetics is culture-bound, like the notion of taste, so that an aesthetic appreciation is itself a product of a particular society which can only be properly applied within that social context. Those who hold that view see others applying this culture-bound aesthetic sense in other societies, but feel that their judgements are misplaced. They may even feel that the sense of universality of aesthetic sense is a kind of faith, held in the context of art as theology is with religion. Alfred Gell, who expressed this view in his paper in the Coote and Shelton book (1992), goes on to suggest that art has become a sort of religion, whose shrines are theatres, libraries and art galleries, and whose priests and bishops are the painters and poets.

The other view is that there exists an aesthetic sense in any society, although it will of course be interpreted and evaluated in socially appropriate ways. This view argues for a human capacity to appreciate beauty and experience a sensory reaction to the physical qualities of an object, such as form and texture, which will be related to non-material aspects of that object within its cultural system of knowledge. In his introduction to the anthropology of art, Howard Morphy (1994) gives an example of the way a particular aesthetic effect, namely that of shimmering or shining brilliance, may be highly valued, but with different interpretations, in three different societies.

Among the people with whom he, himself, worked, the Yolngu of Northern Australia, the shimmering effect applied to paintings with a cross-hatching technique is interpreted as the power of the ancestral beings shining out of a creation which is anyway seen as a manifestation of their existence. The value of brilliance is reiterated in myth and song in Yolngu social life. The Wahgi, too, value a shining effect, this time created on their bodies, as described above, but here the association is with health and fertility, with the power and strength of the group as a whole. Morphy's third example is of the shining effect of a black mask valued by the Mende people of Sierra Leone, particularly during a ritual dance display as an expression of female health.

In all these cases, shining is itself a quality selected for particular note. Elsewhere, efforts may be made to reduce shine, such as when a woman powders her nose, or a set of photographs is ordered with a matt finish. The value of shine has undergone a major change in British society, perhaps reflecting an underlying economic and political shift of values. Hard polished wood is still highly prized in antique furniture, but there has been a shift of appreciation towards the originally cheaper pine which is not only easier to care for, but also more politically correct. In the days of shiny polished wood, and bronze and silver ornaments, their ownership and display was a way of demonstrating the economic resources to engage staff to maintain their quality. Interestingly, the lower quality wood, which has been stripped of its glossy paint, is now quite expensive to acquire!

Definitions of Art

The problem with defining the notion of aesthetics is only part of the wider problem of defining the notion of 'art'. We have been applying both terms throughout this chapter, without pausing to define them, partly because an understanding of some of the issues we have raised is vital to an appreciation of this problem. Many of the books cited below tackle the issue of definition, and the reader may pursue the ideas presented, but in the end the whole endeavour of definition is also so culturally bound that it seemed better not to engage in it at the outset. The next chapter is almost entirely devoted to the problems of defining the term 'religion', which runs into parallel problems and the reader will probably find that exercise taxing enough.

A few words are in order, however, by way of summary, for the main problem centres around the varying and disputed attitudes to the concept of art in the English language. Morphy (1994) points out that in the nineteenth century a Western definition of art involved such a strong notion of civilization that the idea of 'primitive art' was almost a contradiction in terms. Even now, the three aspects of a European definition of art that he identifies are very revealing of European ideas: first, the institutional one, whereby objects are deemed art or otherwise depending on whether they are chosen to be displayed in galleries as opposed to museums, and therefore classified as 'fine art' as opposed to 'folk art' or 'craft'; secondly, a definition in terms of attributes makes reference to aesthetics again, but also skills and semantic properties; and finally, Morphy sees the *intent* of the artist as important:

> art objects are ones that are *intended* to be works of art by their makers. With most types of object, intention is subordinate to functional or institutional specification – the intention to make a boat is insufficient if the object is incapable of floating. In the case of art objects the individual has a little more freedom, since the category is always open to persuasion. (1994, p. 652)

which leads to the extraordinary situation we find in art galleries, where almost anything, or indeed, nothing, can be designated as 'art'.

The boundaries which exist between fine arts, crafts and artifacts are now beginning to break down, however, since no clear distinction, anyway often a product of Western hegemony, is made in all social settings. The garden gloves referred to earlier were part of an interesting exhibition of Japanese 'Studio Crafts' which combined a wonderfully irreverent mix of functional artifacts, sometimes called 'traditional', with a dramatic display of abstract 'modern' artistic constructions, one of which, a steep upward slope, is entitled 'The M25', presumably after the usually clogged London ring-road. As mentioned above, Japan is a country where the beauty of an apparent simplicity of form has for long been recognized among the most mundane objects, as well as in the creations of the aristocracy, a point illustrated in a book now well known in many countries, entitled *How to Wrap Five Eggs* (Oka, 1967).

Intent is therefore also a problem, although this is also cited in Layton's (1991) introduction to the anthropology of art where he gives a possible definition as concerned with objects made primarily to be aesthetically pleasing rather than for a pragmatic functional purpose. He considers discussions of ancient Greek philosophy about the formal properties of beauty, but also the capacity of art to represent the world around us in a way which enhances our perceptions of it and indeed, which induces emotional response. Art historians in the Western world look for innovation in artistic accomplishments, and associate these advances with particular periods in the past. Their approach is premised in an idea of creativity of the artist.

This premise is not necessarily shared by people in other societies whose work has been deemed 'art' by the outside world. In some societies, including those of Australian Aborigines, and the Sepik people discussed above, any one of them is thought capable of creating their painting and sculpture. Indeed, the skills are not thought to be talents given only to certain individuals, but to be revelations of the spiritual world through the human beings involved. Neither is there an indigenous concept of originality in art, for since the source of the works is to be found in the spirit world, it is regarded as vital to replicate them to keep them in good order. Thus, the older Kwoma houses are burned down to be rebuilt, and ancient sculptures sold to early travellers, and now maybe carefully guarded in Western museums, are apparently less valuable to the people whose ancestors made them than some purists might think.

In the Western world, replication of a work of art is considered acceptable as part of the learning process, but passing it off as one's own would be a forgery. Of course, in the past, schools of a single artist produced work now attributed only to that one name, and during certain periods art was also much more closely associated with religion than it is now. Some Western people might still argue that they receive their artistic talent from God, but those whose 'art' is a revelation of the spiritual world would possibly not classify their work as art in a Western sense at all! In the next chapter we turn our attention to what it is we mean by the term 'religion'.

References

Anderson, R. L. (1989) *Art in Small-Scale Societies* (Englewood Cliffs, NJ: Prentice-Hall).

Bowden, Ross (1983) *Yena: art and ceremony in a Sepik society* (Oxford: Pitt Rivers Museum).

Bowden, Ross (1992) 'Art, Architecture, and Collective Representations in a New Guinea Society', in Jeremy Coote and Anthony Shelton (eds), *Anthropology, Art and Aesthetics* (Oxford: Clarendon) pp. 67–93.

Coote, Jeremy and Anthony Shelton (eds) (1992) *Anthropology, Art, and Aesthetics* (Oxford: Clarendon).

Faris, J. C. (1971) *Nuba Personal Art* (London: Duckworth).

Forge, Anthony (1970) 'Learning to see in New Guinea', in Philip Mayer (ed.),*Socialization: The Approach from Social Anthropology* (London: Tavistock).

Gell, Alfred (1992) 'The Technology of Enchantment and the Enchantment of Technology', in Jeremy Coote and Anthony Shelton (eds),*Anthropology, Art, and Aesthetics* (Oxford: Clarendon), pp. 40–63.

Gow, Peter (1995) 'Land, People and Paper in Western Amazonia', in Eric Hirsch and Michael O'Hanlon (eds), *The Anthropology of Landscape: Perspectives in Place and Space* (Oxford: Clarendon), pp. 43–62.

Hirsch, Eric and Michael O'Hanlon (eds) (1995) *The Anthropology of Landscape: Perspectives in Place and Space* (Oxford: Clarendon).

Layton, Robert (1991) *The Anthropology of Art* (Cambridge University Press).

Moeran, Brian (1984) *Lost Innocence* (Berkeley, Los Angeles and London: University of California Press).

Morphy, Howard (1994) 'The Anthropology of Art', in Tim Ingold (ed.),*Companion Encyclopedia of Anthropology* (London, Routledge).

Nukada Iwao (1977) *Tsutsumi* [Wrapping] (Tokyo: Hosei Daigaku Shuppansha; in Japanese).

O'Hanlon, Michael (1989) *Reading the Skin: Adornment, Display and Society among the Wahgi* (London: British Museum Publications).

O'Hanlon, Michael (1992) 'Unstable images and second skins: artifacts, exegesis and assessments in the New Guinea Highlands', *Man* (N.S.) **27**: 587–608.

Oka, Hideyuki (1967) *How to Wrap Five Eggs: Japanese Design in Traditional Packaging* (New York: Weatherhill; Tokyo: Bijutsu Shuppansha).

Williamson, Margaret Holmes (1979) 'Cicatrisation of Women among the Kwoma',*Mankind*, **12**: 35–41.

Further Reading

Banks, Marcus and Howard Morphy (1997) *Rethinking Visual Anthropology* (New Haven, Conn. and London: Yale University Press).

Moeran, Brian (1997) *Folk Art Potters of Japan: Beyond an Anthropology of Aesthetics* (Richmond: Curzon).

Morphy, Howard (1991) *Ancestral Connections* (Chicago University Press).

Novels

Ishiguro, Kazuo, *An Artist of the Floating World* (Harlow: Faber, 1986), is a novel which illustrates the relationships between Japanese artists in the turbulence of pre-Second World War Japan.

Films

The Wodaabe (Leslie Woodhead and Mette Bovin, 1988), a film in the Granada 'Disappearing World' series, is about the nomadic lives of a Fulani people of Nigeria who are described as 'obsessed with male beauty'. A part of the film is devoted to the extraordinary facial decorations they apply.

Parts of the 'Strangers Abroad' film on Sir Walter Baldwin Spencer (see Chapter 2) is about Australian Aboriginal art and its meaning.

CHAPTER 7

Cosmology I: Religion, Magic and Mythology

Religion, Science and Cosmology

Until the last chapter, we were looking rather broadly at the way in which anthropologists observe and make sense of particular societies, the way they try to understand systems of classification and value, and the social relationships into which they enter. In Chapter 6 we began to look at contested ideas about objects and their meaning. It was mentioned at the outset of this book that another important task for anthropologists is the translation back of their findings into their own language and their own system of categories. This is what makes it possible to compare their findings with those of people working elsewhere, or, at least, to present a description capable of comparison with those produced elsewhere.

Important categories of analysis have therefore been those which represented divisions made in the societies of the academics doing the analysis – religion, politics, economics – and broad headings for the chapters which follow include these very three. However, as we have begun to see, problems arise when anthropologists try to fit the indigenous categories of other parts of the world into their own clearly defined notions, and all kinds of other descriptions are needed to describe local ideas. In the pages which follow we shall examine some of these problems as well as some of the descriptions, and we will introduce some analytical notions which have fewer restricting connotations to detract from our understanding of people with very different ideas.

This and the next chapter are concerned with what anthropologists have come to call **cosmology**, or, in other words, broad ideas and explanations which people have about the world in which they live and their place in that world. These include ideas about the creation of the world, or the arrival of the people in question into that world. They include notions of other worlds, worlds from which they may believe they have come, and to which they go after death in this world, or indeed during transcendental experiences in this world. Until now we have concentrated on social relations between living beings, but in all cultures there are notions about beings beyond that living world, about places and events beyond those of the strictly tangible, and these are usually related to explanations about life itself.

We are in the area of **religion**, but as we shall see, some of the theories and practices found around the world make the drawing up of a valid universal definition a virtually impossible task. In this chapter we shall consider some of the problems of definition, and in the next we will turn to examine some indigenous ideas and some actual situations. We are also in the area of **science**, and many readers may feel that this is where we should now turn for answers to all the above questions. A minimal definition of science is 'a body of knowledge', with further qualifications about observation, experiment and induction, but let us examine that concept too.

Definitions and Distinctions

Various attempts have been made to define the word 'religion'. Edward Burnett Tylor, who was the first professor of social anthropology at the University of Oxford, tried to be very broad when he suggested religion be defined as 'the belief in spiritual beings'. (1913, p. 8). A problem arises immediately, however, for there are plenty of people whose apparently devout religious activities involve no spiritual beings. Buddhists, for example, are concerned with achieving a state beyond the spiritual, a state which does not require the intervention of a god or gods. Indeed, a Buddhist specialist working in Sri Lanka enjoys telling people about how two different monks there told him quite clearly that the word usually translated as 'religion' has nothing to do with gods (Gombrich 1971, p. 46).

This statement sounds crazy to a reader brought up in the Judaeo-Christian tradition, but it makes perfect sense in the local language of Sinhala where 'religion', as far as Buddhism is concerned, refers to a path leading beyond this world. Other ideas about spirits and gods are part of worldly life and defined quite differently. The names of some of the gods come from Hinduism, but this set of beliefs is not classified as 'religion' as far as local Buddhists are concerned. As discussed in Chapter 5, a parallel situation was found in post-Second World War Japan, where Buddhism is again regarded as 'religion', but indigenous ideas about gods and spirits, which form part of a complex known as Shinto, were described by many as 'superstition'.

Tylor's definition above may also include notions such as **magic** and witchcraft, which many would object fall outside the area of 'religion' as such, and a category was subsequently developed of **magico-religious beliefs** which was broad enough to include all the above phenomena as well as ideas of pollution and taboo. Perhaps because of their own prejudices, based on deeply felt distinctions, several scholars tried to find ways of distinguishing between magic and religion, however (see Tambiah, 1990, for further reading providing a detailed historical analysis of this propensity from a Sri Lankan anthropologist). Sir James Frazer, whose monumental twelve-volume work, *The Golden Bough*, addresses just these issues, argued for the following distinction:

[**Magic**] assumes that in nature one event follows another necessarily and invariably without the intervention of a spiritual or personal agency. Thus its fundamental conception is identical with that of modern science; underlying the whole system is a faith, implicit but real and firm, in the order and uniformity of nature. (1922, p. 49)

In contrast,

[**Religion**] is a propitiation or conciliation of powers superior to man which are believed to control and direct the course of nature and of human life. Thus defined, religion consists of two basic elements, a theoretical and a practical, namely a belief in powers higher than man and an attempt to propitiate or please them. (Ibid., p. 50)

With an abundance of examples, Frazer demonstrates that there are but two basic principles underlying the practice of magic. The first is that like produces like, so that a magician trying to bring about an effect may imitate the effect he wants to produce, for example by sticking pins into a model of the victim. This is what he calls *homeopathic* or *imitative magic*. The second, *contagious* magic, assumes that 'things which have once been in contact with each other continue to act on each other at a distance'. Thus, acting on something which was once part of a person will still affect that person even when no longer attached to them, leading to spells involving the hair, finger nails and so forth.

Frazer was writing in the evolutionary mode characteristic of his time when he suggested that there had been, everywhere, an Age of Magic, which was followed by an Age of Religion, when at least the more intelligent people realized the falsity of some of these theories and turned instead to superior beings. This move involved an assumption that nature is to some extent elastic or variable, however, subject to deflection by a mightier power, the opposite of the assumption which underpins both magic and science. Close observation proved this to be untrue, he argues, so thinking people moved into a third age, the Age of Science, which rejects both the previous modes of thought. He then makes a wonderfully futuristic statement:

> Yet the history of thought should warn us against concluding that because scientific theory of the world is the best that has yet been formulated, it is necessarily complete and final. We must remember that . . . the generalisations of *science*, or, in common parlance, the laws of nature are merely hypotheses devised to explain that ever-shifting phantasmagoria of thought which we dignify with the high-sounding names of the world and the universe. In the last analysis magic, religion, and science are nothing but theories of thought; and as science has supplanted its predecessors, so it may hereafter be superseded by some more perfect hypothesis. (Ibid., p. 712, my emphasis).

In practice, it seems that magic and religion persist, even in a world dominated by scientific thought, and the 'more intelligent', or 'thinking people', as Frazer would have them, are by no means excluded. Malinowski took up this subject, and argued, moreover, that scientific thought exists everywhere, alongside ideas about magical powers. Based on his own experience with the 'savage' people of the Trobriand Islands, he argued in his essay *Magic, Science and Religion* that they were aware of and distinguished all three modes of thought, demonstrating the existence of rational explanations for technological routines, which form a body of knowledge easily comparable with what we call science.

He argued for a clear distinction between these and ideas of magic and religion to which people turned in times of uncertainty, and explains that Trobriand Islanders fishing in a lagoon, where conditions are known and quite safe, practise no magic, but when they venture out into the ocean, where there may be sudden changes in the weather, they take ritual precautions to seek to avert the possible danger. Furthermore, on the subject of the failure of magic always to succeed, he wrote:

> we should vastly underrate the savage's intelligence, logic and grasp of experience if we assumed that he is not aware of it and that he fails to account for it. (1974, p. 85)

Malinowski's distinction between magic and religion refines Frazer's on two levels. He proposes:

> **magic** as a practical art consisting of acts which are only means to a definite end expected to follow later on; **religion** as a body of self-contained acts being themselves the fulfilment of their purpose . . .

> **Magic** . . . had to be handed over in direct filiation from generation to generation
> . . . it remains . . . in the hands of specialists . . . **Religion**, on the other hand, . . .
> is an affair of all, in which everyone takes an active and equivalent part. (Ibid.,
> pp. 88–9, my emphasis)

One of the problems here is that, according to Malinowski's distinction, some
of the practical aspects of religious worship in Roman Catholic countries look
pretty much like magic: for example the conversion of bread and wine into
the body and blood of Jesus Christ is an act with a very specific end, as are
rites of exorcism, and so forth, and they are both carried out by priests who
have been given much training – in other words, experts whose role is hardly
'equal' to that of their parishioners.

Durkheim had proposed a similar distinction to the second half of
Malinowski's one, however, when he insisted that religion needs a moral
community, whereas in magic, laymen are merely clients. He formulated a
definition of 'religion' as:

> A unified system of beliefs and practices relative to sacred things, that is to say,
> things set apart and forbidden – beliefs and practices which unite into one single
> moral community called a Church, all those who adhere to them. (1915, p. 47)

This definition, while useful, presupposes the acceptance of a universal
division of the universe into the two categories, **sacred** and **profane**, as well as
a very corporate concept of the community, neither of which always hold up
in practice. Indeed, in several societies the sacred, as we might understand the
term in English, is found to pervade all spheres of life, and religious practice,
where there are ascetics and other individuals who seek personal salvation,
may also be found to be a very lonely and isolated pursuit. The case of
Buddhism is a very pertinent one again, for the search for *nirvana* is precisely
concerned with removing oneself from social life, though those who achieve it
may be expected to return to help others along.

It has, over the years, proved very difficult to find an acceptable universal
definition of religion, though there are clearly resemblances between the ideas
of these different thinkers. Before continuing with the examination of
indigenous ideas, let us turn to examine some of the ways in which ideas
about 'religion' have been investigated by those who drew up the definitions.

Origins of Religion

In the nineteenth century people were greatly concerned with the origins of
religion and they looked to the so-called primitive societies for ideas about

how religion might have developed. This approach reflected contemporary scientific advances which were apparently disproving religious beliefs. By their very nature these theories were speculative, but some of them had a great impact on the thinking of the time, and a few influenced social anthropology in quite a profound way. The various theories are discussed in a very readable manner in the book by Evans-Pritchard entitled *Theories of Primitive Religion* (1965), where they are divided into the *psychological* and the *sociological*.

Notable among the psychological were the rather similar, though independently developed theories of Herbert Spencer and Edward Tylor, which argued that notions of the spiritual were derived from the apparent existence of a dual self. There was the self of the waking world and the self of dreams, trances and death, Spencer imagined the primitive person reasoning. He argued that as dead people could appear in dreams, the earliest idea of the supernatural must be associated with ghosts, so that ancestor worship must have been the first form of religion. It was inevitable, he argued, that ghosts would develop into gods, so that the offerings to the dead to please them would gradually become libations and sacrifices to the gods to propitiate them.

Tylor's theory was also rooted in the idea of a self of dreams, but he focused on the notion of a soul which could act separately from the body. He saw primitive people attributing souls also to animals and even to inanimate objects. These ideas constituted a primitive religion known as **animism**, according to Tylor, and these souls became the spirits of his minimal definition, which eventually developed into the gods and God of more highly developed religions in which they took control of the destiny of man. Although anthropologists have come up with detailed descriptions of religions of this sort, which show great differences between them, common parlance still seems to describe animism as a kind of universal earlier form of religion.

Evans-Pritchard points out that in both cases the arguments were mere speculation. Each of the writers simply imagines himself in the shoes of some so-called primitive man, but neither has any evidence at all that things did indeed develop in this way. Dreams might have led to speculations about souls and ghosts, but there is no real way of knowing, and there is no particular reason why these should have developed into gods. There were many other attempts to explain religion in this 'psychological' way, but Evans-Pritchard dismisses them all, pointing out that psychological states vary from one individual to another, and in one individual from time to time, so these states could not serve to explain social behaviour which exists independently of the psychological states it might or might not induce:

in an individual's experience the acquisition of rites and beliefs precedes the emotions which are said to accompany them later in adult life. He learns to participate in them before he experiences any emotion at all, so the emotional state, whatever it may be, and if there is one, can hardly be the genesis and explanation of them. A rite is part of the culture the individual is born into, and it imposes itself on him from the outside, like the rest of his culture. It is a creation of society, not of individual reasoning or emotion, though it may satisfy both; and it is for this reason that Durkheim tells us that a psychological interpretation of a social fact is invariably a wrong interpretation. (1965, p. 46)

Evans-Pritchard goes on to discuss sociological theories, and the most ingenious is that of Durkheim, himself, explained in his book, *The Elementary Forms of Religious Life* (1915), where he also proposed the working definition quoted above. Durkheim was convinced that the simplest form of religion was a system known as a *totemic clan cult*, found among Australian Aborigines called the Arunta, and also in North America. This religion brought together the worship of ancestors with the notion of a **totem** to represent them. The totem was a sacred symbol which stood for the clan that it represented, and rites of worship served to recharge the sense of belonging and solidarity of the clan itself. God, for these people, was simply the clan itself divinized.

Durkheim argued that all the elements of more advanced religions were to be found in this system, which had elsewhere gradually developed over time, so that other religions were simply more complicated versions of the same idea. He marshalled evidence to demonstrate that rites in any religious system served to draw people together and to renew in them a sense of solidarity and communality as they worshipped their gods, which stood for the society, and eventually God, when polytheism gave way to monotheism. These actions were carried out by individuals, but they existed in collective form which transcended individual participation. The driving force was society itself, also the object of worship, so that God was simply society divinized.

Durkheim argued that in secular times, the same function could be performed by patriotism. In the French Revolution a cult had arisen around the notions of the Fatherland, Liberty and Equality, and he hoped that humanitarian values would replace the spiritual ones. Evans-Pritchard admires Durkheim's 'brilliant and imaginative' theory, but he calls it yet another 'just-so story', based on insufficient and atypical ethnographic evidence (1965, p. 64). He chose **totemism** to discuss, assuming people with simple technology would have a similar simple religion, but this is only one kind of totemism, and even in other Australian groups it was quite different, nor was it particularly characteristic of all people with simple technology.

Indeed, as we saw in the previous chapter, the 'totem' poles of North West America, where the word originated, apparently have no such function. Again, the seeking of origins must be little more than conjecture, Evans-Pritchard argues. The theories may be true, but equally they may be false. As for totemism, the whole subject became something of anthropological red herring, eventually dispensed with very firmly by Lévi-Strauss in the early 1960s when he applied his then new form of **structural analysis** to the subject to argue that theories about it said more about the theorists than the people under consideration. In Europe, anyway, the word seems less used now than animism, and totem poles are probably back in place in Canada, in popular thought.

Explanations of Religious Phenomena

Anthropologists eventually turned from trying to establish the origins of religious phenomena to seeking explanations of them within their social context. Durkheim's grand evolutionary religious theory may have foundered, but his insistence on the identification of **social facts** in any study continued to be much more influential. Instead of working out explanations of behaviour by trying to enter the mind of those participating, he urged researchers to seek social constraints which exist outside the individuals. Religious faiths and moral systems provide a rich source of such constraints into which any one individual is gradually socialised, and these also provide the social facts an anthropologist should seek.

The interpretation of these facts within the wider social context falls into various types, two of which have subsequently been described as **functional'** and '**structural**', though they are not completely separate and the latter has at least two distinct forms. Examples of these will be given below, along with an attempt to explain this classification. We shall also examine briefly the association of religious phenomena with moral systems, a subject which will recur in Chapter 9, and we shall look at explanations of some quite extraordinary manifestations of religious phenomena which have apparently arisen in times of great social change. Other examples of reactions to social change will emerge in the next chapter.

Functional Explanations

One set of sociological explanations of religion seeks to analyse religious rites for their capacity to promote social cohesion, to encourage a spirit of co-operation, and to support the social structure of a particular society, just as

Durkheim proposed. These explanations also sought to relate religious systems to the social and political system in which they were found, and as detailed ethnography became available, religious behaviour could be analysed as part of the total set of social facts to form a coherent system. Radcliffe-Brown's work was of this type, and his analysis of the religious life of the Andaman Islanders was a specific example of his more general theory on the subject, later to be dubbed **structural functionalism.**

Malinowski's approach, on the other hand, related religion, magic and the related subject of **mythology** to very specific human needs, providing what became known as essentially *functional* explanations. For example, he explained the magical practices associated with fishing at sea, where sudden storms might bring danger, as efforts to control adverse, unknown factors as opposed to the predictable ones associated with fishing in the safer lagoon. *Mourning rites* he explained as serving to reintegrate the group's shaken solidarity on losing a member, and the re-establishment of the morale of the community. There were personal benefits in comforting the bereaved, Malinowski argued, but he also saw the anthropologist's job as showing the value of phenomena for social integrity and the continuity of culture.

Mythology he saw as a *codification of belief*, which acted as a *charter for ritual*, justifying *rites, ceremonies* and *social and moral rules.* Thus, for example, myths about the points of origin of local groups he explained as justification for the clan hierarchy, and myths concerned with death as a kind of screen between man and 'the vast emotional void' which would otherwise gape beyond death (1974, p. 138). It may sound sacrilegious and somewhat trite to say so, but this line of argument brings the great books of world faiths, such as the Bible and the Qur'an, into the category of mythology, because they serve much the same purpose. We need to recognize that the English language use of the word 'mythology' implies a disbelief which is disrespectful of people who may hold their own myths as truth.

Following the line of argument which sees **science** as another type of faith, we can better understand the conflicts and rows which arose in the nineteenth century when Darwin proposed a theory of evolution which appeared to disagree with the explanation of the origins of the human race propounded in Genesis. Those who took both seriously felt they had to decide which one to 'believe', and this period could be seen as a turning point in the dislocation of security. In complex societies, people have come to live with apparently conflicting world views, and their cosmologies may include scientific, religious, and even magical elements. Indeed, in Japan, a sick person may well consult a diviner as well as a doctor, as we shall see in the next chapter, and she may also visit a shrine or temple to pray for recovery (Ohnuki-Tierney, 1984).

In some ways, Malinowski went too far in making such a clear distinction between magic, science and religion, because his definitions did not always apply elsewhere, as we noted above. However, it is useful, though perhaps sometimes a little alarming, to consider science as part of a wider cosmology, in the same way as magic and religion. They all aim to provide theories about the world, as Frazer suggested, and they all also offer practical, *functional* ways of dealing with problems. After all, for many of us, science is rather mystical, even if we do have more faith in it to offer explanations of illness and disaster than we do in magic or religion – but it is *faith*, rather than knowledge, in many cases!

Even practising scientists are aware of the mysteries which remain to be explained, and the extent to which they make assumptions which may later prove to be unfounded. Much of their learning is of 'theories', which are the best available understanding of a phenomenon at the time it was made, but which may well be disproved as further knowledge comes to light. Medical doctors are aware too of the enormous psychological value of their prescriptions, and they are not averse to offering what is known as a *placebo*, with no specific pharmaceutical value, if they feel their patients will benefit. Practitioners of East Asian medicine tend to allow more time and attention to their patients than Western doctors do, because they see this as an important part of the healing process.

The most frightening diseases are those which appear to have no cure, or worse, no understanding, such as Aids and certain forms of cancer. Once diagnosed by 'scientific' rationale as a hopeless case, sufferers and their families anywhere are often open to suggestions about alternative healers, and they may travel long distances if they feel there is a chance that they could be 'magically' cured. A friend of mine who was told she was suffering from terminal cancer travelled from Oxford to Mexico to learn about a special diet, which has apparently held her symptoms at bay for several years now, and the strength of public support for this kind of venture may be seen when communities raise the funds to send one local child half-way around the world to be treated at a clinic of special renown.

The Structuralist Approach

Another influential approach, which differs quite fundamentally from the structural functional, as it was called (which examined the *functional* role of components of a particular society for maintaining the social *structure*), is the **structural analysis**; of the French anthropologist, Claude Lévi-Strauss, who was more interested in a universal organizational capacity of the human mind. We have mentioned that he applied this method to the subject of totemism, but he developed his ideas most successfully in the analysis of **mythology**, including nursery rhymes, just-so stories and other collectively owned materials, when he noticed amazing similarities in the structure of stories from widely separated parts of the world.

> Mythology confronts the student with a situation which at first sight appears contradictory. On the one hand it would seem that in the course of a myth anything is likely to happen. There is no logic, no continuity. Any characteristic can be attributed to any subject; every conceivable relation can be found. With myth, everything becomes possible. But on the other hand, this apparent arbitrariness is belied by the astounding similarity between myths collected in widely different regions. Therefore the problem: If the content of a myth is contingent, how are we going to explain the fact that myths throughout the world are so similar. (Lévi-Strauss 1963, p. 208)

Lévi-Strauss collected huge volumes of stories, including several different versions of the same tale, divided them up into what he perceived as their smallest elements, and analysed the structure which he felt was common to all, by looking at the relations between these elements. He concluded that they act as devices for apparently mediating important and usually impossible oppositions such as those between life and death, man and god, nature and culture. The analyses are often long, complicated and not always immediately convincing, but to give a flavour of the idea let us examine part of his attempt to explain why the role of a **trickster** is so often played by a raven or a coyote in many native American myths:

> If we keep in mind that mythical thought always progresses from the awareness of oppositions towards their resolution, the reason . . . becomes clearer. We need only assume that two opposite terms with no intermediary always tend to be replaced by two equivalent terms which admit of a third one as a mediator; then one of the polar terms and the mediator become replaced by a new triad, and so on. (Ibid., p. 224)

Through this process, Lévi-Strauss identifies a mediating structure in the native American myths in which the initial pair *life* and *death* is replaced by a triad of agriculture (on the life side), warfare on the death side, and hunting in the middle (as having qualities of each). This is in its turn replaced by a further triad, where herbivorous animals replace agriculture, beasts of prey replace warfare, and carrion-eating animals, such as the ubiquitous raven and coyote, appear in the mediating position, again as having some qualities of each of the others. A story centred around one of these ambiguous characters thus usually appears to mediate the actually irreconcilable opposition between life and death.

Further details of this analysis, and other aspects of Lévi-Strauss's work, may be pursued in his book *Structural Anthropology* (1963), which serves as a good preliminary to the more difficult tomes of mythological analysis which he has also published, with intriguing titles such as *The Raw and the Cooked* and *From Honey to Ashes.* Another good and relatively accessible analysis of myth is to be found in his essay, the 'Myth of Asdiwal' (Lévi-Strauss, 1967). Because the oppositions he considers are usually impossible actually to mediate, characters who appear in the myths tend to be the same anomalous or abnormal beings such as monsters, incarnate deities or virgin mothers which, we noted in Chapters 2, provide the focus for taboos and ritual observance.

Edmund Leach, who introduced those ideas in a consideration of language, also put forward an interesting structural analysis in his *Genesis as Myth*, mentioned in passing in Chapter 5, where he sets out to resolve the paradox that Christians, who forbid incest, are all apparently descended from Adam and Eve. He argues that a series of stories which offer a number of examples of incest, some worse than others, place the tribal neighbours of the Israelites in varying degrees of inferior status. By comparison, the marriage of Abraham to his paternal half-sister seems almost virtuous, he argues. This, and indeed some of Lévi-Strauss's analysis, confirms a functional role, as Malinowski suggested, justifying the status quo in a particular social configuration.

The structural approach to religion may supplement the functional explanations discussed above, which have also been called **instrumental** explanations. As well as looking at the function of certain rites, the idea is to look for *meaning* which may be described as **expressive**, which may tell us something about the delineation of the important categories of society, or, as Radcliffe-Brown put it, 'express . . . their fundamental notions of life and nature' (1964, p. 330). In a more formal structural mode, however, we are back to the identification of systems of classification, and the association of anomalous and abnormal beings with mediation of impossible oppositions is another way to identify the liminal middle ground between these categories.

In the case of **rites of passage** people are moved from one category to another – an **instrumental** aspect of the rite, creating new adults, or members of a particular group, or moving people safely from one area or time zone to another, but the rites themselves divide up life into meaningful chunks, just as they divide up space and time for that particular people. This is the **expressive** aspect. Looking at religious activities in a structural way therefore also means looking for what they can tell us about the dividing up of people and their world.

Many studies since that time demonstrate the structural role of religious activities in any one case. My own work in Mexico revealed a neat parallel between the Holy Family emphasized by Mexican Catholics, which places the Virgin of Guadalupe in a position of greater importance than God, or even Jesus, and the actual Mexican family, where the mother very often plays the dominant role in holding things together. Mexican men sometimes have two or three different nuclear families they have fathered, and they are peripheral in the maintenance of even one. The real source of stability in any particular case is the mother who must find a way to provide for her children, so it is small wonder that Mexicans of both sexes prefer to bring their important prayers to a female source of divine power.

John Middleton's book, *Lugbara Religion* (1960), based on fieldwork in the Uganda/Belgian Congo borders in the 1950s, is an excellent example of an ethnography organized to present the expressive role of religious activities, which centre around ancestor worship held at shrines associated with the lineage groups important in everyday life:

> The cult of the dead is intimately connected with the maintenance of lineage authority. The exercise and acknowledgement of this authority are bound up with the cycle of lineage development. Senior men attempt to sustain their authority against their juniors' claim to independence, and the consequent conflict is conceived largely in mystical and ritual terms . . . I show how the men of a single lineage group manipulate the cult of the dead as a means to the acquisition and retention of authority (Middleton, 1960, p. v)

The chapters of the book are organized in such a way that the background information about Lugbara social and political life is presented first, then the details of the cults of the dead, both material and conceptual, after which the chief focus of the book – the ritual action – may be understood in its proper context. Finally, Middleton addresses the effect of the religious ideas on the moral community. The overall picture is one in which religious ideas reflect the social life of the Lugbara people, which is physically mapped out in the arrangement of shrines within the village compound.

Religion as a Moral System

Clearly in considering large world religions such as Christianity, Judaism, Islam, and the Indian religions, an important aspect of their role in society is to lay out the moral order by which people are expected to live. They are associated with books and teaching, much of which is concerned with spelling out these ethical codes. As mentioned briefly in Chapter 3, giving freely is usually a part of these codes, and it is their basis in **soteriology** or salvation of one sort or another which allows the principles of reciprocity to be applied to this apparent generosity, though it may not be seen in exactly that way. In these cases explanations of this world and the next will be inextricably linked to ideas of behaviour acceptable to the wider society.

In most Western countries, the legal system is based on Judaeo-Christian ideas, though now often tempered with a fair degree of 'humanism', and in the Islamic world much legislation is rooted in the Qur'an. Punishment meted out to criminals and others who break the law is often justified in moral terms, and those who escape the earthly justice system may fear retribution in heaven, or 'the other place'. The idea of 'burning in hell' is still part of common parlance, or at least it was until early 1996 when the Church of England declared hell a much less fiery place, perhaps in recognition of the fact that people may actually be less worried that this will be their fate than they used to be.

Not all religious traditions include such a clear connection with laying out a moral code. Indeed, in small-scale societies, moral values and the ideas we may term 'religious' pervade social life so completely that neither can be clearly separated from the rest of social interaction. Ancestors may be seen as the repositories of moral order, and illness and other misfortunes may be interpreted as an expression of their wrath, incurred almost immediately because of contraventions of moral or social rules. However, there may be no notion of sacredness associated with the activities of these former human beings. Explanations of misfortune may also manifest themselves in other ways, as we will see in Chapter 8. A more detailed consideration of social rules and the various mechanisms for their enforcement will be the subject matter of Chapter 9, on social control, so we will not persist with this subject here.

Cults: The Persistence of Religious Movements

Contrary to the evolutionary expectations mentioned at the beginning of this chapter, and despite the predictions of sociologists and others that modernization would bring with it secularization in the world at large, religion does not seem to be giving way to more 'rational' ways of explaining the world. Indeed, new religious sects are appearing abundantly around the world – and there is quite a variety to choose from. In Japan, people turn from one to another, seeking solutions to problems they may be experiencing, and in Britain, several Japanese new religious groups are quite active. The neighbour in Japan, mentioned in Chapter 3, who introduced me to the niceties of meeting further neighbours, became a Christian shortly after I left, and I came back to find two or three Japanese Buddhists among my students.

New religious movements have often appeared in times of great social change and upheaval, according to another variety of anthropological explanation, and some special **cults** demonstrate an interesting expression of cultural confusion. Typically where the lives of one people have been profoundly affected by the invasion, however peaceful, of another, religious reactions can be shown to express efforts to adjust in one way or another to the new situation. In North America, for example, there was widespread practice of a 'ghost dance' among the Plains Indians whose land and livelihood had been devastated by the arrival of Europeans. The aim of the dance was to rid the ancestral land of these new people and bring about a return of the native buffalo they had hunted, and the medium was prayer to the ancestors through dance.

More spectacular examples of religious reaction to the arrival of outsiders sometimes took place at considerable distance from the new settlement so that knowledge of the invaders was largely second hand. Cults would grow up whose aim was to achieve the greater standard of living which had been observed, possibly only by one or a few prophet-like figures, and the aim was a kind of moral regeneration of society. Usually, there would be a charismatic leader, and the results were sometimes devastating. In one part of South America, for example, a whole congregation of indigenous people jumped off a cliff, believing that they would subsequently be reborn white, with all the advantages they had heard that would bring.

In Melanesia, cults arose which have become known as 'cargo cults', for their practices were aimed at attracting the goods to which they saw white people had access. Some of these have been brought to the attention of the public in film and on stage. A Jacques Tati film showed a group of people building an airport in the hope that they could attract the enormous birds they saw delivering all manner of good things to the white people who had settled nearby. A stage play entitled *Sergeant Ola and his Followers* illustrated even in its title the role of the charismatic leader. In this production, local people dressed up as whites and spent their time trying to replicate their activities, reading newspapers and tapping away at a typewriter, though they were illiterate.

Peter Worsley's book, *The Trumpet Shall Sound* (1970) includes a comprehensive survey of these cults, which were found in various parts of New Guinea as well as in Fiji, the Solomon Islands and the New Hebrides. He also calls them 'millenarian movements' because of their similarity to movements found all over the world, characterized by a belief in the imminence of the end of the world, some of which occurred in Europe in the run up to the year 1000. The expectation is that a cataclysm will destroy everything, but that the ancestors, or some prior god, will return and liberate the people from their new oppressors, incidentally making available all the goods these same oppressors seem to own. Hence the preparations.

These movements are of course not peculiar to Melanesia, as Worsley himself points out, nor are they only to be discovered in the anthropological fieldnotes of the past, especially as we reach a new millennium. The shocking release of poisonous gas in the Tokyo underground in 1995, and the mass suicide/murder of members of the Branch Davidian cult in Waco, Texas, two years before that, may both be seen as examples of the continuing power of people preaching about the end of the world. The tale of the Japanese group, Aum Shinrikyo, which has been blamed for the deaths and injuries in Tokyo, is a text-book example of a millennium cult. In a well-informed study of the group, Ian Reader writes of its leader, Asahara Shōko:

> He . . . achieved prominence because of his frequent, drastic prophecies, which stated that an apocalypse would occur before the end of the century to engulf the vast majority of humanity and sweep away the corrupt material world and destroy Japanese society. He proclaimed that he was a messiah who had come to save his followers from the apocalypse and lead them forward to form a new, ideal spiritual universe that would emerge from the ruins of the old. (1996, p. 2)

Worsley's survey concludes by putting the Melanesian material in a wider anthropological and historical context, where he identifies common features in a wide range of different movements. Resistance to oppression is a common theme, as is the drawing together of a new, and possibly powerful amalgamation of smaller groups. The promise of a better life is of course another powerful characteristic, and the charismatic leader is a virtual *sine qua non*. These cults allow a kind of generalization which is rare in anthropological literature, and Worsley's book is an accessible example of how this may be done. In the next chapter we return to an examination of the more culturally specific, which allows more informed interpretation of the 'magico-religious' phenomena found in any one place.

References

Durkheim, Emile (1915) *The Elementary Forms of the Religious Life*, trans. J.W. Swain (London: George Allen & Unwin).
Evans-Pritchard, E.E. (1965) *Theories of Primitive Religion* (Oxford: Clarendon).
Frazer, Sir James George (1922) *The Golden Bough; A Study in Magic and Religion*, abridged edn (London: Macmillan).

Gombrich, Richard (1971) *Precept and Practice: Traditional Buddhism in the Rural Highlands of Ceylon* (Oxford: Clarendon).

Leach, Edmund (1969) 'Genesis as Myth', in *Genesis as Myth and other Essays* (London: Cape).

Lévi-Strauss, Claude (1963) 'The Structural Study of Myth', in *Structural Anthropology* (Harmondsworth: Penguin).

Malinowski, Bronislaw (1974) *Magic, Science and Religion* (London: Free Press).

Middleton, John (1960) *Lugbara Religion: Ritual and Authority among an East African People* (London: Oxford University Press for the International African Institute).

Ohnuki-Tierney, Emiko (1984) *Illness and Culture in Contemporary Japan* (Cambridge University Press).

Radcliffe-Brown, A. R. (1964) *The Andaman Islanders* (New York: Free Press)

Reader, Ian (1996) *A Poisonous Cocktail: Aum Shinrikyo's Path to Violence* (Copenhagen: Nordic Institute for Asian Studies).

Tylor, Edward B. (1913) *Primitive Culture, Vol. 2,* (London: John Murray)

Worsley, Peter (1970) *The Trumpet Shall Sound: A Study of 'Cargo' Cults in Melanesia* (London: Paladin).

Further Reading

Burridge, Kenelm (1960) *Mambu: A Melanesian Millennium* (London: Methuen).

Lévi-Strauss, Claude (1967) 'The Myth of Asdiwal', in Edmund Leach (ed.),*The Structural Study of Myth and Totemism* (London: Tavistock).

Lindstrom, Lamont (1993) *Cargo Cult: Strange Stories of Desire from Melanesia and Beyond* (Honolulu: University of Hawaii Press).

Morris, Brian (1987) *Anthropological Studies of Religion: An Introductory Text* (Cambridge University Press).

Tambiah, Stanley Jeyaraja (1990) *Magic, science, religion, and the scope of rationality* (Cambridge University Press).

Novels

Endo, Shusaku, *Silence* (London: Peter Owen, 1976), tells the story of two European missionaries whose less than successful work in Japan finds them seeking some sign from God that their work is not in vain.

Hellerman, Tony, *Sacred Clowns* (Harmondsworth: Penguin 1993) is a murder mystery involving two native American detectives and a sacred festival.

Trollope, Joanna, *The Choir* (London: Black Swan, 1992) takes the reader into a fictional world of politics, scandal and social relations in a Church of England community.

Films

The Dervishes of Kurdistan (Brian Moser, André Singer and Ali Bulookbashi, 1973) illustrates some of the extraordinary feats people with strong faith are able to perform.

The Kalasha: Rites of Spring (John Sheppard and Peter Parkes, 1990) is another very good 'Disappearing World' film about a minority people living in the mountains of Pakistan who resist the surrounding Islamic influence.

CHAPTER 8

Cosmology II: Witchcraft, Shamanism and Syncretism

Indigenous Categories of Cosmology

In this chapter we will turn to examine in detail some important categories which have interested anthropologists over the years, and in which they have sometimes engaged in interesting dialogue with European historians. The first subjects are witchcraft and sorcery, which are not without intriguing meaning in the English language, but we will turn for our initial definitions to an African people studied by one of the better known British anthropologists introduced in the last chapter, namely Edward Evans-Pritchard. The people are the Azande, a tribe of the Southern Sudan, for whom the word *mangu*, translated as 'witchcraft', was perhaps the most commonly used in their language when Evans-Pritchard lived among them. It was a matter of daily discussion, irritating rather than frightening, and, as an ethnographer, he could hardly ignore it.

Evans-Pritchard chose this subject for his study because it clearly pervaded the thinking of the Zande people and he realized that an understanding of their social life depended upon an understanding of their ideas about witchcraft. He became aware that their moral universe was not constructed around a Supreme Being, or the ghosts of ancestors, but around their ideas about witchcraft. The practice of witchcraft he found was almost synonymous with bad character, with greed and jealousy:

> witches tend to be those whose behaviour is least in accordance with social demands. Those whom we would call good citizens – and, of course, the richer and more powerful members of society are such – are seldom accused of witchcraft, while those who make themselves a nuisance to their neighbours and those who are weak are most likely to be accused. (1976, p. 52)

The study of witchcraft thus provided an essential key to understanding Zande systems of thought and paved the way to deciphering many other aspects of their social and political life.

Evans-Pritchard's work among the Azande also allowed him to devise theory about witchcraft which proved highly influential among ethnographers making observations in a wide range of other societies. His analysis has thus provided a basis for comparison with almost all the further studies which have been made. Some of these agree with his ideas, providing further examples of the general principles, others offer modifications or alternative types of analysis. None ignore his work, and even if only for this reason, it seems essential to start with his study and the theory it engendered. It is also a fascinating case, written in an extremely accessible style, so it is an excellent introduction for the student of witchcraft phenomena. It is not everywhere that notions of witchcraft were found to be important, however, and other indigenous categories are thought better translated as spirit possession, shamanism, and so forth. These phenomena are discussed in the second part of this chapter, again with an emphasis on local understanding. In the last part of the chapter some attention is paid to places where ideas and beliefs from more than one religious tradition appear to co-exist quite happily, a phenomenon again quite difficult to comprehend from the perspective of Europe and the Middle East, where history would be decimated if it ignored the many times people and places have been ravaged by religious wars. This is another area in which the knowledge acquired by anthropologists might be put to good use, were people convinced to listen.

Terminology

The terms **witchcraft** and **sorcery** were until Evans-Pritchard's time used rather unsystematically to describe a wide variety of ideas held in different parts of the world about mystical powers which people may possess. This power might have been thought to be a psychic one, with which a person is born, or a skill which can be learned, and perhaps passed on through an initiation ceremony. It might have been thought to emanate from the body, perhaps even unconsciously, or to be manipulated consciously through the use of spells. Evans-Pritchard, in his classic book *Witchcraft, Oracles and Magic among the Azande* (1976) made clear a distinction between witchcraft and sorcery, which he saw as an evil form of magic, based on these sorts of characteristics. The distinction includes the following elements:

Witchcraft	Sorcery
• a psychic power	• use of medicines for evil ends
• often hereditary	• anyone can learn it
• may be unconscious	• conscious

This distinction was based initially on the Azande case, where witchcraft was said to be inherited in the male or female line (that is passed from father to son, or mother to daughter) although Evans-Pritchard did notice that this was not always the most important criterion when people were trying to identify a possible witch to accuse. The power was thought to reside in a substance in the belly, but this power could lie dormant or 'cool' indefinitely, and would only be activated if its owner became angry or jealous. People could also be entirely unaware of their power and it was held to be something of an individual quality for it to become active. If the witch died, an autopsy was said to confirm whether or not the substance had been present, but these operations were banned by the British government so Evans-Pritchard was not able to observe them.

Sorcery, on the other hand, was held to be a skill which could be learned, and passed on through conscious study. It was defined as the evil use of medicines, a practice also known as black magic, thereby seen as parallel to white magic used for positive purposes. Anyone with an interest could learn these skills and put them into practice, whereas the activation of witchcraft power was held often to be unconscious as well as limited to those with the substance in their bodies. The distinction is also held to distinguish kings and princes in Zande society from commoners, for the former are said to be both incapable of and immune to witchcraft, whereas they may be subject to the evil effects of sorcery.

Evans-Pritchard's distinction holds up rather well cross-culturally, but it is apparently not always possible to make in every society, and other efforts have been made to delineate the same sort of subject matter. For example, in their book *Witchcraft and Sorcery in East Africa*, the authors John Middleton and E. H. Winter, suggest the term **wizardry** to cover all such mystical activities, and they define it as:

> beliefs which people have about the capabilities and activities of others and the action which they take to avoid attacks or to counter them when they believe they have occurred. (1963, p. 3)

Another suggestion, made by I. M. Lewis in an article he contributed to the collection edited by Mary Douglas (1970), entitled *Witchcraft: Confessions and Accusations*, was that **spirit possession** be included together with **witchcraft** and **sorcery** in a notion of **mystical attack**, which could be classified as *oblique* or *direct*, depending on the perceived motives of the accuser, rather than the accused. Lewis pointed out that it is after all the accuser who initiates the attack of public opinion against the witch, who in the end is the victim of social action, and this is parallel to some of his ideas about spirit possession.

We will return to the subject of possession later in the chapter. In the meantime, however, let us turn to examine further the ideas of Evans-Pritchard gleaned from the Azande.

The Roles of Witchcraft and Sorcery Beliefs

The most influential aspects of the theory about witchcraft which Evans-Pritchard drew up were his considerations of the roles ideas about witchcraft played in relation to norms of good behaviour in Zande society. His discussion about these roles can be laid out under five headings, and in the pages which follow we can draw also on comparisons from other studies of witchcraft and sorcery. Perhaps most widespread of all is the way witchcraft could provide an explanation of misfortune.

(1) Witchcraft as an Explanation of Misfortune

Among the Azande people, witchcraft would be blamed for all kinds of unfortunate events which occurred in everyday life. Crop failure, illness, or simply a lack of fish could all be put down to witchcraft, although Evans-Pritchard emphasizes that the Azande were not unaware of natural causes, such as adverse weather conditions, as well. Perhaps his most famous illustration of this principle is when he describes the Zande explanation of the collapse of a granary on a group of people eating their lunch. They knew that the granary supports had been eaten by termites, he asserts, and they knew that the people sitting under the granary were doing it to take advantage of the shade it offered. It is witchcraft, however, which explains why the granary fell down at that particular time on those particular people.

In Evans-Pritchard's view, witchcraft carries an explanation to its logical conclusion. It explains why misfortune happens to certain people at a certain time, and in this way, explanations are carried one stage further than they may be elsewhere. A common view for someone involved in a car crash, for example, might be to ponder whether if they had left home a few minutes later they would not have been hit by that person jumping a light. Someone missing a plane or bus which crashed might feel strangely lucky or protected. They might wonder about 'fate', 'destiny', 'luck' or 'acts of god', but with less immediate confidence than the Zande have. They are quite sure about why particular people are in the path of misfortune at a particular time – it's due to witchcraft.

Other belief systems have a similar confidence, however. For example, a Muslim's view of misfortune may see it immediately as an act of God. Indeed, an expression commonly used in Islamic circles allows for this intervention when a person modifies an arrangement by adding*insh'Allah*, meaning 'God-willing', to their proposed plans. In Western countries we seem to have a need to find a human cause for misfortune, so that a disaster will be followed by a court of inquiry to see where the blame lies. In an air crash, it is always important to seek the 'black box', for example, and ferry disasters in the English Channel have led to considerable modification to the design and execution of the journey. A disaster seems somehow less destructive in the long run if some action may be taken, and this is another role which notions of witchcraft allow.

(2) Witchcraft Provides Some Action which may be Taken

The second role played by witchcraft is that ideas about it offer clear steps which may be taken to alleviate the misfortune. Just as we feel better about illness if we know what it is and how to treat it, the Azande can take action to find out who is bewitching them and why. They turn to oracles for this purpose. The most famous of these is known as the chicken oracle, when a series of chickens are fed doses of strychnine which are on the borderline of being lethal. Questions are presented as each chicken is given the dose, and the answer is provided by the death or otherwise of the chicken. Less expensive oracles involve putting sticks in a termite mound to see which is eaten faster, and the use of a 'rubbing board'. This last is described, by Evans-Pritchard, as:

> a miniature table-like construction . . . carved out of the wood of various trees. They have two parts, the 'female', or the flat surface of the table supported by two legs and its tail, and the 'male', or the piece which fits the surface of the table like a lid.
>
> When the operator jerks the lid over the table it generally either moves smoothly backwards and forwards or it sticks to the board so firmly that no jerking will further move it, and it has to be pulled upwards with considerable force to detach it from the table. These two actions – smooth sliding and firm sticking – are the two ways in which the oracle answers questions. They correspond to the slaying or sparing of fowls by the poison, the eating or refusing of the branches by the termites. (1976, pp. 168–70)

(3) Witchcraft Brings Social Tensions out into the Open

Questions put to the oracles are usually in a form which requires a yes or no answer, and Evans-Pritchard noticed that those conducting the investigation consider not who is a known witch, but who might bear malice against the afflicted person. Witchcraft among the Azande is supposed to occur spontaneously if a person with the innate power is angry with or jealous of another, so that considering who might feel that way is thought likely to elicit a positive answer from the oracles. There is then a procedure to approach the person, most formally by presenting the wing of the dead chicken. The accused is likely to deny malice, but will probably go through a rite of blowing water on the wing to cool the witchcraft and exorcise any ill-feeling. This procedure serves a simultaneous purpose of bringing underlying tensions between people into the open, Evans-Pritchard argues, and dealing with them in a way acceptable to both parties

(4) Witchcraft has a Normative Effect on Society

These beliefs about witchcraft may serve as a 'corrective to uncharitable impulses', argues Evans-Pritchard, 'because a show of spleen or meanness or hostility may bring serious consequences in its train' (ibid., pp. 54–5). In other words, people will try to curb their jealousy and other forms of unpleasantness for two important reasons:

(i)   to avoid being accused of witchcraft, and
(ii) to avoid incurring the wrath of a witch.

Accusations are usually made to those who are rude, dirty, and jealous, he notes, those with a generally bad character, so the whole system is a discouragement to people to behave in an unpleasant manner. 'Since Azande do not know who are and who are not witches, they assume that all their neighbours may be witches, and are therefore careful not to offend any of them without good cause' (ibid.).

Reactions and other Theories of Witchcraft

Most people who have discussed witchcraft since Evans-Pritchard wrote his classic book have reacted in one way or another to his work, many reinforcing his ideas about the roles played, particularly about the way it provides an explanation of misfortune. An interesting article by the historian Keith Thomas (1970), for example, describes the situation in England in the sixteenth and seventeenth centuries. He points out that misfortune could also be explained by the wrath of God, but witchcraft offered people more scope for action (see (2) above) than the new Protestant church did.

A man who decided that God was responsible for his illness could do little about it. He could pray that he might be cured, but with no very certain prospect of success, for God's ways were mysterious, and, though he could be supplicated, he could not be coerced. Protestant theologians taught that Christians should suffer stoically like Job, but this doctrine was not a comfortable one. The attraction of witchcraft beliefs, by contrast, was that they held out precisely that certainty of redress which the theologians denied. A man who feared that a witch might attack him could invoke a number of magical preservatives in order to ensure his self-protection. If the witch had already struck, it was still open to him to practise counter magic . . . Best of all, the victim could have the witch prosecuted and executed. For the point of such witch trials was not merely that they afforded the gratification of revenge, but that, according to contemporary belief, they positively relieved the victim. (Thomas 1970, p. 57)

The Roman Catholic church had had clearer procedures to be followed, and this difference could account to some extent for the rise in witchcraft trials after the Reformation, Thomas argued. He also offers support for (3) above by suggesting that accusations of witchcraft might well have followed feelings of guilt at having offended a neighbour, or refusing a person asking for alms, and that these ideas might therefore have encouraged neighbourly behaviour and generally reinforced moral standards. As in (4) above, people would try to avoid behaviour which might lead to accusations of witchcraft or the curses of a witch.

Both Keith Thomas and Evans-Pritchard point out, however, that it can sometimes be advantageous to have a reputation of power. In England, old ladies begging for alms could benefit from the fear that their potential benefactors might have of their bewitching capabilities. Among the Azande, those with a reputation for witchcraft were often offered extra meat when the spoils of a hunt were being divided up. This was thought to protect against possible interference during a further hunt; indeed it would be an incentive for the witch to ensure good hunting fortune, they argued.

Writing of the Amba of Uganda (Middleton and Winter, 1963), Winter argues that witchcraft is not always beneficial to society, however. Indeed, he shows how notions of witchcraft tend to disrupt the social cohesion of the village. Witches, in an Amba view, exhibit an inversion of physical and moral qualities of human beings. They hang upside down, eat human flesh, quench their thirst with salt, go about naked, and, unlike the situation in the case of feuds, they take their victims from their own villages and share them with witches in other villages.

Thus if witches in a particular village kill a person they invite the witches from another village to share the ensuing feast. At a later date, the witches of the second village must reciprocate by inviting their previous hosts to a feast at which they will serve the corpse of a victim from their own village. (1963, p. 292)

The behaviour of witches is thus precisely the opposite of that expected of ordinary people, who abhor the idea of eating human flesh, and always go about with clothes on their bodies. The notions of witchcraft should be examined in the context of the whole moral universe, Winter argues, when they can be seen as a *structural inversion* of the social order. This argument is thus an example of an *expressive* role of witchcraft, in the same sense as we used the idea in the previous chapter, in that it tells us something about important categories in society. It thereby goes beyond, and complements the *instrumental* or *functional* role presented by Evans-Pritchard and others, when they identify the normative effect witchcraft has on society.

Other structural interpretations are found in the analyses of sorcery accusations made in South America. Peter Rivière's (1970) article in *Witch-craft: Confessions and Accusations* describes the way lines of sorcery accusation reflect the sociopolitical structure of the Trio Indians of Surinam in helping to demarcate divisions between villages. In the case of the Akwe Shavante of southern Brazil, they reflect lines of division between political factions. In both cases, the groups are somewhat fluid. Allegiances can alter, and people move to rearrange their neighbourly links. Confirmation of a new division is clear when sorcery accusations are made, for these do not occur among people who share a village, or a faction.

In the introduction to the same book, Douglas describes witchcraft as 'essentially a means of clarifying and affirming social definitions' (1970, p. xxv). If the witch is an outsider, there is a reconfirmation of the inside, whatever that may be. If the witch is an insider, witchcraft may have the function of controlling deviants in the name of community values, it may promote factional rivalry, or it may redefine a hierarchy. In *Purity and Danger* (1966) she argued that uncontrolled witchcraft is attributed to people in dangerously ambiguous roles, people who may be potential sources of disorder. They may have their own niche in one group, but be an intruder from the point of view of another: 'Witches are the social equivalents of beetles and spiders who live in the cracks of the walls and the wainscoting' (p. 124). An example she gives is easily recognizable: Joan of Arc, 'a peasant at court, a woman in armour, an outsider in the councils of war' (Ibid.) – small wonder she was accused of witchcraft.

Peter Brown (1970), in another article in the Douglas collection, points to so-called flash points of sorcery accusation at times of crisis and social change, suggesting an increase when areas of the social structure are ill-defined. Some of his examples are the fourth century remains of the Roman Empire, England in the sixteenth and seventeenth centuries which he relates to the undefined position of the poor until the passing of the Poor Law, and a rise of witchcraft in Africa with colonization and missionary work.

It is difficult to say whether current witchcraft practices in England are related to any kind of crisis or social change, or, indeed, whether they have ever really abated over the intervening years. It is certainly true, however, that magic and witchcraft continue to intrigue members of the wider society, and practising witches are found among the most apparently staid and middle-class of professions. These subjects occasionally attract undergraduate students at Oxford Brookes, and those who have gained access to local covens have written very interesting dissertations. A Cambridge PhD thesis which became an excellent ethnography of British witchcraft – *Persuasions of the Witch's Craft* (Luhrmann, 1989, see under Further Reading) – is a good introduction to the subject which also addresses the thorny question of rationality.

Possession and Shamanism

Explanations of misfortune form part of the **cosmology** of a society, and in industrialized societies, science is very often invoked for this purpose. When this is the case, we visit a doctor when we are ill, ask a forensic expert to help solve a murder, examine fingerprints in the case of theft, and seek the 'black box' to explain a plane crash. In other societies people turn to spirits for explanations of all these kinds of eventualities, usually by asking a specialist such as a **shaman**, a **diviner**, or a **witch-doctor** to intervene in communicating with the spirit world. Communication with the spirits may take place on behalf of an individual, it may take place at a large gathering, often with much ribaldry and enjoyment, and ethnographers have commented on the entertainment value of these occasions.

The different words used for these practitioners tend to be associated with particular regions. **Shaman**, for example, is from the Tungus tribe of Siberia, although it is used elsewhere, particularly for practitioners who claim to have a soul which can leave their body and travel to a heaven or an underworld. People of South America often have such practitioners, who may train to go into trances, perhaps by drinking tobacco juice or taking hallucinogens, and then claim to go on trips to visit the spirit world. They may also learn a technique for receiving spirits into their own bodies, which will then speak to the assembled company (in any number of different voices!) about their problems and requests.

Audrey Colson, who worked among the Akawaio people of British Guyana, describes such occasions in lively detail (Wavell, Colson and Epton, 1966). Indeed, one of my strongest memories as a student learning anthropology was listening to Audrey's tape of an Akawaio seance, because the audience is extremely participative and the whole thing sounds immensely exciting. The visiting spirits are asked to deal with misfortune, to help find lost articles, including determining who might have stolen them in case it was a matter of theft, and to identify the causes of sickness, and recommend ways to bring it to an end. People in the audience join in with their own suggestions throughout the procedure, and Colson argues that the shaman, or the spirits who are possessing the shaman, make decisions which reflect public opinion.

In this way, the Akawaio seance plays some of the same roles as described by Evans-Pritchard for witchcraft beliefs, for it provides an opportunity for underlying tensions to be expressed in a legitimate fashion, for people in a contained situation to throw out accusations against others whose behaviour could have brought about the misfortunes – perhaps by upsetting the spirits who would bring about illness, for example. Because names of possible transgressors are brought to the visiting spirits, Colson argues that this is a strong disincentive to people to behave in an anti-social way, and the whole procedure again has a normative effect on Akawaio society.

Diviner is a broader category of people who may address themselves to similar problems. In Japan and other parts of the Far East their roles include divining the causes of illness (perhaps by claiming to enter the body of the afflicted), assessing the suitability of a marriage or a proposed alteration to a house, and determining auspicious days for a venture of any sort. A complicated calendar may be consulted for these purposes, and this is drawn up according to astrological ideas, in association with ideas about the division of the world into *yin* and *yang*. The classification of time, discussed in Chapter 1, is influential here too, so the work of a diviner is not only concerned with communication with spirits.

However, Japanese diviners may also be consulted to explain misfortune, and some of their explanations may involve dissatisfied ghosts and ancestral spirits. Memorials for the dead should be carried out on certain death days, for example, and forgetting these could cause trouble. A recent reaction to misfortune has been to attribute it to the souls of aborted babies, and Buddhist temples have set aside areas for small memorial statues, as well as running monthly rituals to appease these lonely souls. New temples have even opened which cater exclusively to the souls of aborted babies (see

LaFleur, 1992 for more detail). Japanese people anyway think nothing of consulting a variety of diviners *and* doctors about the same ailment, as was mentioned in the last chapter.

Practitioners of this sort are in Africa more commonly described as **spirit mediums** or **witch-doctors**, though their roles may be very similar; that is, divining the cause of illness, and finding out how to appease an offended spirit. In talking of communication with spirits in different societies, Raymond Firth suggested that a distinction be made between:

- **spirit possession**, which is largely involuntary
- **spirit mediumship**, where communication is voluntary and
- **shamanism**, which involves some control over spirits.

There have been many different approaches to this subject, and some of them are discussed in *Ecstatic Religion* by I. M. Lewis (1971) – see below under 'Further Reading'. As was raised in the last section, Lewis (1970) compares the interpretation of spirit possession with that of witchcraft. He considers possession as a strategy employed by a person seeking an outlet for distress. Among the BaVenda of Southern Africa, for example, the treatment for a women's possession involves the husband and family according the afflicted person special respect and kindness, and, perhaps not unexpectedly, this kind of possession is said to recur rather frequently. A similar form of spirit possession apparently occurs elsewhere among men of low status, who thereby have their position at least temporarily enhanced. Persistence of the 'affliction' may lead to suspicion of witchcraft and *'direct'* rather than *'oblique'* mystical attack, in Lewis's terms.

There are several ethnographies that give pride of place to the practice of spirit possession, and some of these are listed below under 'Further Reading'. A useful article which examines Lewis's broader theories about spirit possession in the context of the particular case of the Newar people of the Kathmandu Valley is that by David Gellner (1994), entitled 'Priests, healers, mediums and witches'. A classic collection is that by Beattie and Middleton (1969), which focuses on the role of spirit mediumship in Africa, and a nice introduction to interaction with spirits in Japan is the book by Carmen Blacker entitled *The Catalpa Bow* (1975).

Syncretism

In complex multicultural worlds, different cosmologies must needs co-exist. Tolerance of different faiths is one way of seeking a peaceful life, and people of varying backgrounds do manage to live alongside one another in many cities of the world. In urban schools, these days, children may learn a veritable medley of ideas about the faiths which the teachers find among their charges. They encourage children to share their notions of this world and any other they have been taught to believe in, and the school may play host to all manner of different festivals and rites. The aim is to teach tolerance, but it may also engender a degree of confusion, and some of my students who have been brought up in this climate of opinion are only devout when they talk of environmental issues.

Those who become most serious on this subject may turn to a form of nature worship known as Paganism, which has recently become quite influential in Britain. Although there are many forms of this movement, which has adopted as a name the word used to describe pre-Christian religious ideas which existed in Britain, there is an overarching organization which aims to keep different groups in touch with one another. One of the common themes seems, appropriately, to be the revival of ideas which were prevalent in Europe before Christianity, but there is also a common concern with the conservation and protection of the environment. Anthropologist Charlotte Hardman writes:

> the state of Paganism in the UK has been changing in the last ten years or so . . . Ecologically, although Paganism has always had behind it a romantic view of the land and has always been 'green' philosophically, it has now also become more clearly an activist movement in this area . . . Respect for Nature, being 'green', is no longer just part of the philosophy; the eco-magic of Pagan ritual can be activated towards environmental, social and spiritual change. (1996, pp. xiv–xv)

There is some overlap here with Luhrmann's witches, but she also had informants who did not classify themselves as Pagans, sometimes even practising Christianity (Luhrman, 1989, p. 5).

People who turn to paganism and witchcraft in Britain are revitalizing old categories into new systems of cosmology. They draw on an abundant fund of ancient ideas to create a new way to impose order on an increasingly confusing world. Sometimes in despair at the way scientific discovery appears to ignore the fragility of natural resources, people look back to times which seem idyllic from the perspective of nuclear power and mass destruction. Like the art collectors mentioned in Chapter 6, who seek solace in aboriginal paintings, these people look for wisdom in ancient or disappearing worlds. They reject the excesses of a scientific world view, and seek to find a spiritual life which reflects the concerns of the world in which they find themselves.

Drawing elements of different cosmological systems into a new world view is a practice as ancient as cultural exchange, and the results are sometimes called **syncretism**, literally the co-existence of beliefs, although in practice one set may virtually subsume another, when it may be called *synthesis*. As Christianity has spread around the world, it has often incorporated elements of previous belief systems into its range of varying ideas and practices. The timing of the celebration of the birth of Christ to coincide with mid-winter conveniently replaced previous northern European festivals, for example, as mentioned in Chapter 4, and the celebration of Hallowe'en, now a 'religious' practice only in Pagan circles, is not by chance on days known in the Christian calendar as celebrations of All Saints and All Souls.

In Mexico, these days are among the most important in the calendar, when people remember their departed loved ones and visit their graves. Principally known as the Day of the Dead, the period is marked by the construction and sale of an abundance of goods and sweets with ghoulish themes, such as rubber skeletons and chocolate skulls. It is several centuries since Christianity was introduced to the Mexican people, who previously espoused a number of different belief systems, among them the Aztec and Mayan, so tracing the individual elements back would be a complex and difficult task. However, there is evidence in the writings of the missionaries of the time that efforts were made to incorporate indigenous practices, and it is interesting that the Virgin of Guadalupe made her first appearance on a hill sacred to Tonantzin, an important Aztec Earth Mother.

The 'Disappearing World' film, *The Azande*, noted below, gives a more recent demonstration of how the ideas described above are now finding ways to coexist with newly introduced Christianity.

In Japan, the situation is a rather different, and provides a better example of syncretism. The indigenous Shinto, which literally means 'path of the gods', was a set of rather miscellaneous ancient beliefs without a name, possibly related to Taoism, until they needed to be distinguished from other more established traditions which were introduced from the outside. These now co-exist with ideas and practices from Buddhism, Confucianism and Christianity. These, of course, have their own dogma, teachings and ritual experts, but ordinary Japanese people seem to find little difficulty in drawing on anything available in turning to what we might call religion.

We have already noted that the Japanese language sometimes classed Shinto ideas as 'superstition' in the post-war disapproval of its support for imperial expansion, but the word usually translated as religion (*shūkyō*) is also more appropriately used for the teachings introduced from outside than for these indigenous ideas. The word for 'believer' (*shinja*) is also applied rather to someone who chooses a special (often 'new') religious path than to the many Japanese people who incorporate various strands of religious influence into their life almost imperceptibly. Visits to Shinto shrines at birth, Buddhist funerals, Christian weddings, and the consultation of a (possibly Taoist) shaman may all be practised by the same person in Japan.

Analysis of the practices of the people who lived in the rural community where I carried out fieldwork (Hendry, 1981) coincided with the findings of those who have specialized in looking at religious practises in Japan. On the whole, Shinto is found to be drawn upon in celebrations associated with life and health, Buddhism with death and memorials for the ancestors. The former are usually community celebrations, perhaps held at the community shrine, the latter are household ones which make use of the household altar. Clearly, these practices may again be seen as playing an *expressive* role, one which is reinforced when we notice that the consultation of the less well defined shaman takes place in times of illness, marriage and house-building, when the important categories are threatened or undergoing change.

Christianity in Japan has not made much progress, counting less than 2 per cent of Japanese as practitioners. Perhaps this is because the syncretic system, which now also includes a number of 'new' sects of Buddhism and Shinto, is not only at odds with the more exclusive nature of Christianity, but also still serves to accommodate the changing structures of Japanese society. Looking back over 1500 years of Japanese history, the two major strands of Shinto and Buddhism can be seen to have undergone much separation and assimilation, but certain elements have also continued to persist. Confucianism has been a long-term influence too, but largely in the underpinning of morals and ethics, a subject we shall consider in more detail in the next chapter.

Recent discussions (Stewart and Shaw, 1995) about syncretism have argued that all religions have drawn on different traditions over the centuries, so little is to be gained by using the term, but the notion is useful for pointing out the relatively ethnocentric nature of the idea that one religion should make an exclusive call on its adherents. David Gellner (1997), in a critique of the Stewart and Shaw book, considers different varieties of syncretism, and makes a comparison between the Buddhism found alongside Shinto and Confucianism in Japan and the case of the Newar people of the Kathmandu Valley, in Nepal, who continue to practise Tantric Buddhism in a predominantly Hindu State. His book *Monk, Householder and Tantric Priest* (1992; see under 'Further Reading' below) is a detailed ethnography of the Newar people who live in the Hindu-Buddhist city of Lalitpur, and focuses on the religious activities which provide many good examples of syncretism in practice (see Photograph 8.1).

Photograph 8.1   Three Buddhist *chityas* (cult objects) outside the Bhimsen Temple, Kathmandu. The *chitya* in the foreground is of the style popular in the 17th and 18th centuries, the other two are the syncretic form which became popular in Kathmandu in the later 19th and early 20th centuries, a time of intensive Hinduisation. They incorporate as part of the base a water course that is copied from the most common Hindu cult object, namely the *shivalinga* (photograph courtesy of David Gellner).

References

Brown, Peter (1970) 'Sorcery, Demons and the Rise of Christianity from Late Antiquity into the Middle Ages', in Mary Douglas (ed.), *Witchcraft, Confessions and Accusations* (London: Tavistock), pp. 17–45.

Douglas, Mary (1966) *Purity and Danger* (Harmondsworth: Penguin).

Douglas, Mary (ed.) (1970) *Witchcraft: Confessions and Accusations* (London: Tavistock).

Evans-Pritchard, E. E. (1976) *Witchcraft, Oracles and Magic among the Azande* (Oxford: Clarendon).

Gellner, David (1997) 'For syncretism. The position of Buddhism in Nepal and Japan compared', *Social Anthropology*, **5**(3): 277–91.

Hardman, Charlotte (1996) 'Introduction', in Graham Harvey and Charlotte Hardman (eds), *Paganism Today: Wiccans, Druids, the Goddess and Ancient Earth Traditions for the Twenty-First Century* (London: Thorsons).

Hendry, J. (1981) *Marriage in Changing Japan: Community and Society,* (London: Croom Helm; Tokyo: Tuttle, 1986).

Lewis, I. M. (1970) 'A Structural Approach to Witchcraft and Spirit Possession', in Mary Douglas (ed.), *Witchcraft, Confessions and Accusations* (London: Tavistock), pp. 293–309.

Middleton, John and E. H. Winter (eds.) (1963) *Witchcraft and Sorcery in East Africa* (London: Routledge & Kegan Paul).

Rivière, Peter (1970) 'Factions and Exclusions in Two South American Village Systems', in Mary Douglas (ed.), *Witchcraft, Confessions and Accusations* (London: Tavistock), pp. 245–55.

Stewart, Charles & Rosalind Shaw (eds) (1995) *Syncretism/Anti-Syncretism: The Politics of Religious Synthesis* (London: Routledge).

Thomas, Keith (1970) 'The Relevance of Social Anthropology to the Historical Study of English Witchcraft' in Mary Douglas (ed.), *Witchcraft, Confessions and Accusations* (London: Tavistock), pp. 47–79.

Wavell, Stewart, Audrey Colson and Nina Epton (1966) *Trances* (London: Allen & Unwin).

Further Reading

Beattie, John and John Middleton (1969) *Spirit Mediumship and Society in Africa* (London: Routledge & Kegan Paul).

Blacker, Carmen (1975) *The Catalpa Bow: A Study of Shamanistic Practices in Japan* (London: Allen & Unwin).

Eliade, Mircea (1964) *Shamanism: Archaic Techniques of Ecstacy* (Princeton University Press).

Gellner, David (1992) *Monk, Householder and Tantric Priest* (Cambridge University Press).

Gellner, David (1994) 'Priests, healers, mediums and witches: the context of possession in the Kathmandu Valley, Nepal', *Man*, **29**: 27–48.

Jencson, L. (1989) 'Neo-paganism and the great mother-goddess: anthropology as the midwife to a new religion', *Anthropology Today*, **5**(2): 2–4.

LaFleur, William R. (1992) *Liquid Life: Abortion and Buddhism in Japan* (Princeton University Press).

Lewis, I. M. (1971) *Ecstatic Religion: An Anthropological Study of Spirit Possession and Shamanism* (Harmondsworth: Penguin).

Luhrmann, Tanya (1989) *Persuasions of the Witch's Craft* (Oxford: Blackwell).

Marwick, Max (ed.) (1982) *Penguin Readings on Witchcraft*, 2nd edn (Harmondsworth: Penguin).

Riches, David (1994) 'Shamanism: the key to religion', *Man*, **29**: 381–405.

Novels & Play

Lowry, Malcolm, *Under the Volcano* (Harmondsworth: Penguin, 1962) is a novel about a disillusioned and alcoholic British consul living in Mexico, but it is of interest here because much of the action takes place on the Day of the Dead.

Miller, Arthur, *The Crucible* (London: Methuen, 1996), is concerned with the Salem witchcraft trials in the United States.

Okri, Ben, *The Famished Road* (London: Cape, 1991) is a novel full of African spirits and mysticism.

Films

Disappearing World: The Azande (André Singer and John Ryle, 1982) depicts the world of Azande witchcraft within the new context of widespread conversion to Christianity.

Kataragama, A God for All Seasons (Charlie Nairn and Gananath Obeyesekere, 1973) is another 'Disappearing World' film set in Sri Lanka (then, Ceylon) which, at least at first, illustrates the variety of ways a people may seek to understand the misfortune of losing an 11-year-old son.

The *Strangers Abroad* film about Evans-Pritchard, entitled *Strange Beliefs* (see p. 33 above) includes an examination of Zande material too.

CHAPTER 9

Law, Order and Social Control

Rules and Norms

In this chapter and the next we are again taking as a focus categories from the English language, and we will examine manifestations of behaviour observed in different parts of the world which conform approximately to the specifications these terms encompass. The terms in question – 'law' and 'politics' – overlap in any society. When a formal political system is distinguished from a legal system, it is still the politicians who design and discuss the laws, while a different set of professionals – lawyers and judges – put them into practice. In both cases we deal, on the one hand, with persons in positions of power – the subject matter of the next chapter – and, on the other, with the constraints imposed on members of the society at large by the mechanisms of control. In most societies, too, the people themselves constrain the acts of others among them in a variety of less formal ways.

In this chapter we will focus on the constraints. Any society needs mechanisms which ensure that its members behave for the most part in a reasonably ordered fashion. In the cosmopolitan world, there are laws, together with systems of policing and courts which execute the enforcement of these laws. There are also prisons and other institutions to exact punishment or rehabilitate offenders. There are also **norms** of behaviour, which may or may not coincide with these laws, that people learn as they grow up within social groups, and everywhere there is some kind of reaction on the part of most other people if these norms are transgressed. Details vary from one group to another, indeed, within one group, but some form of **social control** is found everywhere.

At a local level, and within specific communities, informal constraints on the behaviour of individuals are rather effective, sometimes more effective than the laws of the land, and in this chapter, we will concern ourselves particularly with these mechanisms for 'keeping order' in society. The experience of anthropologists, working for long periods among smallish groups of people, sometimes very isolated from any wider legal system, has given them a special insight into the workings of these informal methods of

148

social control. They are able to observe the kinds of pressures which induce people to conform to certain norms and standards, and they can identify incentives people cite for complying with the expectations of their friends and neighbours.

Actually, we have already considered several methods of social control in previous chapters. In the last one we looked at the shaman's seance, where we noticed that the likelihood of being picked out as a possible transgressor was thought to induce people to behave within accepted norms among the Akawaio of British Guyana. It was also suggested that ideas about witchcraft and spirit possession had a normative effect on the behaviour of the Zande people of the Sudan and the BaVenda of Southern Africa respectively. In Chapter 7, on religion, we talked of the prospect of salvation, or divine retribution, as well as the wrath of ancestors and fears of burning in hell as incentives to conform with the behaviour expected by the moral system.

During my own first fieldwork in Japan, when I was focusing on patterns of marriage, I noticed an interesting mechanism of social control in the way people would check up on the families of prospective spouses. Meetings are often arranged by relatives so that young people can meet likely candidates for marriage, and if there is serious interest between them, each family will take steps to find out about the other. In the country this may involve a visit to the village where they live, and simple enquiries among neighbours and in the local shops. The owner of the general store in my village told me that she was regularly approached in this way. She also explained that she felt a moral obligation to tell the truth as she saw it. If a family were to set up a marriage with a family she knew to be difficult or unpleasant, she would forever feel responsible.

There was also an economic element at play here, since the shopkeeper would clearly lose custom if she protected people who turned out to make life miserable for a new housewife and potential customer. For the existing village families, well aware of the system, it was a powerful incentive to keep on good terms with the shopkeeper, again bringing her custom, especially as one's children approached marriageable age. Among neighbours too it could be very difficult if one were to acquire a bad reputation, and two families in the village had had to set up a marriage between themselves, although marrying out of the village was usually preferred, because of their reputation for rudeness and bad temper. There is clearly an element of social control at play here.

There have been several attempts to make general statements about social control, and in this chapter we will examine two of these in some detail and make reference to a third. In all three cases, the anthropologists have drawn heavily on material from small-scale societies, but their findings may also be usefully applied to segments of more complex societies. First, we will look at the approach of Radcliffe-Brown, who sought an understanding of this subject by looking at **social sanctions**, which he defines as follows:

> A **sanction** is a reaction on the part of a society or of a considerable number of its members to a mode of behaviour which is thereby approved (positive sanctions) or disapproved (negative sanctions). (1952, p. 205, my emphasis)

The standards of behaviour by which people judge one another are based on the norms of that society, ideas of right and wrong, which are learned early, as we discussed in Chapter 2. These may be highly complicated, however, and quite situationally specific. Indeed in some societies the situation may be a more important consideration than any absolute rules, as is sometimes argued for Japan. To take an example which will be recognizable in most societies, there is usually a rule or law against killing another human being. However, under certain circumstances this rule may be broken. In most, war is a sufficient excuse, in some societies, vengeance or legal retribution is another, and in Japan, people are sometimes admired when they take their own lives.

In any society it is possible to learn about the norms which people share by observing the sanctions which come into play to encourage some kinds of behaviour and discourage others, and Radcliffe-Brown drew up a system for classifying these, which we shall shortly consider. It must also be remembered, however, that different members of any one society will have somewhat differing views, and the degree to which variation is tolerated is another aspect of this subject of social control. In some societies, it is possible to live quite an idiosyncratic life, in others the leeway is far less broad. The examination of sanctions is not so good at identifying this kind of range of acceptance, or, indeed, the possibility of contested norms within one society.

The second approach we will consider can be more effective in this respect. Laid out in detail by Simon Roberts in his book *Order and Dispute* (1979) there are some areas of overlap with looking at sanctions, as we shall see, but Roberts decided to focus on the resolution of disputes. He starts with the assumption we made above, that there must be order in any society, and he also takes as given that disputes are inevitable. His interest is in the variety of methods which come into play to resolve them, and we will examine these in some detail. In our third example, we will turn to a collection of papers which considers actual disputes from a detailed ethnographic perspective (Caplan, 1995), and here we will encounter the ability to detect contested norms in a specific case.

Sanctions

Radcliffe-Brown (1952) drew up a very useful list of different types of sanctions which come into play as part of the regulation of social behaviour. He first made an important distinction between *positive* and *negative sanctions*, helping us to identify some of the positive forces for action which are present in any society, but particularly in places like Japan and Melanesia where a strong emphasis on harmony discourages open disputes. These positive sanctions include material rewards such as prizes, titles and decorations, but they also include things less easy to define, such as the good opinion of neighbours and workmates, prestige and status within the community, and general support and success in social activities.

Negative sanctions are those which form some kind of penalty for stepping out of line, for behaving in a way which is unacceptable to members of the wider society. These include definite, regulated punishments such as the fines and prison sentences meted out by courts of law, and those of other constituted organizations such as the Church, which may defrock a priest, or excommunicate a parishioner, and professional bodies which may strike off a medical or legal practitioner. They also include more spontaneous expressions of disapproval through gossip, avoidance and ridicule within the local community. Radcliffe-Brown's second distinction, between *organized* and *diffuse sanctions*, corresponds to these two extreme sets of examples, as well as to the different types of positive sanctions mentioned above.

Organized sanctions are characteristic of large-scale, anonymous societies, but diffuse ones are found among any group of people who live in face-to-face contact. They are particularly effective in small-scale societies where it is difficult for people to move away if they fall out with their neighbours, for these are people whom one must meet constantly. In an agricultural or horticultural society, where a good deal of time and effort has been invested in the cultivation of land, they are strong, but they work effectively among the employees of large companies in industrial society too, if people want to keep their positions. In practice, sanctions may fall on a continuum between the highly organized at one end and the totally spontaneous at the other in almost any situation. Let us look at a few examples.

Japanese people discussing their own society often turn to the cultivation of rice as an explanation for the strong emphasis on harmony and co-operation, for much mutual support is necessary for a successful crop. The fields must be flooded when the rice seedlings are planted out, and complicated irrigation networks have been built up over the years to ensure this process. However, the water supply must be shared out, so villages work to a rota, and families used to help one another to do the planting, and later the harvesting, to gain maximum advantage from the period when they are allocated sufficient water, on the one hand, and when the ears ripen on the other. Now that there are machines to do many of the tasks, it is not so vital to share out these roles, but people still turn to this process to explain the co-operative nature of Japanese society.

The most severe sanction which could be brought into play in a Japanese village, especially during the pre-modern period when it was forbidden to move from one part of the country to another, was called *mura-hachibu*. This means 'village eighth-part', and it restricts neighbourly co-operation to only enough for the family to survive, that is one-eighth. Otherwise, members of the whole household were totally ostracized. No one was to speak to anyone concerned, not even the children, and no one was to invite members of the family to participate in village meetings, celebrations or festivals. Personal events such as birth, marriage and death would receive none of the usual support, indeed arranging a marriage with such a family would be well-nigh impossible. This was a highly organized sanction, arranged by the village assembly and limited to a specific period, after which the offending behaviour would supposedly be curtailed, although the only case I know personally involved the expression of disapproval about the building of a factory, which is in fact still in place.

Ostracism may also be a much more diffuse sanction, of course, and the avoidance of a person who has offended in some way is a common occurrence in many societies. In English, there is an expression 'sending to Coventry' which is a relatively organized arrangement made by some people to cut off communication with another. The expression probably dates back to the historical decision of the people of Coventry (in Warwickshire) to pull their curtains and look away when the unpopular King of Mercia's wife, Lady Godiva, was forced to ride around the streets naked to achieve the pardon she had sought for some local prisoners. In the Irish film *Ryan's Daughter*, there were impressive scenes where a family was ostracized because of the association of their daughter with a British soldier.

House-burning is another sanction which may be more or less organized. In the Highlands of Scotland, where it was for long the custom to close down all forms of business on Sundays, including cafés, restaurants, and even bed-and-breakfast establishments, to all those who were not booked in on the Saturday, a few places were apparently burnt to the ground when they began to try to alter the custom. No one was arrested, and the police could find no witnesses. Word had it that the fires were clearly 'an act of God', although somehow this custom now seems to have become outdated and God has apparently soothed his wrath.

In the almost abandoned village of Hampton Gay, just outside Oxford, a ruined house is said to stand witness to a similar occurrence (see Photograph 9.1). It is very close to the railway line, and local people say that the nineteenth-century occupants were extremely angry when their peace was shattered by this ugly innovation in travel. When an accident took place nearby, and nine railway carriages fell into the river, it is said that they refused to open their doors to help the injured, and they would lend no blankets to keep them warm. The house burnt down some time later. Historical records show that the fire actually happened several years after the accident, so the stories relating the events may be apocryphal, but their existence can in itself be seen as a potential form of social control.

A third kind of more-or-less diffuse sanction is of a type described by Radcliffe-Brown as *satirical*, usually involving some kind of public mockery. In the film mentioned above, *Ryan's Daughter*, the British soldier's woman has her beautiful hair cut off in a manner reminiscent of the 'tarring and feathering' practised in earlier times. A custom known in part of Spain as the *vito* brings neighbours round to sing abuse outside the house of a person of whom they disapprove, typically for a transgression of a sexual nature, such as adultery (see Pitt-Rivers, 1971, pp. 169–77). A similar custom in rural

Photograph 9.1   The ruined house at Hampton Gay, near Oxford (photograph: Joy Hendry)

England is known as 'loud-shouting' or 'rough music' (Thompson, 1991, pp. 467–533) – and some evening-class students I taught in rural Oxfordshire described singing repeatedly: 'we know you're in there' outside the house of an adulterous couple of whom they all roundly disapproved.

Under these circumstances, in an English village, the recalcitrant(s) may see such a display as unreasonable, but if they want to stay together, their only option would probably be to move out of the community. Fear of such unpleasant sanctions is an even more powerful force for social control in countries where the avoidance of ridicule and laughter is tied up with strong values of honour and shame. An excellent ethnographic example of this situation is to be found in an article by Juliet du Boulay, about rural Greece, where she analyses in some detail the relationship between mockery as a force for social control and the use of lies to conceal misdemeanour in the maintenance of family honour in the community where she worked.

Social relations in the community are characterized by competition between different families over wealth and reputation, and people constantly seek faults in others apparently in order to maintain their own relative superiority:

> On discovery of some offence, the discoverer immediately relates it to his or her friends and relations, and in no time at all the story is all round the village and everyone is, as they say, 'laughing' (*gelame*). The more serious or ludicrous the offence is, the more people mock the principals of it. The more they laugh, the more the victims of the laughter are humiliated, because the chief ingredient of laughter is lack of respect, and it is this above all that is the enemy of reputation and self-esteem . . . Mockery, therefore, may be said to work through shame to preserve honour. (1976, pp. 394–5)

Clearly nobody can be perfect at all times, however, and as a form of defence in this hostile environment, the local people use lies in a systematic way to protect their reputations. Du Boulay identifies no fewer than eight different kinds of lies, and she makes very clear that some forms of lying are not only tacitly accepted, but almost expected, especially when they become opposed to betraying another family member. Others are quite taboo, however, and understanding the system is evidently an important aspect of the maintenance of honour. As du Boulay puts it:

> Because the reputation for which everyone strives is something which is given by the community, this reputation, and, in the last extreme, honour itself, in a very literal sense only has reality if the rest of the community grants it that reality . . . it is [thus] more important to be thought to be in the right than it is

> actually to be in the right, and . . . deceit comes to be regarded as an
> indispensable element in social relations . . . Deceit, therefore, and the
> avoidance of public mockery, appear as phenomena ultimately connected with
> the structure of the value system and as part of the legitimate means by which
> the honour of a family is preserved and the prosperity of a house maintained.
> (Ibid., pp. 405–6)

This value system is quite difficult to understand for those brought up in a
society where frankness and honesty are granted high value, though they may
think nothing of telling a 'white lie' in a social situation where 'politeness' is
called for. 'Lies' are assigned negative value is many societies which have a
high regard for diplomacy, but most peoples have acceptable forms of indirect
communication which could also be described as a type of deceit. We shall
return to this subject in the next chapter, but du Boulay's paper is an
interesting examination of these issues as well as providing a good example of
mockery as a form of social control.

Radcliffe-Brown also talked of *religious* and *ritual sanctions* which depend
on a system of belief. Some people avoid certain types of behaviour because of
the fear that ancestral ghosts will take retribution, others may regulate their
lives in a way conducive to a favourable position in a life after death. The
terrible threats of hell preached in Christian, Muslim and Buddhist faiths
alike are certainly strong forces for social control, as are the positive images of
heaven and *nirvana*, and here a further distinction is made between *immediate*
and *delayed sanctions*. In many societies, illness and other misfortunes are put
down to the wrath of god(s), spirits or ancestors, as we saw in the last chapter,
and it is the role of priests, shamans and other mediums to intercede and find
ways to make retribution.

The reciprocal principle which may underpin such recourse is also to be
found in *economic sanctions*, which were picked out by Malinowski as
particularly important because they were often related to survival. In the
Trobriand Islands, people are careful to get on with their neighbours because
they are involved in the exchange of goods essential to their diet, he argued,
and this must be the most important sanction of all. The 'do as you would be
done by' principle is part of many forms of religious and moral dogma,
although it may not always be practised. Nor are economic sanctions always
effective, as we see from time to time when countries express disapproval of
one another by cutting off certain supplies, or by boycotting goods. A
worldwide avoidance of French wine and other goods apparently had no
effect whatsoever on nuclear testing in the Pacific.

However, reciprocal principles are useful in bringing about a neutraliza-
tion of the infringement of rules and norms of society. The payment of

compensation may go some way towards appeasing an angry customer, or a person hurt by another, and there are societies where a recognized form of 'blood-money' is to be paid in the case of murder. There are also all sorts of ritual ways of cleansing people and bringing them back into the fold, as it were, and many peoples have some way or other of giving their recalcitrants at least a second chance, as long as they appear to be sorry for what they have done. In Japan, judges try to bring about a reconciliation between parties to a dispute, rather than deciding clearly who is right and wrong, and this undoubtedly again reflects the emphasis on maintaining, where possible, a harmonious front for social relations.

Order and Dispute

Simon Roberts (1979) takes a slightly different approach to the subject of social control, as we outlined above, and his focus is on possible reactions to **dispute**. He assumes it to be inevitable that disputes will arise in any society, and he identifies different types of reaction which come into play. Of course, the expression of dispute will vary from one society to another too, but this is something we shall leave until the last section of this chapter. Here Roberts is concerned with 'legal anthropology', or the reactions he sees as in some way equivalent to or comparable with the exercise of law. However, he is at pains to point out that there may be quite different ways of keeping order, which involve nothing like the application of law, and his aim is to seek these mechanisms.

The first he discusses is the permitted exercise of *interpersonal violence.* Here, the principle is very often the reciprocal one, discussed above, where a limited amount of interpersonal violence is seen as an appropriate response to the suffering of the same. Thus, vengeance is approved in some societies, although usually only up to the limit of the hurt received, as in an 'eye for an eye, a tooth for a tooth'. Of course, in practice, the side suffering the vengeance may perceive things quite differently from that meting it out, and the continuation of such disputes into a long-term feud between groups is not at all uncommon. Indeed it forms the stuff of well known dramas such as *Romeo and Juliet* and *West Side Story*, and it may underpin a wider political system as we shall see in the next chapter, when we consider the Nuer people of the Southern Sudan.

In some cases, an organized arrangement of interpersonal violence may divert attention from the original object of the dispute and bring about a resolution. In New Guinea, among the Minj-Wahgi people, for example, there is an institution known as the *tagba boz*, which involves men from two opposing sides lining up, clasping their hands behind their backs, and kicking at each others' shins until one side withdraws. Another example is apparently found among several Eskimo groups, who either sit opposite one another and engage in head-butting, or stand up and deliver straight-arm blows to each other's heads. In either case, the battle continues until one side falls over.

In case this sounds uncivilized behaviour, the reader might like to consider the dawn duel between gentlemen, or the trenches of the First World War, as ways of resolving quarrels in Europe. In the cases cited by Roberts, on the other hand:

> An essential feature of controlled conflict of this kind is that there are recognised conventions which delimit the struggle, and ideally have the effect of preventing death or serious injury on either side . . . thus making continuous and escalating violence unlikely. (1979, p. 59)

There is an element of ritualization of the dispute in these cases, but a complete representation of the violence forms a second type of reaction, which Roberts calls *channelling conflict into ritual*. Another good example he gives is also taken from Eskimo societies, where a *'nith*-song contest' allows both sides to enunciate their grievances at a public gathering, but only through the medium of song and dance. After each side has exhausted itself in hurling as much melodious abuse as it can at the other, one party apparently usually emerges in receipt of greater public acclaim, but in any case each has had plenty of opportunity to get the problem off their chests. A similar practice is apparently found among the Tiv people of Nigeria.

The practice of sport may be seen to some extent as a ritual form of channelling conflict, for it allows in the same way representatives of two opposing groups to exercise skills in the enactment of a battle. People living in neighbouring towns and villages very often build up resentment against each other, and a weekly sporting event allows the expression of competition between them usually to be carried out in a controlled fashion. Of course, *interpersonal violence* may still break out, and it could be argued that the sporting event incites this violence, but such a breakdown of control is then subject to considerable censure on the part of the wider society. When the popular footballer Eric Cantona crossed 'the magic line' dividing the field and the fans to kick a member of the audience who shouted abuse at him, he was roundly condemned, even by his own supporters.

A side-effect of the *nith*-song contest is that it makes public all the aspects of a misdemeanour, which may well shame the guilty party into future compliance, and it is this *shaming* which forms Roberts' third type of reaction to dispute. He cites various examples, but one of them, the public harangue, will illustrate the point. In parts of New Guinea, a person who feels he has been mistreated will stand at his door, usually in the middle of the night or very early in the morning, and simply deliver a harangue against the person or persons he believes responsible. The villages are apparently compact enough, and the night sufficiently silent, for all to hear clearly what is said. The response is typically absolute silence, the guilty party to be found 'with his head bowed under the imagined stare of the whole community' (Roberts, 1979, p. 62, quoting from Young, 1971, p. 125).

The next two types of response discussed by Roberts are very similar to examples of sanctions cited by Radcliffe-Brown, namely the appeal to *supernatural agencies* and *ostracism*. The latter we have already discussed in some detail, and Roberts gives further examples of the principles involved. The former includes consideration of societies which hold ideas about witchcraft and sorcery which were the subject matter of our last chapter. Where misfortune of one sort or another is put down to witchcraft or sorcery, the response either involves identifying the witch or practising retaliatory sorcery. Various ordeals may be administered to suspected witches, as they were in Europe, and very often the ordeal itself becomes a punishment if the person accused is proved guilty. In West Africa, for example, an accused person is made to drink a concoction prepared with the poisonous bark of the Sasswood tree. If they vomit and survive, they are pronounced innocent. If they die, they were clearly guilty.

The last type of dispute resolution discussed by Roberts is *talking*, and this common form of response he considers under three further headings, namely

(1) *bilateral negotiation*,
(2) *mediation*, and
(3) *umpires*.

In the first case, the two parties concerned address one another directly, to air and try to iron out their differences; in the second case a third party becomes involved, perhaps to carry the grievances to and fro between them, perhaps to set up a meeting. The role of the mediator is to ease communication and to advise, but if a third party is engaged to make a decision about the dispute, this Roberts classifies as being an *umpire*. He also distinguishes two types of umpire, the first an *arbitrator*, who is someone the disputants ask to make a decision on their behalf; the second an *adjudicator*, a person who already holds authority in the society concerned.

The last case will of course cover most systems of courts, where the judge and jury play the role of umpire, but we should remember that the punishment they mete out for a misdemeanour may represent forms of the other types of response discussed above. Imprisonment is an example of formal ostracism, for example, and capital and corporal punishment are clearly examples of interpersonal violence, though this time removed from the disputants themselves and carried out by the wider, impersonal state. Nor are courts confined to industrial societies. In small-scale communities, there may be formal trials for those accused of misdemeanour, and the classic work of Max Gluckman (1955) is an excellent illustration of such a case.

In a monograph entitled *The Judicial Process among the Barotse of Northern Rhodesia*, Gluckman analysed the processes used by this indigenous people, identifying and illustrating concepts parallel to English notions invoked in legal situations, and describing methods used in the examination of crimes, the interviewing of witnesses, and the application of the notion of 'a reasonable man'. Another classic work is that of Paul Bohannan (1989), in his book *Justice and Judgement among the Tiv* (first published 1957), about a Nigerian people, which emphasizes the motives and rationale of the individuals involved rather than the overall structure of the system which comes into play. Both provide good further reading on this subject.

Contested Norms and Social Control in a Context

A more recent collection of papers, entitled *Understanding Disputes: the Politics of Argument* (ed. Caplan, 1995) examines in various contexts the work of a man, Philip Gulliver, who spent much of his life observing disputes. The papers move from national disputes over access to water sources, through 'gentlemanly values' in two sets of political circles, to family wrangles over failed marriages, intra-family strife about death and funerals, and concepts of passion and compassion. The contexts considered are also extremely various, and the reader is introduced to discrepant values in locations as far apart as Ireland in the nineteenth and twentieth centuries, rural Nepal, London, Lagos, and more specific African locations in Kenya, Tanzania and Uganda.

Some of the broader themes covered include discussion of a move from judicial institutions to negotiation as the more 'civilized' means of dispute resolution, including a realization that both these systems still favour the more powerful partner, despite ostensible efforts to incorporate approaches previously more characteristic of weaker peoples. There are also examples of resistance, and some of these illustrate the way different parties draw on different values and methods of approach.

An excellent example is a paper by Stephen Gaetz (1995) about disputes between the leaders and members of an Irish youth club, where the latter resort to violence because they feel excluded from decision-making. The leaders respond to this plea by setting up committee meetings, and then cannot understand why the youths do not turn up, or fail to air their views. From the point of view of the youths, who have no experience of committees and little confidence that they would make a difference, these are just another way for the leaders to exert their authority. Here the important point is illustrated that the disputing *process* may be more significant than any resolution.

Most of the papers follow Gulliver's emphasis on understanding the political and historical context of any dispute and the 'categories of meaning by which the participants themselves comprehend their experience' (Caplan, 1995, p. 156). Sometimes the parties to a dispute do not even share these categories of meaning, and each seeks to manipulate the situation to suit their own understanding. In another case, different sets of norms may be invoked by the same people under different circumstances. Pat Caplan shows how the three sets of Islamic law, Tanzanian law and local custom available in Mafia Island, Tanzania, where she did her fieldwork, make possible a continual negotiation of rules and behaviour, allowing a situation of contested norms to be counterpoised to relations of unequal **power**. Those who are at ease with the three possibilities have a distinct advantage over those who know only one.

In this detailed discussion of a specific long-term dispute, Pat Caplan, who is also the editor of the papers, illustrates her contention at the start of the book that the study of disputes leads us:

> straight to the key issues in anthropology – norms and ideology, power, rhetoric and oratory, personhood and agency, morality, meaning and interpretation – and enables us not only to see social relations in action but also to understand cultural systems. (1995, p. 1)

What her paper also illustrates very nicely is the fluidity of norms, and their manipulative possibilities, an issue which we raised in the introduction to this chapter.

Attempts to classify responses to dispute, and sanctions which come into play, are extremely useful in the understanding of methods of social control which people exercise upon one another in different parts of the world. The work of anthropologists is also particularly valuable for a deep understanding of the constraints which inform the organization of undisputed life, for it is only with long-term observations that strongly held, underlying forces of influence may be identified and evaluated. In the case of Japan, a study of child-rearing methods revealed to me some of the complicated mechanisms of peer pressure which profoundly affect the lives of Japanese adults and the decisions they make about how to behave.

One of the overt aims of kindergarten education, for example, is to inculcate an understanding of the way that subordinating self-interest to the needs of a wider group will have long-term benefits to all involved. Teachers use various means to encourage children to discipline one another in this endeavour, thus imparting a principle which underpins the success of the whole education system and later working life. When I set out to study child-rearing, I had no idea of the extent of the importance of the findings I would make, which illustrates the advantage of long-term study and an open agenda.

We will end this chapter by looking at a book which focuses on social control in a particular society, and which approaches it from an angle which might not at first have been anticipated. In *Power and Persuasion*, subtitled *Fiestas and Social Control in Rural Mexico*, Stanley Brandes (1988) examines in minute detail the events and processes leading up to annual festivals which find the villagers relaxing in a frenzy of fun and fireworks. The villagers almost certainly enjoy themselves, for each fiesta is a culmination of months of arrangements and planning, financing, purchasing and allocation of tasks, and the successful accomplishment of the various elements of the event demonstrate that things in the village are operating in an orderly fashion.

Various aspects of the moral universe are played out during the course of a festival, and power relationships are expressed in the relative financial contributions made by each household in the village to the huge pyrotechnic displays of material wealth and influence. Masked figures in a dance performance known as 'La Danza' portray in symbolic form the system of religious and moral values which underpin social life. They break normal social rules in the way they dance, but the figures they portray, such as Death and the Devil, are so abhorrent that Brandes argues that they actually exert and demonstrate a strong force for social control.

Fiestas in general are expected to find people reversing the expectations of normal everyday life, and turning upside down the moral system. This they do, but their production offers an excellent window on the workings of social and political relations within the village. In Brandes' words:

> To be successful, fiestas of all types depend on two predictable circumstances: cooperation among leaders and order among the participants. When a fiesta is over, and both order and co-operation have prevailed, villagers know that their society is intact. Perhaps the constant threat of disorder and uncooperativeness . . . actually keeps the whole fiesta cycle in motion, as people demand periodic affirmation of cooperation and social control. (1988, p. 165)

In another location, the details might be different.

We have now seen several examples of approaches identified by anthropologists as important for understanding systems of social control. We have looked at witchcraft among the Azande, shamanism among the Akawaio, marriage in Japan and fiestas in Mexico. The anthropologists concerned could possibly have chosen a different focus and come up with something equally interesting, but they could not easily have anticipated all that they would find before they got to the field. Unearthing a system of social control is a long-term endeavour, but it is a satisfying one, and it is one which demonstrates the value of the kind of qualitative research engaged in by anthropologists.

References

du Boulay, Juliet (1976) 'Lies, mockery and family integrity', in J. G. Peristiany (ed.),*Mediterranean Family Structures* (Cambridge University Press).

Brandes, Stanley (1988) *Power and Persuasion: Fiestas and Social Control in Rural Mexico* (Philadelphia: University of Pennsylvania Press).

Caplan, Pat (ed.) (1995) *Understanding Disputes: the Politics of Argument* (Oxford: Berg).

Gaetz, Stephen (1995) ' "Youth Development": Conflict and Negotiation in an Urban Irish Youth Club', in Pat Caplan (ed.), *Understanding Disputes* (Oxford: Berg) pp. 181–201.

Pitt-Rivers, Julian A. (1971) *The People of the Sierra* (University of Chicago Press).

Radcliffe-Brown, A. R. (1952) 'Social Sanctions' in *Structure and Function* (London: Cohen & West).

Roberts, Simon (1979) *Order and Dispute* (Harmondsworth: Pelican).

Thompson, E. P. (1991) *Customs in Common* (London: Penguin Books).

Young, Michael (1971) *Fighting with Food* (Cambridge University Press).

Further Reading

Blythe, Ronald (1972) *Akenfield* (Harmondsworth: Penguin).

Bohannan, Paul (1989) *Justice and Judgement among the Tiv* (Prospect Heights: Waveland Press; first published 1957).

Cohen, Abner (1980) 'Drama and politics in the development of the London Carnival',*Man* **15**: 65–87.

Gluckman, Max (1955) *The Judicial Process among the Barotse of Northern Rhodesia* (Manchester University Press).

Moore, Sally Falk (1978) *Law as Process: an Anthropological Approach* (London: Routledge & Kegan Paul).

Nader, Laura and Harry F. Todd (1978) *The Disputing Process: Law in 10 Societies* (New York: Columbia University Press).

Novels

Gulik, Robert van, *The Chinese Maze Murders* (London: Sphere, 1989) is a series of detective stories which demonstrate the value of an understanding of indirect and non-verbal cues, rather in the manner of Sherlock Holmes, but in a more openly culturally specific mode.

Mo, Timothy, *Sour Sweet* (London: Hodder & Stoughton, 1990) is a novel about a Chinese family which settles in Britain, and the social constraints they experience more from the Chinese community than the wider British one.

Ouzo, Mario, *The Godfather* (Greenwich, Conn.: Fawcett, 1969), is a classic novel about the social control exercised among members of Sicilian/American mafia groups.

Films

The two 'Disappearing World' films, *The Mehinacu* (Carlos Pasini and Thomas Gregor, 1974), about a people of the Brazilian rain forest, and *The Kirghiz of Afghanistan* (Charlie Nairn and Nazif Shahrani, 1976), about a people virtually imprisoned on a mountain top between Russia and China, which they may not legally enter, both illustrate aspects of social control discussed in this chapter.

CHAPTER 10

The Art of Politics

Political Possibilities

It was pointed out in the introduction to the last chapter that it is not always possible to make a clear distinction between the concepts of 'law' and 'politics', but our discussions there fell more into the realms of 'law' than politics. However, we took pains to broaden our approach to include mechanisms of social control which could hardly be described as 'legal', even in the broadest sense of the word, although our approach was certainly not confined to societies which have no overarching legal system. In this chapter we shall turn to areas more usually associated with what the English language might term 'politics', though again the reader must be prepared to have a broad and flexible mind.

We shall start with the internationally familiar, however, and we will move gradually into examples of societies whose political systems, if we may call them such, were at first quite impenetrable to observers from European nations. Much of the early work in the area of British political anthropology was first carried out by anthropologists in a colonial situation, where ethnographers were inevitably caught up with helping their own government to maintain order in unfamiliar circumstances, though they may also have found themselves acting as advocates for the people they came to know better than any other outsider, and criticizing aspects of colonial rule. They were also dependent on the goodwill of the local administrators for their continued presence in a fieldwork location, however.

The influential early British examples were African, and they were classified under two main headings, namely *centralized* and *acephalus* systems (Fortes and Evans-Pritchard, 1940). The first were known as *kingships*, with relatively stable hierarchical units, and the second were apparently 'headless', the Greek meaning of the term. Two famous anthropological studies which are cited to illustrated these types are again by Evans-Pritchard, both of peoples of the Sudan. The first, the Shilluk, exemplify a kingship, and the

Nuer people of Southern Sudan have been held up as a model for the second, *acephalus* type. We will discuss both cases so that the reader will become aware of the base line in this area of the field.

As ethnographic material became available from different parts of the world, however, it became clear that these two approaches were actually better described as opposing ends of a continuum of types of political system, with interesting and sometimes rather recognizable cases in the middle. We will consider some cases from the Latin American rain forest as an example of the middle ground, in a section entitled 'leadership', but we could have chosen to look at people from any number of other locations for all these sections. It is a good exercise to read a complete ethnography to get a feel for the intricacies of a particular political system, and the books listed at the end of the chapter by Ahmed, Barth, Maybury-Lewis, Leach and Strathern are excellent examples.

This chapter is named 'the art of politics' in deference to the stunning ingenuity of human beings in creating and manipulating relations of **power** and authority in a rich variety of ways in different parts of the world, so after the examination of classic political 'types' we turn to consider some of this variety and ingenuity at the level of human interaction. The importance is noted again of guarding against carrying assumptions about behaviour from one political system to another, particularly where the unspoken is almost as important as the spoken word. By its very nature politics often involves disputed ideas of the type we discussed towards the end of the last chapter, and anthropologists are well placed to contribute to this arena too (for example, see Shore, 1990, listed under 'Further Reading' at the end of this chapter).

In the end this chapter must be a cursory glance at a huge subject, for political science forms an academic discipline in its own right, and anthropologists themselves devote whole books to the political branch of their subject (for example, Balandier, 1967; Bloch, 1975; Gledhill, 1994; Godelier, 1986, all listed under 'Further Reading'), but it is useful to examine some of the findings of anthropologists in this sphere for two reasons.

(1) In the classic works we can identify an interesting range of ideas about the distribution of power in society, which may now be interpreted within the context of colonial endeavour (Gledhill is particularly good on this subject).

(2) We can identify in all the variety some persistent themes which run through the gamut of political life, which can inform for anyone the familiar exercise of power, but with unusual twists.

Types of Political System

(1) Centralized Systems

The political system which was most familiar to European nations setting up colonies was a centralized one with various forms of hierarchical arrangements. There are clearly a great number of possibilities for how such a system may work, but we can identify some characteristic features. First, in its most organized form, a centralized system will have a *head* at the top and layers of lesser positions with degrees of authority and dependence below that. The position of the *head* may be *hereditary*, and it may even have some divine qualities, or it may be filled by a person elected by the people at large. These two possibilities may seem quite different within conventional approaches to politics, but they are both part of centrally organized systems. Several countries, including Belgium, Britain, Nepal, the Netherlands, Norway and Sweden manage to maintain both types of centralized system, as indeed does Japan, and the two types play different roles, but they are both *centralized*.

In both cases, the people indicate submission to the system, willingly or unwillingly, by paying **tribute** or tax, and this makes available public funds, which allows for certain other possibilities, for example:

   (i)   a *ruling class* with officials to carry out activities on behalf of the group
   (ii)   *protection* in times of dispute
   (iii) *courts* for dealing with disputes
   (iv)   buildings and other *facilities* for public use
   (v)   *feasts* and *aid* for the needy
   (vi)   *ritual* support, perhaps in dealing with spirits.

A classic example from the anthropological literature is provided by the case of the Shilluk people, who have a hereditary **kingship**, legitimated by the idea that the spirit of their god, Nyikang, passes from one king to another. The king symbolizes the people and the changeless moral order, but his role is sacerdotal rather than governmental. He reigns, and others do the ruling. The Shilluk nation is divided into settlements, each with a chief and council, and further subdivided into hamlets, each with a head, usually of a lineage. Myths validate the overall hierarchy, as all can trace their descent from characters in a saga which tells of Nyikang dividing up the land on conquest. Lineage heads have ritual duties to the king, who is a mediator between man and god. He must keep ritually pure and healthy to avoid natural disaster. If he falls ill or senile, he should be killed for the sake of the people.

When British colonists encountered a society such as this, they had relatively little difficulty in understanding the political arrangements, and they were able to incorporate the system under their own overarching umbrella. By respecting the king, and his entourage, for something akin to their own, they could communicate in a relatively troublefree manner, from their point of view, though things did not always proceed smoothly, as history has taught us. The case of India is a particularly good example of where things at first fell neatly into place to provide 'the jewel in the crown' of the British Empire, but then became more complicated, as Paul Scott's Raj Quartet (see p. 45) made clear in an anthropologically interesting manner.

In some cases potential colonists were understandably opposed in their efforts to impose a new order, but a centralized system is relatively easy to defeat. If the head is deposed, and the new rulers observe most of the niceties of social life as far as keeping the underlying hierarchy in place, they can simply rely on existing mechanisms to impose their new regime. This is what happened in many cases of centralized systems, and the pre-existing culture became gradually eroded. One well-known example is the case of the Aztec Empire in pre-colonial Mexico, a highly organized centralized system, under the rule of the Emperor Montezuma. However, it espoused a set of beliefs which happened to place the arrival on their shores of the Spanish conquistadors as fulfilling a legend that one of their gods would return.

It was therefore relatively easy for Hernando Cortez to step into the position of supreme ruler in the Aztec court, and he and his party could set about colonizing Mexico for Spain. It was not long before Aztec culture was destroyed, although some of the other indigenous people remained. This is the society we mentioned in Chapter 1 where the curtailment of the practice of human sacrifice, seen as a way to keep the gods content and the society prosperous, coincided as predicted with the end of the culture. The other example of a centralized system in South America was the Inca Empire and this suffered a similar fate in the country which became Peru, but not all of South America was so easy to colonise, as we shall see in the next section.

Meanwhile, the centralized case of Japan may be cited to illustrate some of the complications of the too easy application of a 'political type' for understanding the locus of power in any situation. Although Japan has never been colony to another power, it was occupied after defeat in the Second World War, when the Allied Forces insisted on 'democratizing' the political system, already modelled on European prototypes when Japan prepared to 'modernize' in the latter half of the nineteenth century. Japan's system thus has recognizable elements such as a parliament, political parties, and constituencies, as well as full adult franchise and free and fair elections. According to the political observers from the outside world, this is a system they can analyse and understand.

In practice, in a large part, Japan's system still works according to principles which predate even the first modernization process. The confrontational nature of the chambers of the parliament is not a mode of communication in which decisions are easily reached in Japanese discourse, large political parties tend to operate at a factional level more reminiscent of social relations found elsewhere in Japan, and voting is not always an individual decision in a society where reciprocity and loyalty to local benefactors counts highly. This is a good example of why it is useful to examine politics in the context of a wider social system, rather than making assumptions about categories such as 'centralized', and we will return to consider some strategies for the exercise of power in the last part of this chapter.

(2) Leadership

Among the peoples who inhabit the tropical rain forests of Latin America, politics is much less clear cut than the centralized systems we have sketched above. Nevertheless, their leaders have recognizable qualities and their arrangements are still open to comparison with the politics of the industrialized world. Some people become **leaders** and others are content to follow them. There are many societies we could consider here, but the work carried out by anthropologists on the Yanomamö people of Venezuela and Brazil, encountered in Chapter 3 (see also Ferguson, 1995), and the Akwe Shavante, also of the Brazilian rain forest (Maybury-Lewis, 1974), provide good cases for examination. The following characteristics are generally common of the area.

(i) No Central Administration

Here is the first major difference to the societies we have been considering so far, because these peoples have no formal system of authority, and they have therefore posed many problems to the governments of the countries where they are found. Typically, such governments will try to appoint a local chief among indigenous people and work through that chief to maintain communication. They will offer remuneration to such a chief, and possibly a uniform or some other badge of office. Those who accepted such an incentive to represent their people to outside bodies very often found themselves the laughing stock of the community, however, and any pretensions to leadership they might have held before such an arrangement would soon disappear. In some areas only a person regarded locally as an idiot would contemplate such a role.

(ii) Village Autonomy

One of the reasons for this situation is the strong value placed on village autonomy in this part of the world. Leaders can come and go, and if there happened to be two in conflict within one community, the community itself may well split and redefine itself. We referred in Chapter 8 to Peter Rivière's argument about how, among the Trio of Surinam and the Akwe Shavante, these divisions may be initiated through sorcery accusations. Ultimately, the villagers follow a leader only as long as they see it to be in their interest, and they are not inclined at all to be dictated to by outsiders, even if the latter do try to work through their own people.

(iii) The Leaders Lead

As the word implies, leaders in this area have none of the coercive power or accepted authority of the 'chiefs' discussed in the previous section. They simply lead, and if others approve, they follow. Thus, if the leader thinks it time to clean up the central square he will start doing it, perhaps calling to his companions to join him. He has no power to instruct others to carry out such tasks for him, and if others fail to see the sense of his plan, he will be left unsupported. It is even said among the Akwe Shavante that they are likely to kill bossy leaders! Putting on airs would also clearly be unacceptable, and this would explain why the provision of a uniform and a salary might disrupt an otherwise effective relationship.

(iv) Environmental Factors

These are undoubtedly important in the political life of these communities. This is an area where slash and burn cultivation is the norm, requiring commitment to a particular patch of land for only a few years at a time. A smallish area of the forest is cleared for cultivation (see Photograph 10.1) but its nutritional value is limited, so communities are small and where possible people move on regularly. The diet is supplemented with sporadic hunting and fishing, but none of these economic activities requires much managerial organization, as was pointed out by Anthony Leeds in a consideration of the Yaruro people of south-central Venezuela:

> Given the techniques and tools of the Yaruro, all the subsistence activities . . .
> can conveniently be done by one person . . . the logic of tools and techniques
> concerned demands utilization by single persons. Activities of all sorts may be
> done by aggregates of persons, each utilizing his own tools and techniques

Photograph 10.1   Trio Indians in Surinam clear the rain forest for planting in the 'slash and burn' cultivation style (photograph courtesy of Peter Rivîere)

> individually but neither the activity, the tools nor the techniques entail the aggregation of individuals. Thus, from the point of view of human organization, the technology, by itself, entails no managerial functions, no coordination of tasks which must be overseen by someone occupying an appropriately defined status. (1969, p. 383)

The major co-operative venture is choosing and clearing land and setting up a village to administer it. Decisions must be made about when and where to move, and a potential leader is able to judge his support by the response he gets to an initiative to seek a new site. The length of a long-house, which is shared by the men in the group, is a spatial indication of a leader's support, for it will be tailored to suit the size of the community, although people can of course leave if they grow tired of a particular leader, and moving is a time for realignment, as we have seen.

The qualities required by an aspiring leader in this part of the world are interesting to observe, for they are mostly quite recognizable. First of all, a leader is usually an example of a successful person by local standards, so an athletic, well-built person who is good at hunting would be an appropriate type. A leader needs to display *generosity* with goods, and a good hunter is well placed to share his spoils as well as to attract several wives so that he can maintain a surplus of cooked food. *Oratorical skills* are admired here as elsewhere, and they are sometimes used in formal negotiations between villages known as 'ceremonial dialogue', for resolving potential disputes as well as for trade, to arrange marriages, and so forth. These skills are also important to resolve disputes within the local group, and the skills of a *moderator, mediator* and *peace-maker* are highly regarded. Among the Nambikwara, for example, the word for leader is, literally, 'one who unites'.

Among the Akwe Shavante, who are a large enough group to be split into factions, their leaders are permanently in a state of competition over minor disputes, and their skills need to be flexible. The leader of the dominant faction at any one time may emphasize his skills of impartiality, tolerance and wisdom to maintain peace and harmony within the wider community. If threatened, he needs to be ready to become more assertive and aggressive. As Maybury-Lewis notes, using the term 'chief' for the most dominant Akwe Shavante leaders:

> A chief is therefore in a difficult position. The qualities ideally required of him and the behaviour expected of him while he is in office are diametrically opposed to those of which he had to make use when he aspired to the chieftancy. Indeed, in a community where the dominant faction is not firmly established, they are opposed to the talents he must display in order to maintain himself in office at all. . . . chiefs [therefore] tend to veer from one type of behaviour to its opposite. Sometimes they handle seemingly intractable situations with great patience and forensic skill. At others they deal summarily and ruthlessly with only incipient opposition. (1974, p. 204)

Finally, some leaders may need to have **shamanistic** qualities, although this may be a separate but influential role. This split between the *sacerdotal* and the *governmental*, also noted above for the Shilluk, is actually found in many societies. A system found in ancient Japan, for example, held a brother and a sister at the top of the hierarchy. The sister was a religious figure in constant touch with the deities, while the brother took care of everyday political matters. The twin imperial/governmental system still in practice in Japan evidently has ancient roots. Other contemporary monarchies become quite commonplace too in view of these examples, although the role of the monarch is usually more symbolic than religious for most people.

Other examples of leadership and how it may be acquired abound in the ethnography, but the Latin American case gives a good example of the importance of placing a particular political system in its local environmental, ecological and demographic context. This is also an area where anthropologists can hardly fail to get involved in helping the people with whom they work to represent themselves to the outside world. The rain forest habitat is constantly threatened by developers, most recently seeking oil, and anthropologists need to address questions of compatibility between the different political strategies involved in the negotiations. According to Laura Rival, an anthropologist specializing in this area:

> We need to study ethnographically how, when communities encounter the oil transnationals, they come to think in a new way and to take decisions about their futures; and how they come to abandon their self-reliant marginality as they envisage their sustainable integration into wider spheres . . . We need to understand how, in the course of unequal negotiations, emerging forms of political agency are built up through the strategic use of particular rhetorical styles. Under what conditions can the abstract notion of 'equal partnership' become a reality. (1997, p. 3)

The film cited below (p. 180) about the Kayapo people of the Altamira region of the Xingu valley, is an excellent illustration of such negotiations. Thanks to the help of an anthropologist who had worked in the area, and the film crew who helped the Kayapo to record their deals with the Brazilian authorities, the outcome was relatively positive. Others are not so fortunate, and there is still much work to be done, according to Rival. This is a serious and urgent area of applied anthropology. In the following section, we return briefly to Africa, where the anthropologists' work undoubtedly helped the former colonial authorities. An understanding of the ecology is again vital to making sense of an apparently headless society.

(3) Acephalus Societies

(i) Segmentary Systems

Anthropologists from states with highly centralized political systems for a while found it difficult to understand how some African societies were organized at all. They seemed to have very little in the way of political organization, and yet retained order in everyday life. Detailed field research eventually revealed some of the principles underlying this order, and Evans-Pritchard made a breakthrough in describing the **segmentary system** of the Nuer of southern Sudan, a people who hate authority, and who 'strut about like lords of the earth . . . equals who regard themselves as God's noblest creation' (1940, p. 182). It is important in the description which follows to distinguish between the *ideal* system and that which operates in practice.

The Nuer are a cattle-keeping people who live a **transhumant** life, spending the dry season in camps by the rivers, where they also fish, and moving away to villages on high land, where they also grow millet, during the wet season when the river floods. They thus spend part of the year in territorially defined communities separated from each other by flooded land, and part in larger, more fluid settlements when people can move amongst each other. The basic economic unit is conceptually, or *ideally*, a group of relations who move to and fro together, but each move is also an opportunity for *political* realignment, and some members of a village may thus be together for political reasons and not in fact be related. This *territorial* unit is therefore described by Evans-Pritchard as the smallest political **segment**, which in turn belongs to larger segments occupying a particular region.

The whole tribe or clan is made up of people related in this way. However, Nuer men *think of themselves* very much in terms of belonging to a group which shares **descent** from a common ancestor. They *ideally* share living arrangements with close relatives, described by Evans-Pritchard as a minimal **lineage**, and carry out economic and ritual activities of various sorts with larger groups of relatives, which he describes as minor, major or maximal lineages. The largest group defined in this way is a *clan* of people ultimately descended from one founding ancestor, who is described as related to the founding ancestors of the other clans in a way that binds the whole Nuer people.

This *ideal* model is distinguished in Evans-Pritchard's description from groups which align themselves in practice into what he calls *political segments*. The smallest, the villages, belong to *tribes*, which correspond approximately to the *clans*, but they may also align themselves for particular political issues with segments of varying sizes which Evans-Pritchard calls *primary*, *secondary* and *tertiary* (see Figure 10.1). The moral universe varies depending on a specific issue which may arise, and people may only conceive of themselves as members of a particular segment in opposition to others in a different one.

To give an example, if a dispute arises between members of two different villages, their relatives will support them according to principles of common ancestry, which in practice is translated into common territorial segments. Thus, in reference to Figure 10.2, if a member of Z^1 fights with a member of Z^2, the quarrel is between the two Z groups. If a member of Z^1 fights with a member of Y^1, then the differences between the two Z groups will be put aside as the two align in opposition to Y^1 as Y^2. Similarly if a member of Y^1 quarrels with a member of X^1, the whole of Y will align in opposition to X, overriding their previous differences. A common political phenomenon in Nuerland is the feud, and it is more difficult to resolve the larger the groups

Political Units	**Kin Terms**
(Territorial)	(Groups who trace descent from common ancestor)

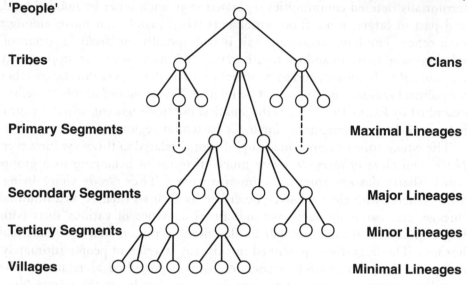

'People'

Tribes   Clans

Primary Segments   Maximal Lineages

Secondary Segments   Major Lineages

Tertiary Segments   Minor Lineages

Villages   Minimal Lineages

Figure 10.1   A representation of the social and political organization of the Nuer

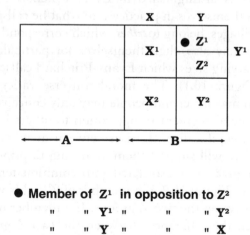

● Member of Z^1 in opposition to Z^2

"   " Y^1 "   "   " Y^2

"   " Y "   "   " X

"   " B "   "   " A

Source: E. E. Evans-Pritchard, *The Nuer* (1940), p. 144, by permission of Oxford University Press.

Figure 10.2   The segmentary system

involved. A feud may be between camps, or villages, or any larger group up to the whole tribe, versus neighbouring people like the Dinka.

This description forms the basis of what has been described as a **segmentary system**. Evans-Pritchard described such a political system as a 'set of structural relations between territorial segments'. A man is a member of a group by virtue of opposition to another group, and thus group membership is relative to the situation.

> political values are relative and . . . the political system is an equilibrium between opposed tendencies towards fission and fusion, between the tendency of all groups to segment, and the tendency of all groups to combine with segments of the same order. The tendency towards fusion is inherent in the segmentary character of Nuer political structure, for although any group tends to split into opposed parts these parts must tend to fuse in relation to other groups, since they form part of a segmentary system. Hence fission and fusion in political groups are two aspects of the same segmentary principle, and the Nuer tribe and its divisions are to be understood as an equilibrium between these two contradictory, yet complementary tendencies . . . the tendency towards segmentation must be defined as a fundamental principle of their social structure. (1940, p. 148)

Similar principles were found among other African peoples, after Evans-Pritchard had published his study, but these principles can be used in other parts of the world too. Consider the case of sporting activities where people alter their allegiances depending on the magnitude of the occasion. Thus supporters of a local town team in any country would oppose another town in a match between the two, but would join forces to support a larger team drawn from both towns to represent a wider area. In an international event, supporters of all these teams would become supporters of their national team against another country.

(ii) Age Sets and Age Grades

The Nuer also divide themselves up into **age sets** and **age grades**, but Evans-Pritchard did not think that these had much political importance. In other African societes, it is the system of age grades which is seen as the basis of the political system. Examples are to be found in the books cited below by Paul Spencer (1973) and Monica Wilson (1963). Typically, all men in the society participate in such a system, women less often. All those born during a particular period of time are automatically members of a particular age set, and they share this membership with their **age mates** throughout life, moving gradually through **age grades** as they get older. Typically, these will include:

- *elders* – who will be responsible for political decisions and dispute resolution;
- *warriors* – who will be responsible for defence and protection; and
- *youths* – who will be learning the ways of their people.

In some larger tribes, the members of age sets will co-operate with their contemporaries in other groups to form *age regiments*. The Southern African Zulu people had such a system.

Examples of people with an age grade political system are the Nandi and the Masai people of East Africa. The Nandi, for example, have no fewer than seven age grades, and each age set recruits for about 15 years, so there is some overlap in practice with the functional roles they are able to play. The youngest group is *small boys*, the next one is *initiates*, who have free sexual access to girls of the equivalent group, the next is *warriors*, who are expected to get married, and there are four groups of older men, each of whom is expected to defer to and obey those above them. Members of the same age set are seen as equals and should help one another, even to the extent of sharing wives. The names of the age sets circulate so that each new group takes the name of the last oldest group, who would by then usually have died out. Important political roles may thus be allocated throughout the society on the basis of age.

Again, this system uses a principle of social order which is found in any society, whether or not it is part of the political system. A cohort of young men may be called upon anywhere to take part in the defence of a nation, or smaller group, although the extent to which age brings greater respect is more variable, especially in the industrialized areas, where people are expected to retire from active work at a certain age. In some parts of Japan, there are age grades, just as in Africa, with functions which operate in a rather similar way at a local level, and this provides an opportunity to keep even the oldest members of the community valued. These consist of:

- *children's groups* – which meet for sports activities, entertainment, and to play a **ritual** role in festivals;
- *youth groups* – which also have ritual roles at festivals, meet each other for sports tournaments, and go on trips together, sometimes as a kind of *ordeal*;
- *fire brigades* – which are groups of young married men who are responsible for *protection* in times of danger or local disaster;
- *adults in the prime of life* – who make *decisions* about community affairs, resolve *disputes* and plan *festivals*;
- *old people* – who also meet for sports, travel together, and carry out tasks in the local community.

In some parts of Japan there are also age sets who meet regularly for social events. They may collect money regularly, help out in times of need, and make journeys together. These groups have little to do with the political system, but they are important for interpersonal relations in everyday life. In general, in Japan, people are expected to defer to their elders, using polite language to address them, and they can only be really relaxed with members of their own age group, hence the importance of age sets and other age-related groups such as old classmates. This is a factor which feeds indirectly into political life in Japan.

Acquiring and Achieving Political Power and Status

Age is in fact a universal way of measuring **status**, and determining people's **roles** in social life. This is an **ascribed** status, which we cannot choose, like gender and inherited qualities such as membership in a lineage or a royal family. **Achieved** status is that gained through one's occupation, skills and success in other fields. In democratic societies, this latter is generally regarded as the more important and acceptable type of status, although acquired characteristics may in practice be vital to achieving success in political circles. In age-set and lineage societies, formal status is ascribed, though informal status may be acquired through oratory and other interpersonal skills.

In any society people interested in the acquisition and manipulation of power will need to negotiate the system as they find it, and anthropologists have adopted different approaches in understanding the rich variety of material they encounter in the field. Evans-Pritchard's studies, cited above, set out an abstract 'structural' system only really accessible to someone who is not caught up within it. He is trying to make clear the way in which the world is classified by the people involved, and thus help a reader to understand the social background within which the behaviour of the individuals he observed may be interpreted.

Others have focused directly on the point of view of the individual members of a society in practice in everyday life. One well-known example of the latter is the work of Fredrik Barth (1965) on the political leaders of the Swat Pathan, which emphasizes the way individuals make choices, usually in their own self-interest, in order to *achieve* status and power. This approach is called 'transactionalist', and it has been criticized for failing to lay out the important categories within which the Pathans were working. Ahmed's (1976) subsequent work sets out to rectify some of this by placing the Swat Pathan material within the context of the state.

A ground-breaking study which emphasized again the importance of looking at people in the wider context in which they found themselves was carried out by Edmund Leach (1970). His book, *Political Systems of Highland Burma*, involves members of several different language groups, and he lays out the formal possibilities for political action by presenting important categories of a system of classification shared across the area in all the languages. This is a structural overview again, and Leach has been criticized for presenting the situation as if it were static, but he argues that he is describing *ideal* systems. As we saw above, it is important to distinguish these from practice, and since this case involves marriage alliances as a vital part of the system, we shall discuss it further in the next chapter.

Opposing principles of equality and hierarchy underpin much of Leach's study, as we shall see, and these also form the focus of a collection of papers, edited by Brenneis and Myers (1984), which examines the situation in a variety of Pacific communities. Entitled *Dangerous Words*, this study approaches the subject of politics through the use of language (c.f. Bloch, 1975), and indeed, through the suppression of language, or the use of non-verbal and other indirect means of communication in the pursuit of political power. Many of the communities under consideration place a high value on harmonious interaction and great pains are taken to avoid direct and open confrontation. Such an avenue to political power is quite unfamiliar to people who have been brought up in a society where government is carried out through debate between a party in power and others in open opposition, but it is precisely an anthropological approach which can reveal the mechanisms of political interaction in societies which do not prize the dialectical means of resolving issues.

In my book *Wrapping Culture*, referred to in Chapter 3, I set out to demonstrate some of the layers of indirect communication which could enter into a struggle for power, and although Japan was the main ethnographic focus, and gifts and their wrapping the prototype, there are many other examples. We considered cases of the power of 'wrapping the body' in Chapters 5 and 6, when we looked at the adornment of the Wahgi people of New Guinea and the political implications of the body tattoo. The use of castles and palaces to express authority as well as demonstrating physical power, is an example of the 'wrapping of space', and I have also suggested a notion of 'wrapping time' to the subtle forms of organization and presentation which may be used in meetings.

In all these cases there is political advantage to be gained by those who can exploit these indirect forms of communication. In a society such as Japan which apparently has a rather fixed set of principles ordering people into hierarchical frames, the skilful use of various forms of 'wrapping' allows considerable manipulation of the status quo by people who understand the system. In Japan, these different layers of operation are clearly recognized,

conception for the development of the new human being, and the father may be expected to keep 'feeding' the foetus with further sexual encounters. This may sound quite bizarre, but one of the concerns of the British public, and therefore the Warnock Committee, was certainly about how a child should be treated once it is born if it is to develop into a well-balanced member of the society in which it lives, as mentioned above in the case of the 'single-parent family'.

Rivière discussed the further complications which arise if all three roles – provision of an egg (the role of the *genetrix*), the carrying of the child, and the subsequent rearing of that child – are separated. The need to use Latin words for these roles already indicates the linguistic problems which arise in English, but there are all sorts of other issues related to cultural constructions of the family, legal ideas about legitimacy and inheritance, religious, scientific and social ideas about the nature of a human being, and the rights of men and women to be in control of their bodies.

There has been much debate among anthropologists on this subject since that time (for example, see Franklin, 1997; Shore, 1992; and Strathern, 1992, all listed under 'Further Reading' below), but Rivière wrote rather cautiously,

> I am not advocating . . . that we should therefore adopt the ideas and practices of other people. I am merely suggesting that it might help if we removed our cultural blinkers and saw our problems in a wider perspective. If we did this, the surrogate mothers might not appear to be the threat to civilization that some people make them out to be. (1985, p. 6)

In a sense, this is a plea which could apply to many social issues, but as we have already seen in our examination of the work of anthropologists, we too see the world though 'cultural blinkers'.

Some anthropologists have tried to draw up typologies of 'kinship systems' which would eventually encompass all possible varieties, others have concentrated on developing often very complex theories about logical possibilities for kin relations. In the 1970s, as part of a 'rethinking' vogue within anthropology, a book entitled *Rethinking Kinship and Marriage* (Needham, 1971) focused on basic difficulties, first about defining something universal which could be called **kinship**, and then about isolating such a thing from wider aspects of the social system in which it was found. The authors suggested that early anthropologists were somewhat blinded by their own expectations of kinship, based on deeply engrained ideas about biological links, and later ones became caught up following their lead without enough reflection about what they were doing and how they might be taking some aspects of social life out of its context. The editor, Rodney Needham, wrote:

There has been a fair amount of discussion about what 'kinship' really is. My own view is that much of this debate is pretty scholastic and inconsequential . . . Let me simply adopt the minimal premiss that kinship has to do with the allocation of rights and their transmission from one generation to the next. These rights are not of any specific kind but are exceedingly various: they include most prominently rights of group membership, succession to office, inheritance of property, locality of residence, type of occupation, and a great deal else. They are all, however, transmissible by modes which have nothing to do with sex or genealogical states of transmitter or recipient. (1971, pp. 3–4)

In Britain, kin relations are often relatively isolated from the rest of social life, and an overlap of family loyalty into economic and political life may be perceived negatively as nepotism, or regarded with great suspicion. The rise to wealth of Mark Thatcher, son of the former British Prime Minister, is a good case to illustrate this point. If he became wealthy in his own right, taking advantage of his mother's name, that is one less than highly admirable thing, but a hint of overlap with political decision-making was totally unacceptable to the British people. In everyday life, we may turn to our kin to help us get on in the world, but there is a clear dividing line between acceptable family support and confusing the needs and desires of ones relatives with one's wider, public duty.

In the previous chapter we began to discern an example of a situation where kin relations were entirely bound up with political life, indeed it would have been impossible to understand one without an idea of the other. Although actual neighbourly relations among the Nuer may be more important than kin when people work out who to support in a particular political situation, they use the genealogical vocabulary to classify one another. **Lineage** membership is a most important principle for calculating relationships, so if a man dies without issue, a **ghost marriage** may be arranged between him and a woman who takes a living man as *genitor*, providing children to continue the line through the dead man (known as the *pater*). In this case the child inherits group membership without a 'biological' relationship.

In the world at large, there is huge variety in the way in which people classify others around them, and relations which we might at first think of as **kin** may actually have little to do with genealogical connections. They may also be inextricably tied up with economic transactions, the political system and the religious beliefs of the people concerned. It is thus very important to understand how people's *relations* fit into the wider society in which they are found before trying to isolate them. It is for this reason that the whole subject of kinship has been left until we have covered other areas, and in this chapter we shall consider a specific case to illustrate this point, but first we need introduce some of the terminology.

Within multicultural societies, people from specific ethnic backgrounds still grow up within their own families, and it is here that they learn to look out at the social life within which their family is lodged. The great variety mentioned above is not now confined to certain defined locations, it is scattered throughout the industrialized world. It is thus not only possible for a wide range of people to broaden the assumptions and expectations associated with relatives by simply taking an interest in those around them, it is also vital for neighbourly understanding. The material presented here is now not only curious and interesting; it is part of everyday life in towns and cities around the world.

In this chapter we will introduce some of the conventions used by anthropologists to describe kin relations by examining first what we shall call a *standard English family*, a kind of model of how people using the English language classify one another as relatives, wherever the language is used. We shall then place this system in a wider context by turning to look at **unilineal descent groups** as a completely contrasting way of classifying relatives, found in various forms in different parts of the world. We will then give a concrete example of how relatives may be perceived in a multicultural situation by focusing on the Pakistani community in Oxford. This case study will lead us into the last part of the chapter, where the focus will be marriage.

Classifying Kin Relations

In order to discuss family relationships at all, various conventions have been adopted. Some of these are familiar to those who take an interest in family trees, others are understood readily only by the professional anthropologist. If we start with the so-called *standard English family*, we can draw a diagram which depicts people in terms of their nearest relations, namely parents and siblings, and by extension, to their more distant aunts, uncles and cousins. We can place marriages on this diagram, and there is a convention for depicting serial marriage in the case of death or divorce and remarriage.

Figure 11.1 is a representation of this 'standard English family'. It uses a small circle to represent a woman and a triangle to represent a man. An equals sign represents a marriage or an informal union which results in offspring, and a line joining a circle and a triangle from above stands for a brother–sister relationship. It is important to remember that this is not a representation of an actual situation, but a set of logical possibilities. Thus, there is only one brother and sister in each unit, because these stand for the two possible positions that children may occupy terminologically. This becomes significant in the next generation, when the pair would take on new roles to each others' children.

By examining the diagram which results, we can work out a number of implications which can be drawn from the English-language system of designating relatives. The terms used separate off units of parents and children from more distant relatives by having unique terms for each category of member – mother, father, son, daughter – as opposed to blanket terms like uncle, aunt and cousins which cover a wide range of people outside that unit. These marked family units are technically called **nuclear families**, and in many English-speaking and other countries people live in units which express degrees of closeness in a similar way.

Up and down Figure 11.1, the terms used in the **nuclear unit** are qualified for the people outside it by adding the prefix 'grand' to the four distinct terms (as in grandmother, grandson, and so forth) or a number of 'greats' to

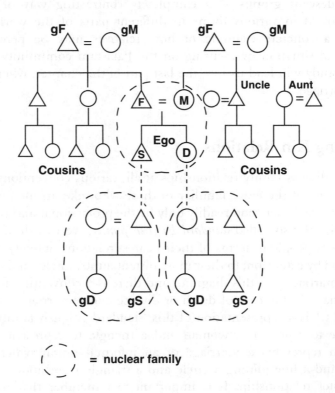

Figure 11.1   A standard English family

indicate further generational distance (as in great-grandmother and so on). These terms distinguish the **lineal** relatives, named after the line which can be traced through the generations, from uncles, aunts and cousins, essentially related through siblings, which are termed **lateral**, after the Latin for 'out to the side'. This use of terminology suggests another marking which may have practical implications too.

Rights and obligations concerned with **inheritance rules** are one example, and these are usually determined by family relationships in any particular legal system, which will distinguish different degrees of proximity, though the details vary from one country to another. In some cases, there is a system of **primogeniture**, for example, which indicates a special role for an eldest son. In Japanese, where terminology makes distinctions otherwise rather similar to the English case, there are terms to mark the eldest son from the other children, and in Nahuatl, an indigenous Mexican language, it is the youngest son who is denoted in this way.

Terminology does not always indicate practice, however, and an interesting aspect of our 'English' diagram is the lack of a distinction based on gender, let alone birth order. From the point of view of a child in the middle nuclear family, a reference point often termed 'ego' by anthropologists, no terminological distinctions are made between relatives on the mother's or father's side, although in practice children's surnames are usually taken from the father in English-speaking societies, and women may well turn to their mothers for help with their own children, for example, and perhaps to pass on certain material objects, such as jewellery.

Inheritance is of course important in all societies, and in many other languages distinctions of this sort are made. Anthropologists have devised a system of talking about inheritance using Latin terms, whether the language concerned makes the appropriate distinctions or not. Thus, when something is passed through the male line, as is the case for most English names, and when the system of **primogeniture** is practised, it is said to be passed **patrilineally**. When it is passed through the female line, it is called **matrilineal** inheritance (see Figure 11.2 for a way of depicting these lines).

In some societies matrilineal inheritance is still passed from man to man, that is a man receives his share of inheritance from his *mother's brother* (rather than from his father, as in a patriline), and, likewise, a man passes it on to his *sister's son*. (In Figure 11.2, the share would then pass between the triangles on the left-hand side of the second diagram). Where this latter preference predominates, the whole society has sometimes been termed a matrilineal society. It is important to consider *property*, *status*, *titles* and *group membership* separately, however. In the following section the last will be the focus of attention.

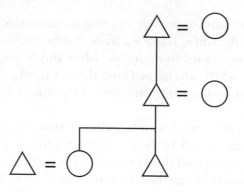

Patrilineal Descent

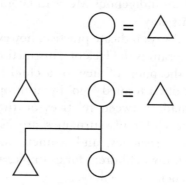

Matrilineal Descent

Figure 11.2   Patrilineal and matrilineal descent

Unilineal Descent Groups

Principles of **descent** are particularly important in societies where they lead to the formation of groups descended from one common ancestor. In Figure 11.3 the situation is depicted of a **patrilineal descent** group, where the shaded brother and sister pair at the bottom are again in the position of 'ego'. This time their relatives are worked out by virtue of membership in a group traced through men, as shown in the diagram. Women who are born into the group, like the female 'ego', usually marry out, so they are not shown. Wives of the males are members of other groups, as shown in the case of the example of a wife at the right-hand side of the diagram.

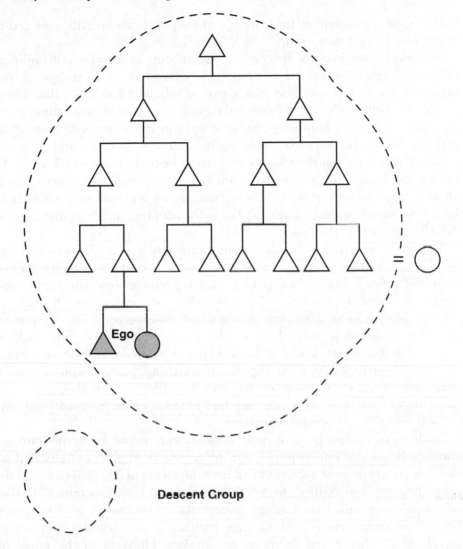

Descent Group

Figure 11.3 A unilineal descent group

Groups of this sort may be *clans* such as those of the Ancient Romans, Hebrews and Scots, or they may form a complicated **lineage** system like that seen among the Nuer and discussed in the previous chapter. Membership in such a group may determine residence possibilities, as well as economic partners such as companions for herding, hunting and agriculture, and it may define political allegiances and obligations in case of war, although the latter may also be affected by one's membership in an **age grade**. It is also very likely to affect possibilities for marriage, since people are usually expected to marry out of their own group.

Ancestors who preceded the present incumbents as members of unilineal descent groups may appear as important characters in local legend and mythology, and they may also play a part in religious and ritual life. These may be the beings who are blamed and consulted in case of misfortune, as we have seen, and their help may also be sought in times of need. Association with particular ancestors may bring rights and/or obligations, and they will certainly play a part in the identity of a living being in their social world. In return, the living will perform rites for the care of their ancestors in their afterlife, and arrangements are very often made for a person with no issue to have descendants through some kind of social adoption, or ghost marriage, as described above for the Nuer.

In some relatively closed societies everybody may be classified as a member of a lineage, and the relationship with everyone else in the society determined by relationships between these groups. Naming terminology will reflect these allegiances, and appropriate behaviour follows depending on the type of relationship involved. Members of one's own lineage would be in a more intimate relationship than those of the lineage into which one had, or expected to be, married, and in-laws might be treated with special respect or even avoidance. Anthropologists approaching such people found it necessary to adopt a group of relatives in order to communicate in a meaningful fashion at all. Once they had found a niche, everyone was able to work out the appropriate behaviour.

Such arrangements make it quite difficult to translate kin terms into the English language. For example, the term which might be translated as 'brother', refers in some societies to all male members of one generation in the same lineage, and 'father' to all those of the senior generation. Earlier anthropologists called such usages *classificatory terminology*, to distinguish them from terms which applied more exclusively to categories they recognized, which they called *descriptive terminology*. However, if the range of people denoted by the term is understood, the terms are *descriptive* in each situation, and they may indicate some important social categories, so seeking to identify the descriptive significance of a term is a good way to proceed.

Terms of address may also carry further significance in making sense of the system of classification in a particular society. For example, in a society where group membership is inherited **matrilineally**, but passed from man to man, as discussed above, there may be a lineage term for 'father's sister' which literally means 'female father', and similarly 'mother's brother' may mean 'male mother'. Here the terms for father and mother will be less concerned with gender than with group affiliation. The 'male mother' will simply be a male of the senior generation in one's own lineage, and the 'female father' a representative of the group to which a father owes his allegiance and inheritance. To the first a young person may owe obedience and respect, to the other deference and distance.

Siblings usually form a unit related to others in the same way, and many people make terminological distinctions between **matrilateral** (related through one's mother) and **patrilateral** (related through one's father) relatives, sometimes because these are automatically members of different clans, and one might have to marry out of one's own clan. **Cross-cousins** (related through siblings of the opposite sex) are also very often distinguished from **parallel-cousins** (related through siblings of the same sex). These distinctions are illustrated in Figure 11.4, where the sibling pair in the centre of the diagram take the positions of 'ego', and their matrilateral and patrilateral cousins, on the right and left of the diagram respectively, are marked as parallel or cross, depending on their parents' relationships.

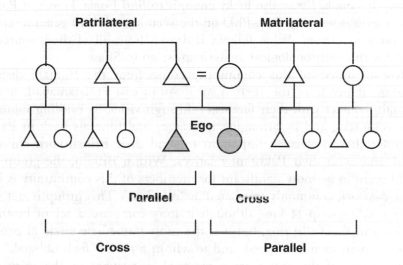

Figure 11.4 Cross-cousins and parallel-cousins

Kinship in a Multicultural Context: A Case Study

To pick up the point made earlier by Rodney Needham about the advisability of looking at 'kinship' in its social context, this section will be devoted to a detailed examination of one particular case. The example has been chosen to illustrate another earlier point about the multiplicity of systems now found in many parts of the world, and the need to understand our neighbours. The case is the Pakistani community in Oxford, and the section is largely based on the ethnography of Alison Shaw (1988), with some personal insights from second-generation members of the community.

Throughout her book, Shaw makes comparisons with the situation of continuing relations in Pakistan and elsewhere, and argues that the similarities between the old and new communities outweigh the differences brought about by co-existence of the new one with the wider community in England. She is also at pains to break down prejudices and assumptions which are commonly made by the wider community about the Pakistanis in Britain, and sometimes vice versa, and her study nicely strives to present the point of view of the people with whom she worked.

As she points out at the end of the book, however, the second generation of this community was only just growing up, and many had still to negotiate the contentious trial of accepting or otherwise the usual arranged marriages, so I have consulted a few of these young people ten years further on, at the time of writing this book. I was also lucky enough to find Fozia Tenvir, a Pakistani teacher who is working for a PhD on the second and third generation young Pakistanis in Oxford. What follows is drawn from all of these sources, but credit for the anthropological analysis must go to Shaw.

Most members of this community come from the Punjabi district of Pakistan, many from the Jhelum area, south-east of Islamabad, and they maintain contact with their forebears through visits, by sending money and other resources, and by arranging marriages and funerals back in Pakistan. Many families also feel it important to send their British-born children to spend time with their Pakistani relatives. Within Britain, the group which would seem to be most significant for members of this community is known as the *birâdari*, commonly translated as 'relations'. This group is not clearly defined as a group of kin, although it may comprise a set of brothers or cousins and their offspring, but it is the most immediate circle of people on whom a member may depend, and to whom a person feels obliged.

The limits of the group are contextual, somewhat in the spirit of the segmentary system of the previous chapter, and the whole Pakistani community in Oxford could be described as *birâdari* in contrast with the wider cosmopolitan citizenship. In other situations, the *birâdari* is conceived to include members of the family who have remained behind in Pakistan, on whom one can call to put up one's children, and to whom one may well be expected to send goods and money. In practice, in everyday life, this group will consist of a set of people who live together, or in close proximity, and it is the women of the group who seek to preserve the strength of the immediate set of close relations through the explicit exchange of gifts.

The composition of a Pakistani household in Oxford sometimes confuses their non-Pakistani neighbours, as may their arrangement of rooms, and Alison Shaw works from the plan of a typical house in Pakistan to explain the modifications of more traditional British use to the often Victorian houses. The most important distinction is between the male and female worlds, for these are Muslim families who seek to preserve Islamic ideals:

> A notable feature of all east Oxford Pakistani houses is that despite the different physical layout of the houses considerations of purdah are very important. This is best illustrated by the arrival of visitors. If male visitors arrive and a male family member is at home, the visitors may first be detained at the door while the women of the household, modestly adjusting their *dupattâs* over their heads, leave the front room and retreat to the backroom or kitchen. For as long as unrelated men are present, the women of the household will not usually enter the front room; instead the men of the household will go or send children to the backroom with requests for food and tea for the guests. The men may themselves carry the food or drinks from the kitchen to the front room, though sometimes the women will do this, without speaking to the male visitors. (Shaw 1988, p. 63)

The children of a house come under the guidance of the women, but young married couples very often live with the parents of the husband, and the grandmother is sometimes addressed with the same term as mother in Urdu and Punjabi, namely *'ammi'*, which can be confusing when the children begin to translate things into English. Similarly, they may use the same Urdu/Punjabi terms for brother and sister in reference to their cousins, especially if they are co-resident, because the strict terms are simply 'aunt/uncle-born brother/sister', with distinctions for matrilaterality and patrilaterality. On the male side, too, the term for father may also be used for grandfather, and the term for father's brother is appropriate for father's cousins and apparently also for friends' fathers and father's friends, as a sign of respect to the senior generation.

Clearly the view of a child growing up in this community will be somewhat different from that of a child whose first language defines the 'standard English family' detailed above, although that was of course only a model. When a small child from the Pakistani community goes to school and is asked about his or her relatives, the response of an unsympathetic teacher could be withering, but it could also be creative and helpful – a good reason for welcoming students of education on anthropology courses. In practice, the Pakistani children living in Oxford have adapted some of their relationships to make more sense when they speak in English, and my young informant gave me the terms which fitted a 'standard English' view as well as his own indigenous one.

Expectations of behaviour within the Pakistani family are sometimes quite shocking to outsiders in British communities, especially on the touchy subject of gender. Men are in a position to order their female relatives to attend to their needs, it seems, and my informant reported gleefully that his sister is obliged to bring him things in the home. He also noted that this expectation only starts as the girls grow up, however, and if he tries to get his younger sisters to wait on him he is given short shrift. This expectation is part of a wider view still maintained in the more conservative families that men are the ones to earn the money and women to take care of the home, but a stronger constraint on all family members is usually to play an appropriate part in contributing to the wider needs of the *birâdari*.

Alison Shaw starts her book with an example of even her own initial misunderstanding of the decision of a promising member of the community she had studied to turn down a place at university. She goes on to present his rationale in terms of the expectations of the wider Pakistani community, and compares this with her own reasons for being disappointed on his behalf. She uses this example to illustrate the difficulties of undoing ones own pre-conceptions in looking at those of people brought up with a different set, but also to introduce the value of belonging to a wider group such as the Pakistani *birâdari*.

Later in her book, Shaw details several cases of real material help people have received from their relatives – for house purchase, building, education, marriage and so forth – and this is of course the positive side of the commitment which imposes the constraints. Being part of a large social group, such as we have described here, clearly involves fitting in, at least to some extent, with the wider expectations of the group. Those who wish to receive the benefits must also make a contribution. They will be continually involved in the exchange of gifts, and they will participate in the perpetuation of the society through marriage as well as in maintaining economic security.

Within the family, youngsters are expected to defer to the wishes of their elders, and it is the elders who make arrangements for the marriages of their children, both boys and girls. Some children have rebelled and made their own marriages, occasionally successful, outside the community, but all can also cite cases where a second marriage has had to be arranged for such tearaways when the first one broke down. Whether an outside spouse is accepted depends partly on the extent to which they are prepared to adopt and contribute to the social life of the community.

Marriages are usually arranged between members of the same*birâdari*, very often between first cousins, and one important criterion is that the families should be compatible.

> In most cases the question of caste status in marriage does not arise explicitly because of the traditional Pakistani Muslim preference for marriage with first cousins. This stated preference is sometimes justified with reference to the Qur'ân, which permits first-cousin marriage, and the life of the Prophet Mohammed whose daughter Fatima was married to her cousin, the Prophet's nephew. It is also justified in terms of maintaining 'purity of the blood' and in this context the particular qualities of the family or caste are emphasized. In a society in which a dowry must be given by the girl's family when a daughter is married, the preference for first-cousin marriage is also important as a means of keeping property within the family. (Shaw, 1988, p. 98)

Alison Shaw investigated the extent to which younger members of the community, particularly those of the second generation, resented having their marriages arranged for them, and she found only a small amount of real dissent. In most cases, people felt that the system was good for them, and they preferred being part of the community which they seem to see as more caring and meaningful than the 'free' outside world. It seems from the more recent work of Fozia Tenvir, and Shaw herself, that this situation continues into the third generation, and families are less worried than they used to be about letting their daughters go to mixed schools. Three girls whose outside marriages failed have proved a strong negative example, and although Pakistani boys sometimes have relationships with white girls from the wider community, they see these as playful, and argue that the girls do not mind, as their own sisters might.

Marriage

One of the reasons that Pakistani girls in Oxford prefer to marry within their own community is because they will be able to continue to count on the support of the wider *birâdari*. Marriage for them is more than a relationship between two people, and there may be reasons for making a match which go beyond personal choice. They also observe the fragility of some of the unions made in wider British society, as divorce rates increase, and remarriages complicate the lives of the children involved (see Simpson, 1994 for further reading). There are also religious differences, of course. Perhaps these alternative marriages do not seem very impressive?

It must be part of this chapter, then, to consider what exactly we mean when we talk about **marriage**. Let us start again by looking at the word in the English language, as an element in the 'standard English family' we used as a model above. Something called 'marriage' clearly played an important part in the construction of the **nuclear** unit, and it is 'marriage' which moves people from the family of their birth to a new one for procreation and continuing the lines of descent. However, what do people need to do in order to make this transition? And is it actually necessary for people to marry at all, if they simply give birth to children of their own?

First of all, there is a legal definition of marriage, and this will vary from one system to another, affecting the way that people are permitted to behave within any particular society. Inheritance rules are affected by the legal situation, and so may be the status of children. In some systems of legislation, it is only possible to have one legal spouse at a time, whereas in others **polygamy** is not only possible but sometimes a preferred arrangement. The laws with regard to divorce will indicate the possibilities for breaking a union once formed, and arrangements for children will also be part of the legal framework.

There are also often strong religious ideas about the state of marriage, and these may even be at odds with the evolving legal system. In a Christian Church, for example, a couple makes a solemn undertaking to spend the rest of their lives together, through thick and through thin – 'in sickness and in health, until death us do part'. Not everyone gets married in church, but many of the couples getting divorced have done so, and some are now seeking to do it again, permitted by the Church of England as this book goes to press. Clearly there is a difference between the ideals expressed in the ceremony and the practice of real life. In other societies marriage may have little to do with religion, but it is not uncommon to find a discrepancy between ideals and practice.

This brings us to a third definition of marriage, namely the customary one. Here we enter the area of social control again. A couple wishing to marry is expected to comply with legal regulations, and they may choose to formalize their union with a religious ceremony, but it is also quite possible to set up a family without doing either of these things. It may not be the preferred arrangement of the parents of the couple concerned, but neighbours may well treat them in much the same way as they would people with a more conventional union.

In all these examples, however, whatever their variety, we are making certain assumptions. First of all, we are expecting marriage to be a union between a man and a woman, and we are probably also assuming that this man and woman have chosen to be together, preferably also that they are, or have been 'in love'. These are some of the fundamentals which have remained relatively unchanged in the English use of the term. Homosexual unions are not unheard of, and we know that ethnic groups like the Pakistani one described above practice 'arranged marriage', but these are considered to be exceptions. Marriage, on the whole, is considered to be a union entered into freely by a man and a woman wishing to share a major part of their lives together.

Elsewhere, these underlying assumptions about marriage may be rather different, and it is necessary to think again carefully about what the institution means. It may, for example, be seen as something much closer to a political or an economic alliance, enabling the uniting of potentially hostile groups, or the consolidation of a vital means to trade. In rural Japan, the written character used for a bride (or wife) is a combination of one for 'woman' and one for *ie*, or 'house', suggesting that the bride is seen as married to the house as a whole, not just to the young husband with whom she shares a bed. In some societies unions between ghosts, or between two women, are also quite possible, and it may certainly be thought less necessary for the couple to make choices than for social expectations to be fulfilled.

As was the case with kinship, marriage means different things in different societies, and in an article about the problems of defining marriage in *Rethinking Kinship and Marriage*, Peter Rivière even went so far as to write that 'marriage as an isolable phenomenon of study is a misleading illusion' (1971, p. 57). Again, he recommends, we must look at marriage as part of the wider society where it is found, at how it fits into wider systems of exchange and political allegiance, and then we can understand the role it plays in a particular case. Anthropologists have developed theory around the term **'alliance'** to examine some of the examples found in a way which does not imply underlying notions associated with the term 'marriage'. In this final section, however, we shall simply introduce and explain terms which have been used in describing arrangements in various societies, and try to give some idea of the variety which is possible. This will lay the groundwork for readers to understand any more specific ethnography they might find.

(1) Endogamy, Exogamy and Incest

In most societies there are some limits, broadly agreed, about whom one may or may not marry:

- rules of **exogamy** define groups *out of which* one should marry; and
- rules of **endogamy** define those *within which* one should marry.

Rules of exogamy sometimes, but not always, coincide with rules of incest, in other words those who are prohibited for marriage are usually the same people with whom it would be inappropriate to have sexual relations. These groups vary from one society to another: they may include only the nuclear family, they may comprise a lineage to a certain distance, or even a whole clan sharing a name. The Chinese character for 'incest' literally means 'confusion of relationships', and this is a nice expression of the way rules of incest and exogamy often help to define important groups in any particular society. However, they must be separated as concerned with sexual relations and marriage respectively.

Anthropologists have pointed out that *marrying out* creates **alliances** between groups which may not otherwise have a great deal of contact, or whose contact may be hostile. Tylor even went so far as to suggest that people 'Marry out or die out'. Others have written that in Africa people 'marry our enemies' in order to create peaceful ties, although in the tropical forest of South America, marriage is no insurance of peace and there are even people whose word for 'brother-in-law' is synonymous with that for 'enemy'. However, as was pointed out in the section on **exchange** (pp. 54–6), marriage is one means of maintaining **communication** between peoples, whether it be friendly or hostile.

Rules of endogamy, on the other hand, put an outer limit on the range of marriage partners. Even where there are few explicit rules, marriages may provoke disapproval if they cross lines of class, race, religion or nationality. We saw that members of the Pakistani community in Britain choose to arrange marriages with their own people, preferably cousins of a similar caste background. In the Indian sub-continent, there may be more explicit **caste endogamy** since members of different castes are often regarded as different kinds of people. At the same time there may be **village exogamy**, so the two categories are by no means mutually exclusive.

(2) Marriage as Exchange – Dowry and Bridewealth

Another phenomenon found in India is **hypergamy**, which refers to the fact that those who receive a wife, the *wife-takers*, are regarded as superior to the *wife-givers*. This system must be seen in the context of the payment of **dowry**, which is wealth which travels with the bride to her new family. The Jains of Jaipur (northern India), a religious community concentrated mainly among business and trading castes, provide an example. According to Josephine Reynell (1991), the dowry here includes furniture, kitchen utensils and electrical goods to equip the bride's new home, as well as clothes and jewellery for the bride, and money for the bride's new parents-in-law. The practice of religious and caste endogamy, as a way of maintaining control over economic resources, limits overall hierarchical difference, but a bride's parents would not eat with her new family after the marriage (Photograph 11.1 was taken at a Jain marriage ceremony).

In other societies this system is reversed and *wife-givers* will be seen as superior to *wife-takers*, when the situation is described as **hypogamy**. In this case, it is more likely that goods called **bridewealth**, or **brideprice**, will be travelling in the opposite direction. Whenever imbalances of this sort occur, exchange must be *indirect*, or *generalized*, to use Lévi-Strauss's terms mentioned in Chapter 2; in other words, there must be at least three groups involved, as people can not be seen as superior and inferior at the same time.

Photograph 11.1 **A Jain marriage ceremony, in Jaipur, northern India. The father of the bride (right) has formally handed his daughter over into the safekeeping of the groom and his family. The bride holds her hands over the right hand of the groom. Their right hands will be bound, symbolising their lifelong union (photograph courtesy of Josephine Reynell).**

A more straightforward exchange, where women move on a regular basis between two different groups (see below), Lévi-Strauss called *direct exchange*, which can also refer to a situation where women are apparently being exchanged for labour or for bridewealth.

Missionaries and other visitors from outside societies where such systems operate condemned these arrangements, as they appeared to represent the purchase of women, or, perhaps worse, the persuasion by the use of wealth to have women taken away. A deeper examination reveals much more significance, however, and bridewealth in different locations may also play one or more of several important roles. It is also very likely to initiate or continue a series of exchanges which ensures long-term **communication** between the groups involved who will of course both be related, as kin, to the children of any union set up.

Bridewealth may also play the important role of *validating* the marriage. In the absence of any other kind of legal contract, a couple setting up home without prior payments could well be seen to have an improper, illegitimate union. The payments also act as a kind of *security*. If a husband and his family treats the wife badly and she returns home, they will lose the payments they have made. Conversely, if the wife behaves badly, her husband may ask for a return of his payments. Since the bride's family may already have handed on the bridewealth to marry one of their menfolk, it is likely that they would put pressure on the woman to fit into her new home.

In Japan, there is no term for 'bridewealth', as such, but wealth in various forms is paid over by the groom's family in betrothal gifts which the bride uses in turn to prepare her **trousseau**, usually worth much more than the payments received. She receives goods from her own family and, like some cases of dowry, she takes these away again if the marriage breaks up, for they also represent a share of her family's inheritance. In families with no inheriting son, the initial payments may be made from the bride's family to that of the groom, who will join the house as potential successor. In both cases, as in situations in societies where a substantial dowry is paid over with a bride, the goods become part of the security of the new family.

Particularly in Africa, where bridewealth is often paid in cattle, the movement of animals may be seen as marking out a kind of map of human relationships. Bridewealth received for a daughter will be used for the wives of sons, and many relatives will make contributions to each other's weddings when they have beasts available in the knowledge that they will be able to draw on reciprocal support when they need it. Writing of the Nyakyusa of Malawi and Tanzania, Monica Wilson (1963) thus noted that cattle are continually driven down the paths of human relationship. Beattie suggested going a step further when he said, 'they tread out these paths' (1964, p. 125).

The movement of wealth made in connection with marriage can clearly play roles which go way beyond the nuptial link being made.

Direct sister exchange (see Figure 11.5) is another type of marriage discussed by anthropologists as a way of describing long-term arrangements of alliance between two groups in which men who think of themselves as 'brothers' set up reciprocal links through their wives and sisters. In practice, the men involved probably share a lineage group, as described above, where the category 'brother' includes all males of the same generation. As the relationships continue through the generations, a girl from a man's mother's lineage, a mother's 'brother's' daughter (MBD in Figure 11.5) would be an appropriate partner, who would also be classified as a 'father's' sister's daughter (FZD).

Such a situation would be compatible with the system of exogamy, which ensures communication between different groups of people, but it is a very male-orientated view and allows the women involved less say in the matter than they may in practice exercise. In Figure 11.5 I have also shown the

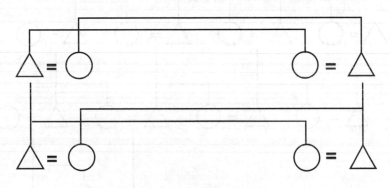

Men marry MBD = FZD

Women marry MBS = FZS

May be Prescriptive or Preferential

M = Mother
F = Father
B = Brother
Z = Sister
D = Daughter
S = Son

Figure 11.5 Direct (sister) exchange (for example, the Amba of Uganda)

relationships from the point of view of the wives. Direct exchange is found in situations where this type of alliance is *preferred*, perhaps to keep goods within a family group, but not necessarily *prescribed*, as would need to be the case for an interesting form of *indirect* exchange known as **matrilateral cross-cousin marriage**, where men *must* marry their mother's brother's daughters to make the system work (see Figure 11.6).

It is important again to remember that the triangles and circles here represent categories of people in particular relationships to one another. It will be noted that men in such a system move in one direction and women in the other, so direct exchange of sisters would not be possible. There may also be an element of hypergamy or hypogamy here, where the wife-givers are considered superior or inferior to the wife-takers, and this may have ramifications for the political system. An interesting example of this is the case of the Kachin people of Southern Burma, described by Edmund Leach, in *Political Systems of Highland Burma*. He writes:

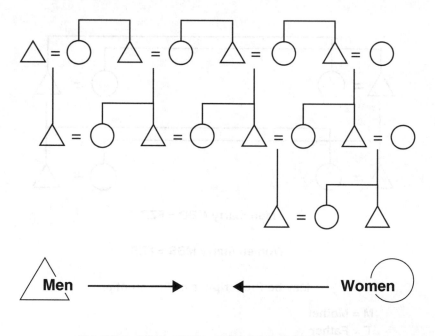

Men Marry MBD = Mother's Brother's Daughter
Women Marry FZS = Father's Sister's Son
for example, the Kachin of S. Burma

Figure 11.6 Matrilateral cross-cousin marriage (example of prescriptive system)

Much the most important set of relationships in any Kachin community are those which establish the mutual status relations between the various*htinggaw* groups that exist in that community. From the individual's point of view every *htinggaw* group within the community falls into one or other of four categories:

i.   . . . lineages which are treated as being of the same clan as Ego's own and are near enough related to form an exogamous group with Ego's . . .

ii.   *mayu ni* are lineages from which males of Ego's lineage have recently taken brides.

iii. *dama ni* are lineages into which females of Ego's lineage have recently married.

iv.   . . . lineages which are recognised as relatives . . . but with which the relationship is distant or indefinite . . .

The essential feature of the system is that the [first] three categories . . . are distinct. A man may not marry into his *dama*, a woman may not marry into her *mayu*. From an analytical point of view the system is one of matrilateral cross cousin marriage, but it needs to be stressed that a Kachin, in marrying a girl from his *mayu ni*, does not normally marry a true matrilateral cross cousin but only a classificatory cross cousin. (1954, pp. 73–4)

The practicalities of such a system are discussed in great detail by Leach, who demonstrates in this now classic study an example both of the ingenious possibilities of structural analysis to make sense of social and political behaviour, and the way that such an abstract construct works in the practice of real life relationships. Another extract, this time laying out more clearly the political elements of this system, also illustrates this point:

This account of Laga village has brought out the fact that within the village the more permanent *mayu-dama* links serve to display the formal political status relations between different *htinggaw* lineage groups. In this formal system it is assumed that the *dama* are the political subordinates of the *mayu*; but let it be stressed that even within the village this subordination may be theoretical rather than actual. Any nominal inferiority can, in practice, be largely compensated by strategic marriages outside the village. (1954, p. 81)

(3) Locality of Marriage Residence

Decisions about where a couple will live after they are married are very often decided by custom, or by a practical economic or political consideration, in a particular society. Anthropologists have terms to describe various arrangements. For example, where a man moves in with his wife's family, or into his wife's community, the marriage is said to be **matrilocal** (from the point of view of the next generation) or **uxorilocal** (from the Latin for 'wife'). If the woman moves to the man's former residence, the marriage is said to be **patrilocal** or **virilocal**. A completely new residence would be **neolocal**.

Factors like this may have very important ramifications for future relations, and again may play a part in the political system of the people concerned. In a society with patrilineal descent and patrilocal marriage, strong stable descent groups are likely to result, and these can form the basis of the political system, as is found among the Nuer. In Japan, during a period between the ninth and thirteenth centuries, there was a family known as the Fujiwaras who dominated the political scene through a continual series of matrilocal marriages with the Imperial family which for generations ensured that the child emperors grew up in a Fujiwara household. They were thus subject to the influence of their Fujiwara grandparents from an early age, and usually married into another Fujiwara household where they would be close to Fujiwara in-laws as they came to the throne. The Fujiwaras occupied a series of positions in the court, but the influence they exerted through marriage is widely acknowledged by historians of the period today.

(4) Monogamy and Polygamy

So far we have talked little about forms of marriage which involve more than two partners. A system involving *one* person marrying *one* other is known as **monogamy**, where 'mono' stands for 'one'. In a society where this is the law, if one of those partners wishes to marry someone else, they must first divorce their existing spouse. If a person thereby takes several spouses over a period of time, this is called *serial monogamy*. In some societies, however, it is perfectly acceptable for a man to maintain marriage to more than one wife (**polygyny**) or a woman to have more than one husband (**polyandry**). In either case, the system is described as **polygamy**, or multiple marriage.

In some ostensibly monogamous societies, where it is illegal for people to have more than one spouse, it is nevertheless fairly institutionalized that a man may maintain more than one household, one with a legal wife, others with his mistresses. The *casa chica*, or 'small house' is a phenomenon of this sort found in Latin America, and the situation is also well known in Japan. A man's wealth will determine his ability to do this, of course, as it would in a society which accepts polygamy, and his status will also be affected. In the case of the leaders of the tropical rain forest, discussed in the politics section, an abundance of wives was mentioned as a distinct advantage. The living arrangements for women in polygamous marriages, often in separate units with their children, may thus be rather similar to the 'single-parent families' we mentioned at the start of the chapter.

The Nayar and the Anderi, of India, are examples of peoples who practice polyandry. In the first case, women grow up and continue to live with their brothers, receiving visits from one 'husband' at a time. He leaves a spear at the door to deter any other who might think of calling while he is there. In the second case, one woman may be expected to take care of a whole group of brothers single-handedly, as a mechanism to avoid dividing up the family land. This will also have the effect of limiting the number of children they might collectively produce. Small wonder that polygyny is much more common!

This chapter has brushed rather cursorily over some of the abundance of work anthropologists have produced on the subject they call 'kinship'. Since it was emphasized in the book edited by Needham that the great variety of arrangements found around the world might be better understood by looking at them in their local context, the volume has abated somewhat, attention turning instead to the consequences of new forms of technology on family and reproduction. We have therefore focused on equipping readers with a conceptual framework to make sense of other studies they may find. In the following chapter, we turn to do something similar with economics.

References

Beattie, John (1964) *Other Cultures* (London: Routledge & Kegan Paul).

Leach, E. R. (1954) *Political Systems of Highland Burma* (London: Athlone).

Needham, Rodney (ed.) (1971) *Rethinking Kinship and Marriage* (London: Tavistock).

Reynell, Josephine (1991) 'Women and the Reproduction of the Jain Community', in Carrithers, Michael and Caroline Humphrey (eds), *The Assembly of Listeners: Jains in Society* (Cambridge University Press).

Rivière, P. G. (1971) 'Marriage: A Reassessment', in Rodney Needham (ed.), *Rethinking Kinship and Marriage* (London: Tavistock) pp. 57–74.

Rivière, P. G. (1985) 'Unscrambling Parenthood: The Warnock Report', *Anthropology Today*, 1(4): 2–7.

Shaw, Alison (1988) *A Pakistani Community in Britain* (Oxford: Blackwell).

Wilson, Monica (1963) *Good Company: a Study of Nyakyusa Age-Villages* (Boston: Beacon).

Further Reading

Bremen, Jan van (1998) 'Death Rites in Japan in the Twentieth Century', in Joy Hendry (ed.), *Interpreting Japanese Society*, 2nd edn (London: Routledge) pp. 131–44.

Franklin, Sarah (1997) *Embodied Progress: a cultural account of assisted conception* (London: Routledge).

Goody, Jack and S. J. Tambiah (1973) *Bridewealth and Dowry* (Cambridge University Press).

Holy, Ladislav (1996) *Anthropological Perspectives on Kinship* (London and Chicago: Pluto).

Shore, Cris (1992) 'Virgin Births and Sterile Debates: Anthropology and the New Reproductive Technologies', *Current Anthropology*, **33**: 295–314 (including comments).

Simpson, Bob (1994) 'Bringing the "unclear" family into focus: divorce and re-marriage in contemporary Britain', *Man*, **29**: 831–51.

Strathern, Marilyn (1992) *Reproducing the Future: Anthropology, Kinship and the New Reproductive Technologies* (Manchester University Press).

Novels and Other Works of Interest

Achebe, Chinua *Things fall Apart* (London: Heinemann, 1962).

Ariyoshi Sawako, *The River Ki* (trans. Mildred Tahara, Tokyo: Kodansha, 1981) is a moving tale about several generations of a Japanese family.

Jung Chang, *Wild Swans* (London: HarperCollins, 1991) is the much celebrated account of three generations of Chinese women who lived most actively through the tremendous changes of the cultural revolution.

Tanizaki, Junichiro, *The Makioka Sisters* (London: Mandarin, 1993) is a novel which details the problems which arise for a Japanese family trying to arrange appropriate marriages for a group of four sisters.

Films

Life Chances: Four Families in a Greek Cypriot Village (Peter Loizos, 1974) is a classic film about social change and its effect on families living in a Greek community in Cyprus.

Secrets and Lies (Mike Leigh, 1995) is a feature film illustrating problems which can arise when people reared in an adoptive family take steps to make contact with their parents of birth.

Strangers Abroad: Everything is Relatives (André Singer, 1985) is a film about the anthropologist W. H. R. Rivers, whose work we discussed in Chapter 1, focusing on his study of kinship and genealogy among the various people with whom he worked.

Under the Sun: The Dragon Bride (Joanna Head, 1993) depicts the preparations and marriage of a 16-year-old girl of the Nyinba people of Nepal to four brothers from another village. Personal interviews flesh out and illustrate this unusual example of fraternal polyandry.

CHAPTER 12

Economics and the Environment

Drawing to a Conclusion

In the last two chapters we dipped our toes into some of the deeper issues anthropologists address, but we also glimpsed a little of the way an anthropological approach can contribute to an understanding of subjects of wider interest. In this final chapter we take up this theme again in reference to the contribution anthropologists can make and have made to the study of economics and the environment. While doing this, we shall draw together elements of anthropological work that we have considered throughout the book, and demonstrate how a good understanding of social (and economic) life depends on an understanding of the systems of classification and notions of exchange which we introduced at the outset.

We will start with a very basic part of the study of any society, and draw up a fairly crude classification of social groups according to their means of subsistence. Most classic anthropological studies actually started out by describing the economic base of a particular people and the environment in which they lived, for this is usually a highly influential part of social life. Even at the most basic level, the environment is also socially constructed, however, and understanding the constructions of others can be quite informative at a time when environmental concerns are a vital part of global discourse. Leaving this subject to the end helps to demonstrate the extent to which these issues are embedded in social life.

Over the years anthropologists have learned a lot about social life by focusing on small groups, and those who live at a basic economic level provide interesting information which is not irrelevant in a more complex, multicultural world. In the end, one person can only operate socially within a limited number of family, friends and associates, and there are certain rules of behaviour which pervade life in these micro-level groups, wherever they are found. In Chapter 3 we discussed Sahlins' ideas about forms of generalized reciprocity which he argued operate within the closest circles; in Chapter 9 we examined methods of social control effective in such groups; and in the last chapter, we looked at the specific example of the Pakistani *birâdari*. Here we glimpsed the important idea, continually aided by developments in information technology, that groups geographically separate can easily keep in touch.

This approach, then, brings together the various topics we have pursued, and demonstrates that however basic or elaborate the means of subsistence, people still need ways of classifying and ordering themselves and their environment, they still have to organize means to defend and reproduce themselves, and they have views of the world in which they live. They have **collective** ways of 'seeing' the world, or **collective representations** of that world. In relatively isolated communities, people are more likely to share ideas about these things, whereas in a multicultural society, many views of the world co-exist, and any one individual may be influenced by several of them. In all cases, anthropologists have something to offer in making sense of social life.

The process of drawing towards a conclusion will be completed in the last section, where different elements of social life will be specifically related to the environment in which they are found, and some final remarks will be made about systems of classification. We shall only have begun to see what social anthropology is all about, but it is hoped we shall have demonstrated its continuing value for grappling with the world of the twenty-first century, and the reader will have acquired the basics for building up a greater knowledge. In recent years, anthropologists have been so prolific in their writings in a variety of different directions that there is plenty for an enthusiast to read.

Subsistence and Survival

Economics is first of all concerned with the means of *survival* and how this is achieved. It is concerned with the way food is produced, shelter is provided, and with other everyday activities essential to life. Exchange, and specifically markets, are a further development of economic life, made possible when subsistence is secure. Small-scale societies were divided into three types by early anthropologists making sense of the world they observed (for example, Forde, 1934), and these divisions are still used to describe forms of basic economy of both isolated contemporary peoples and earlier forms of social life described by archaeologists, though evolutionary schemes and generalizations about social interaction have been severely challenged. The three types are:

- hunter-gatherers or 'gatherer-hunters'
- pastoralists
- agriculturalists.

(1) Hunter-gatherers or 'Gatherer-hunters

People described in this way collect food from their immediate environment, and they have been characterized as picking or catching only as much as they could eat at any one time to avoid problems of storage or transport. They were said to be usually **nomadic**, since they must move about to avoid exhausting their supplies, and to seek foods when they are in season and abundant. They were also said to have little role specialization, the chief division of labour being made along lines of age and gender, so that the healthy and capable collect for the very young and the very old and infirm, and, typically, men hunt, while women gather.

Economists had described this life as hard and difficult, but ethnographic material indicated that many such people only 'worked' for long enough to provide themselves with sustenance, leaving the rest of their lives to relax and enjoy each others' company. Marshall Sahlins thus described hunter-gatherers as the 'original affluent society':

> Hunters and gatherers have by force of circumstances an objectively low standard of living. But taken as their *objective*, and given their adequate means of production, all the people's material wants usually can easily be satisfied [a common understanding of 'affluence', Sahlins, 1974, p. 1] . . . The world's most primitive people have few possessions, *but they are not poor*. Poverty is not a certain small amount of goods, nor is it just a relation between means and ends; above all it is a relation between people. Poverty is a social status. As such it is an invention of civilization. (Sahlins, 1974, pp. 36–7)

Sahlins' argument is worth following up, for he makes the interesting point that if people want no more than their food, and that is available, then they have all they desire. In other words, they have not been corrupted by the addictive and competitive traps of property ownership and capitalism. This idea became somewhat romanticized, however, using as a classic example the !Kung or San Bushmen of the Kalahari Desert, whose warm and abundant surroundings made life comparatively rather easy. The feature film, *The Gods must be Crazy*, cited below, illustrates this view when it tracks the events following the arrival of an empty Coca-Cola bottle into a Bushmen camp, thrown carelessly out of the window of a small plane, but forthwith corrupting the otherwise innocent lives of these formerly apparently idyllically happy people.

In practice, there are many and varied peoples in different parts of the world who sustain themselves largely through hunting and gathering techniques, or 'gathering and hunting', as some feminists have argued they should be called, in deference to the female provision of gathering as the basis of their economy, with hunting supplementing the diet only for special or sporadic occasions. Some own property and store food, and others live very tough and difficult lives in regions much less hospitable than that of the continual African sunshine. They have a range of interesting sets of power relations and ideologies, and they also produce some highly skilled art and material culture.

Anthropologists of peoples who fall under the category of 'hunter-gathering', or 'gatherer-hunting', tend to meet and compare their findings, despite this diversity, and a very useful two-part collection justified this practice, as follows:

> In some ways hunter-gatherer societies have developed independently of other branches of social anthropology. Yet we believe that they are not simply in tune with social anthropology more generally: they are the backbone of the discipline. They are often much more in touch with the essence of what it is to be human than are trends in virtually any other branch of the subject. (Barnard and Woodburn, 1988)

Examples of surviving hunters and gatherers, apart from the rather well known !Kung Bushmen and Mbuti Pygmy peoples of southern Africa, include some Australian aborigines, such as the Yolngu people whose art was discussed in Chapter 6, and the Inuit or Eskimo people of the extreme Northern hemisphere, whose methods of social control were described in Chapter 9. There are also several groups in North America, and some of these challenge the original definition by also having settlements. The Kwakiutl, Tlingit and Haida, whom we considered in Chapter 3 as practising exchanges described as **potlatch**, are settled during part of the year, and rely on fishing for a substantial part of their diet, but are also important hunters, so their activities help to confound the definition.

Many more people lived from hunting and gathering in the distant past, and they used to be seen as technologically the most primitive people (as Sahlins suggests above), but anthropologists who specialize in contemporary hunter-gathering peoples are keen to point out the social and cultural complexities that may go along with this means of subsistence, and argue that it is not necessarily possible to learn about ancient societies by looking at the modern ones. Few of the latter are now completely out of contact with the wider world, and they have anyway changed themselves over time, apart from adapting to technological change. A good collection about hunter-gatherers is to be found in Ingold, Riches and Woodburn (1988).

(2) Pastoralists

'Pastoralist' is the term used for people who live off the produce of herds of cattle, sheep, goats and so forth. They also generally need to move about to find fresh grazing for their animals, so they may be nomadic, but they could also be **transhumant** – that is, moving between fixed locations, as we saw in the case of the Nuer. The splendid tents (known as *yurts*) constructed and occupied by various nomadic peoples of Central Asia, and displayed in many ethnographic museums around the world, demonstrate the extent to which 'mobile homes' may be substantial and highly decorative, however. Some people in this part of the world now own houses in the towns, but at certain times of the year, prefer to live in their *yurts*, even erecting them in their back yards when they are not in the desert.

Some pastoralists satisfy almost all their requirements – food, shelter, clothes and fuel – from their animals, as well as finding aesthetic appreciation in them, as we saw in Coote's discussion of the Nilotic peoples, such as the Nuer and Dinka, in Chapter 6. They may also create semi-permanent relationships of exchange with their neighbours, however, for example giving cheese to secure grazing rights.

An example of this type of situation is described in an excellent ethnography by John Campbell (1964) about the Sarakatsani, Greek shepherds whose view of the world also demonstrates a system of classification based on different degrees of trust, a scheme of relations rather similar to that outlined by Sahlins for his cycles of reciprocity (discussed in Chapter 3). The greatest trust is with the family, but lesser degrees of trust are established with 'patrons' on whom the Sarakatsani depend for grazing, both sets distinguished from other outsiders. Campbell writes:

> Sarakatsani are deeply concerned about three things; sheep, children (particularly sons), and honour. It is a common feature of many pastoral peoples with simple material cultures that they are highly dependent on their physical environment and that the care of herds, the structure of the community, and its social values, form a coherent pattern of activities and sentiments which present few inconsistencies. The three concerns of the Sarakatsani are mutually implicated. The sheep support the life and prestige of the family, the sons serve the flocks and protect the honour of their parents and sisters, and the notion of honour presupposes physical and moral capacities that fit the shepherds for the hard and sometimes dangerous work of following and protecting their animals. (1964, p. 19)

Campbell goes on to present the social and spiritual life of these shepherds, within the wider Greek community, as totally constructed around the sheep who form the economic base of their lives. It is also an excellent example of another society where the values of honour and shame underpin the system of social control so that fear of gossip and ridicule are strong sanctions for compliant behaviour, as we saw in Chapter 9.

(3) Agriculturalists

The earlier evolutionary economic arguments turned to the development of agriculture and horticulture as requiring a more sedentary lifestyle, and a longer-term investment in the land, which could then support larger populations. This, they argued, allowed a greater division of labour, specialisation became feasible, and a complex political system could be sustained, freeing some people from the needs of survival to rule, fight, judge and so forth. Differences might still be based on age and gender, but there could develop further possibilities for gaining status and more ways to develop an aptitude, for example for oratory, or divination.

A sedentary population is in a better position to accumulate surpluses, it was argued, which allows the greater development of systems of **exchange**, and as the extent of these spreads out from the immediate surrounding community, the beginnings of a **market economy** may be observed. As a society becomes more and more complex, any one individual is less likely to provide for his own survival directly, and more likely to be engaged in exchange and specialization. Food is mostly purchased, and the wherewithal to purchase it is earned through specialist employment. It was from this point of perceived complexity that it seemed appropriate to apply and develop economic theory, and a branch of anthropology developed called Economic Anthropology (for example, see Firth, 1967).

In fact, people who grow crops may also move about, as we have seen in shifting agriculture, such as the *slash and burn* type of cultivation found in the tropical rain forest of South America, and the millet growing of the transhumant, predominantly pastoral Nuer, and we have looked at some of the social implications of these systems in Chapters 8 and 10. We have also seen that property and exchange may characterize the lives of peoples in simpler economic circumstances, such as hunter-gathering and pastoralism. Thus the evolutionary economic argument is not particularly helpful, though we did see in Chapter 9 the greater effectiveness of certain social sanctions in a co-operative rice-growing community, than where people could easily move in and out. In the next two sections we shall consider some of the contributions ethnographic studies have made and can still make to an understanding of economic ideas.

Property and Land Tenure

Important aspects of economic life are related to notions of**property** and **land tenure**, and anthropologists have gathered interesting material on these subjects. Ideas about the ownership of land have been variable throughout the world, with subtle differences eventually causing horrendous long-term problems between neighbouring and colonizing peoples. Hunters and gatherers are dependent on using land as they need it, which is fine as long as there is abundant land available. Pastoralists, too, need to seek pasture for their animals, and if this is scarce, they may have to seek grazing rights. Even agriculturalists, such as those who cultivate by the slash and burn method, may just expect to move around as they need to, but such freedom has become rare in the modern world.

A scarcity of land for the people trying to use it leads to the development of rules, which may become more and more complex as the pressure increases. In some parts of Africa and North America, there was a concept described by anthropologists as **usufruct** which granted rights to use land, but without overall ownership. The land may have been perceived of as belonging to a tribe, a lineage, or a king, perhaps, and if it was not in use it would revert to a central pool. So long as a family used it, they could pass it on through the generations, but it was not seen as theirs in perpetuity. This was one of the areas of greatest misunderstanding and conflict between Europeans and Indians in North America, where the latter granted rights to use land, which the former then thought they had purchased.

Throughout the colonized world, and particularly since the raising of local awareness during the United Nations' Year of Indigenous Peoples in 1993, problems such as these have become hot political issues. Anthropologists have had a role to play in helping indigenous people translate their point of view into terms which could be understood by the wider authorities, and the Kayapo Indians of the Xingu Valley in Brazil were aided in this way, as we saw in Chapter 10. In Australia, where land rights issues have become internationally well known, some anthropologists have become involved in helping the government solve apparently irreconcilable demands.

Important rules have also developed about the inheritance of land, as we have already glimpsed in the section on kinship in the last chapter, and about keeping land within a family, as may be a consideration in the setting up of a marriage. If land is constantly divided between children, the areas will become smaller and smaller, so there are very often institutionalized ways of avoiding this. The solution of the Anderi, where a group of brothers work together, marrying one wife between them, is rather unusual. In Japan, the *ie*, or 'house' was until post-war legal changes seen as owning the land, but only one person inherited the position of head of the house, with the right to cultivate the household property. Other children left to set up their own houses, or to marry into pre-existing ones. In Mexico, there is a dual system, with owned land, known as *huerta*, and village land which is leased to families to use, known as *ejido*. The latter reverts to the common pool if it is not cultivated.

Moveable property, on the other hand, may be exchanged, and passed on, and there may be separate inheritance rules for this, as was mentioned in the section on kinship. It may also be given as **tribute** to a leader, which helps to perpetuate a centralized political system, as we saw in Chapter 10. In societies without money or recognized currency, people would give away perishable goods as a kind of insurance for future needs. They trust that those who receive the goods will return the favour when they have a surplus. Similarly, the payment of tribute to a chief may be seen as a kind of investment, and chiefs have even been described as primitive bankers. Some of this form of exchange has economic aspects, then, but much of it is social, and it is difficult to draw a hard and fast line.

Market Economics

We discussed the social aspects of some simple *market economies* in Chapter 3, where we talked of the villages in Mexico and Guatemala which specialize in the produce of specific goods, such as bread, pots, woollen garments, flowers and fireworks, and we suggested that the markets serve to maintain communication over a wide area and offer entertainment as well as providing for basic needs. This system works because people marry **endogamously** within their communities, passing on the skills required for their trade through the generations. The economic aspects of these markets are thus best understood within the context of social arrangements through time.

These endogamous villages were contrasted with those in Africa and elsewhere where rules of **exogamy** can be seen to ensure communication over a particular cultural areas. In this case, women apparently become commodified as objects of exchange, at least according to some interpretations, but this idea was modified in the last chapter, where we saw that bridewealth transactions were misunderstood by outsiders such as missionaries and colonial administrators. In practice, they embodied important social elements like the validating of the union, the legitimizing of offspring and the provision of security.

Anthropological studies of markets and exchange usually throw up social factors which economists are inclined to overlook, and this emphasis affects the principles of analysis too. The concept of value, related to the cherished idea of *supply and demand*, is an interesting aspect of economic theory to consider. It is usually associated with scarcity, and very often related to the degree of access to resources. It is no good offering gold to someone dying for lack of water in a desert, for example, but in global terms water is much more abundant than gold, and the latter has acquired a widely recognized exchange value. Once subsistence is secure, food too is assigned differential value. The avocado, an expensive luxury in British supermarkets, lies rotting in superabundance in Mexico. Apples, which often do the same in Britain, are highly prized in Japan, where an aubergine, or eggplant, again something of a treat in Britain, is regarded as a poor food.

Serving a food made expensive like this is a way to gain status, however, and even a contemporary visit to palaces built and decorated by European monarchs during the periods of discovery and exploration of the New World (as far as they were concerned) illustrates some of the social reasons why they were prepared to make enormous investments of their resources in ships and sailors. The example of gold also demonstrates the idea of aesthetic value, and a consideration of the use of gold for the production of jewellery can lead us into its symbolic value. Wedding rings denote a social relationship which, as we have seen, may have a variety of particular connotations, and gold and silver are commonly used for gifts to mark rites of passage. The loss of such objects means more than a reduction in wealth.

The conversion of wealth into status was demonstrated forcibly in Chapter 3 by the case of the potlatch feasts, but another Mexican example illustrates a different element of constraint in this type of transfer. Here fiestas are financed by one person known as a *mayordomo* who pays for the whole event, thus winning a position of respect and power within the community. So unpopular are those who gain wealth but fail to do this, that people will bankrupt themselves for several years to put on a good show when their turn comes. George Foster's (1965) 'Image of Limited Good' relates this practice to a collective idea that if one family gets too rich others believe they are being deprived. Financing a festival not only redistributes wealth, then, but also offers a means to avoid jealousy and bitterness.

We briefly discussed social ideas about money in Chapter 3, where we gave examples of how cash may be converted into a gift. The use of any type of currency requires a certain agreement about its value, and the locally symbolic nature of this value is immediately evident when we return from a holiday with a pocketful of foreign coins. Out of the country where they are recognized, they might as well be pebbles, for all the use they are. A credit card, likewise, has little intrinsic value, but it has acquired some very useful global symbolic status. In the end, the global value of 'money' is determined in international markets in a system which looks remarkably like the barter which economists called primitive. We also showed in Chapter 3 that barter may be imbued with morality, and the lack of a shared system of morality at a global level may be a factor that bothers critics of the system.

In Sahlins' cycles of reciprocity, the generalized end of the continuum is the area of most social and moral implication, and thus another problem for *Western economic theory* when it assumes that people are always trying to *maximize their gains.* Even if the gains of prestige, power, status and divine benefits are added to material gains, there still remain the personal ties of that closest group, expressed in culturally specific notions like love, friendship and loyalty, even just a shared system of classification. At all levels of economics social factors play a part, and one of the reasons why foreigners doing business in Japan find themselves so well wined and dined is because their Japanese counterparts assign great value to making a business relationship a social one.

Anthropologists have now ploughed several ragged edges into the universalist furrows economists had previously presented so straight and clear, and the use of words such as **commodity** and **consumption** abound in *their* recent discourse. An influential work entitled *The Social Life of Things: Commodities in Cultural Perspective* (Appadurai, 1986) sought to shift attention from the forms of exchange and reciprocity, such as gift-giving, barter and trade, to the objects themselves, and how they are understood and appropriated in different ways, with different values and interpretations in the different situations in which they find themselves. We saw examples of this type of approach in the last section of Chapter 3.

An earlier influence was *The World of Goods: towards an Anthropology of Consumption* (Douglas and Isherwood, 1979) where an anthropologist and an economist together focused similar questions on the reasons behind the purchasing and acquisition of goods. The focus on consumption as a means to understanding social behaviour has recently become very popular among anthropologists. This includes not only the behaviour of shoppers in supermarkets and other retail outlets, but on subjects formerly seen as ritual and symbolic, such as weddings. In Japan, a wedding package may be purchased in its entirety, including every detail of dress and bridal coiffure, ceremony and feast, through to the arrangement of a suitable honeymoon location – the consumption of all of which Ofra Goldstein-Gidoni has interpreted in the global marketplace as an expression of Japaneseness (1997).

Social Views of the Environment

In this final part of the book, we have come full circle back to thinking about classification. In the early chapters we discussed anthropologists who classified themselves at the pinnacle of the developed world. At the time of writing, our **environment** is thought to be under threat from too much development, and the same people whom our forebears thought primitive are admired for their techniques of conservation. In practice, problems arise in thinking about the environment because of apparently incompatible views, and an anthropological approach can help to formulate less fiercely opposed alternatives. This, in turn, can help decision-making bodies to take account of all the people involved when they devise plans to make economically advantageous developments.

In a book entitled *Environmentalism: The View from Anthropology* (1993), Kay Milton has collected together a series of articles which offer various contributions to the debate. She points out, in the introduction, that concerns with the preservation of the environment are by no means new in small-scale societies:

> The Australian Aborigine who avoids hunting animals on sacred sites, and performs ceremonies to ensure the continued existence of edible species, is, like the Greenpeace campaigner, implementing environmental responsibilities. The rubber tappers of Amazonia, the Penan of Borneo, the subsistence farmers of northern India and many other communities have attempted to defend their traditional patterns of resource-use against what they see as the destructive consequences of large-scale commercial exploitation. (1993, p. 3)

Milton considers the advantages some local discussion and interpretation could have when governments and international NGOs (non-governmental organizations) formulate their environmental policies. An understanding of each other's motives and expectations would go a long way towards easing in changes perceived as globally important at a local level, but a greater understanding of local views might even offer an opportunity for a better system of conservation to be put into place. As Milton explains, ideas about the environment are constituted through discourse, and this draws on all kinds of ammunition depending on the point of view being advocated. Aboriginal people may be credited quite falsely with environmental concerns if it suits an argument for them to be so cited. On another occasion, the same people may be painted in a negative light for the same set of practices. Before we pursue this line of discussion, it is important that we try to see how complicated the issues may be.

In industrialized Britain, for the most part, people are able to transcend environmental limitations, except in extremes of weather, such as snow, floods and excessively high wind, and even then they get upset that the forecasters did not warn about the problems in time, or that the railways seem unable to cope. British concerns with 'the weather' reflect the unpredictable climate, and its sudden changes may interfere with plans, but on the whole, it is at most irritation at the vagaries of the physical environment, and except when severe conditions remind people of their vulnerability, they hardly adjust their usual routines to accommodate it.

It is usually only on television that they watch the damage caused by environmental phenomena in other parts of the world, and the tornado that tore a strip of complete devastation through Florida in early 1998 shocked the British people for whom this part of the world is known as an idyllic holiday zone. In other areas, chaos is caused by earthquakes and volcanos, and the ineptitude of the British government's response to the volcanic eruption on the island of Monserrat illustrates their lack of familiarity with such disasters. The British were also stunned by the stark contrast between technological achievement and the indiscriminate damage caused by the mighty earthquake which hit Kobe, Japan, in January 1995.

People in less-developed regions live in much closer contact with the physical environment, and their view of the world will reflect this intimacy. The various Inuit or Eskimo groups have a multitude of ways of dealing with the snow and ice in which they spend so much of the year, reflected in their words for different forms of it, and the Bedouin of the Sahara desert have a similar understanding of the sand. An anthropologist living among such people must consider environmental factors as a prime feature of their study, but novelists and film makers have sometimes better captured the feel of a way of life so alien to a cossetted twentieth-century city dweller. The novel by the Danish writer, Peter Høeg, *Miss Smilla's Feeling for Snow*, presents a Greenlander's view of the snow, for example, and some passages of Michael Ondaatje's book *The English Patient* forcibly illustrate the importance in the desert of understanding different types of wind. Both of these works have now been made into films which well illustrate the environmental exigencies of life in these extreme circumstances, and an ancient but classic anthropological film known as *Nanook of the North* makes clear the stark daily life of an Inuit family.

Anthropologists must look at environmental conditions wherever they work, but they realize that the world view of the people they live with may involve quite different perceptions to those which they themselves classify as 'the environment'. The anthropologist must aim to unearth this view, and in Chapter 6 where we showed how perceptions of the landscape could be unlike anything familiar to proponents of Western, or even Eastern art, we began to approach the potential complexity of the problem. Another aspect of the subject is the way in which people place themselves in the context of their surroundings, and in this environmentally conscious contemporary world, the extent to which their ideology is reflected in practice.

In the opening of a book on *Japanese Images of Nature*, the authors write:

> It is often claimed that the Japanese have a particular love for nature, a love often reflected in their art and material culture. But today equal notice is being given to the environmental degradation caused by the Japanese at home as well as abroad. How can these phenomena be reconciled? The aim of this volume is to address this question through an in-depth analysis of the human–nature relationship in Japan. (Asquith and Kalland, 1997, p. 1)

In the book, much attention is devoted to Japanese ideas which are translated as 'nature', demonstrating again the problems of definition, as well as conceptions of human interaction with the rest of the world.

In another article in Milton (1993), Tim Ingold makes a point very apt in this context about our whole notion of the environment as a **global** phenomenon. To think of the world we live in as a **globe** implies a view taken from the outside, as opposed to an earlier (European) view of humankind being part of a series of *spheres* which surrounded as well as included human activity. We learn of the world at school in global terms, although few of us have seen more than a photograph of this version of our environment, and we also study maps which colour the land masses in nation states which represent a history of colonialism and voyages of discovery and exploration.

Ingold refers to an idea that this view represents a triumph of technology over cosmology which, in contrast,

> places the person at the centre of an ordered universe of meaningful relations . . . and enjoins an understanding of these relations as a foundation for proper conduct towards the environment. (1993, p. 41)

Seeing the world as a globe puts human society *outside* what is residually construed as the "physical world" and furnishes the means for the former's control over the latter' (Ibid.). Ingold concedes, however, that each view contains the seeds of the other, and this is the basis of the approach taken up by some of the contributors to Asquith and Kalland (1997), mentioned above. Japanese often argue that they think of themselves as 'one with nature', an idea which they oppose to a Western desire to control it, although in practice, the Japanese clearly make efforts to control natural forces too.

In an indigenous system of Indian thought, too, a person is seen as integrally connected with the cosmos. According to Tambiah:

> The Ayurvedic system we have in mind postulates that the constituents of nature and of man are the same, and that processes such as the ingestion of food and medicine and the excretion of bodily waste products are part and parcel of the flow of energies and potencies between man and nature. Physical illness is the result of imbalances that can be corrected by exchanges at various levels – by the ingestion of the right substances and diet, by exposure to or protection from climatic conditions, by maintaining proper relations with other persons – family, kin, and the gods. (1990, p. 134)

It is important not to fall into the temptation of explaining the whole of social and political life in environmental terms, however. Several explanations of Japanese idiosyncratic 'character' seek causes in the rugged mountainous scenery, or the predominance of rice cultivation. There are mountains elsewhere, however, and plenty of people grow rice. It is important to avoid a **determinist** view. The physical environment undoubtedly limits the social arrangements a people are able to make, but it can not be said to *determine* them. If it could there would always be the same social system in the same environment and this is by no means the case. A glance at the variety of Mexican ethnography will illustrate the point, for there have been highly centralized, artistically and technologically advanced peoples living in precisely the area now populated with societies much more diffuse in political organization, and much less developed in technological terms.

To take one environmental factor, one 'problem' for a people to solve, usually reveals a variety of solutions, and these will depend on cultural differences. Everyone needs water to live, and a shortage of water can be a serious issue. The hunter-gatherer and pastoralist people discussed in the previous section generally solve the problem by moving around, by seeking water sources to resolve their needs immediately. Their response to the 'problem' is the nomadic way of life, and the transhumance of people like the Nuer is a more stable possibility. Elsewhere, a long-term response to the same 'problem' may be achieved through the building of irrigation systems, which in turn involves a social organization capable of maintaining and administering them, as well as sharing out the supplies. Rules of land ownership are then likely to characterize economic life, and access to water will very likely be regulated. Edmund Leach's book *Pul Eliya* (1961) is about the system of land-ownership in a community in Sri Lanka, and it gives an abundance of detail about the social consequences of such a system (see under 'Further Reading' below).

The environment cannot be said to *determine* the social system because the environment is no objective reality. It is always categorized by the people who live in it and make use of it, according to their view of the world. One last example of different views, which has become a highly contentious international issue, involves the varying perceptions of the problems of *whale conservation* found in Japan and among members of different Western nations. According to a Japanese view, based on their own independent research, a view which is shared by Norwegians and Icelanders, there are enough whales to be harvested for consumption, indeed, if they are not, they will eat up food supplies of fish which could otherwise also have been caught to feed the Japanese population. Whale meat is a valuable source of protein, and the catching and preparation of whales are specialist occupations which have been passed down through generations.

The predominant Western view, however, is that the whale population is threatened with extinction, and if the Japanese (and others) keep catching them, they will soon be no more. Many of the people who take this view have been brought up on stories about affable whales such as Moby Dick, and Jonah, and very few of them regard whale meat as part of their diet. One Japanese commentator remarked that if the whales were called 'cows' there would be no problem, and criticized the Western world for being sentimental. A very similar, but measured, anthropological view is presented by Niels Einarsson (1993) who sets out the case of Icelandic fisherman who are losing their entire livelihood for reasons seen locally as quite indefensible. A Norwegian anthropologist, Arne Kalland, has even taken a place on the International Whaling Commission to try to present a more objective viewpoint.

I have no idea whose scientific figures are more accurate, and this is not the place to take up the issue. A demonstration of differing perceptions is the aim at this point. The whaling issue emphasizes the importance of seeing how the environment is **classified** by those who live in it, and also how views of the environment may be created through discourse about it. Greenpeace can be commended for its commitment to many important issues, but it can hardly be denied that it has made use of, nay even exploited, the romanticism of the 'intelligent, singing' whale in attracting support. If these words are making the reader angry, then turn to consider the plight of the people around the world who rely on whales and other sea animals for their livelihood (for example, see Barnes, 1996, and Photograph 12.1).

Photograph 12.1   Villagers in Lamalera, Indonesia divide up a whale they have hunted – a good source of protein (photograph courtesy of R.H. and R. Barnes)

Environmental Influence in Social Life

The *environment* does of course influence economic, political and ritual life in most parts of the world, although in industrial societies this relationship may very often be neglected, especially from the reciprocal point of view. However, as we have seen in the case of the whale, all apparently economic resources may not be regarded in the same way. Among Hindus, the cow is regarded as a sacred animal, and though perfectly edible in objective terms, it is forbidden for consumption by local custom. Cows wander rather freely in some parts of India, damaging crops and impeding traffic, possibly even competing with human beings for the limited resources available. In 1995 a serious rail accident was caused by a cow wandering onto the line.

As we have seen elsewhere in this book, it is also possible to point to relationships between the environment and political arrangements. In the first section of this chapter we saw that the choice of economic activity affects the possibilities for political development. Hunter-gatherers and pastoralists live in groups limited in size by the availability of food for themselves and, in the second case, their cattle, whereas sedentary agriculturalists are better able to develop larger populations and more complex political systems. The case of

Nuer politics, sometimes called *fission/fusion politics*, is clearly influenced by the transhumance of their lives, since allegiances can be adjusted twice a year.

The article by Anthony Leeds in the book edited by Andrew P. Vayda, called *Environment and Cultural Behaviour* (1969), discusses the relationship between ecology and chieftainship among the Yaruro Indians of Venezuela, illustrating the view of leadership found in the tropical forest of South America, which we have already considered in the chapter on politics. In the same book, Stuart Piddocke brings an ecological perspective to the practice of potlatch which we discussed in Chapter 3, and a series of other authors consider environmental influences on political arrangements in a variety of different societies.

Ritual and religious activity is also undoubtedly influenced by environmental features. Festivals are often associated with changes of seasons, planting and harvest, or the depths of winter and summer. Even where the agricultural cycle has been superseded by the wonders of scientific technology for bringing goods to the supermarket, seasonal goods such as pumpkins, strawberries and sprouts are still drawn upon for celebrations. In Japan, whose land area is 90 per cent mountainous, mountains are the sites of religious shrines and pilgrimages, as well as often being regarded as mystical in particular ways. In a land where irrigation is important, water festivals are to be expected, and long spells of dry weather may still be punctuated with rain-making dances.

The very cosmology a people hold is often quite unintelligible without an understanding of attitudes to the environment, its limitations, and associations that have been created with it. Christmas in Europe and North America is inevitably associated with snow, for example, whereas the same feast in Australia is held in mid-summer. It is interesting the way that some of the symbolic associations have persisted through this inconvenient climatic difficulty, and in parts of Australia there is a 'seasonal Christmas' festival, probably largely a commercial venture, but allowing the use of northern symbols such as blazing fires and snowmen at the appropriate time of year.

A visit to the opposite hemisphere, or a completely different climate is a good way to realize how environmentally orientated one's language is. For those of European stock who have grown up in Australia, New Zealand, or other southern climes, daily language contains some wonderful anomalies imported from a completely different ecosystem. The four seasons used in Australia are sometimes only illustrated by the deciduous trees planted by the colonizers and the agricultural cycles imposed by their farmers. Australian indigenous trees flower in the winter and the climate is very often rather warm, especially in the north. Map 12.1 illustrates a possible view of the world, from an Australian point of view.

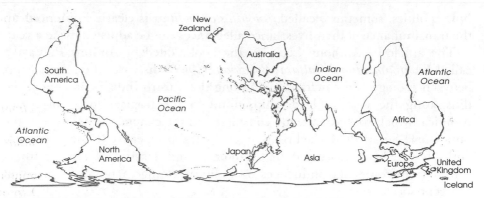

Map 12.1   A view of the world from the Southern hemisphere

In global parlance, too, we have adopted some originally directional words to take on meanings now quite inappropriate in orientation. 'The Far East', like the 'Middle East', was measured from the point of view of Europe, actually west from America, and north from Australia and New Zealand. 'The West' is an expression used to describe an amorphous collection of non-Eastern countries, now rather different from each other, but sharing the language which perpetuates these directional idiosyncrasies. I hope that this book, though it emanates from the original source of these misnomers, will have made way for a more acute examination of 'the other'.

Conclusion

In this last chapter, I have made a point of referring back where possible to previous sections of the book in order to bring areas we isolated to consider separately into a more overarching scheme. In the end, economic and environmental factors are anywhere part of a social and cultural system which they influence, but by which they are also influenced, shaped and defined. Indeed, each of the chapters of this book is an artificial separation of certain subjects for analytical purposes, all of which will influence and affect the others in any particular social situation.

A reader who feels inspired to pursue an interest in social anthropology may choose from the further readings at the end of any of the chapters, but there are also few better ways to gain a deeper feel for the subject than to return again and again to the ethnography of a particular people, and relate the findings to the general principles we have been outlining. It may even become possible to see how the writer might have approached the subject matter differently, or managed to bring out different aspects of social life.

Imagine yourself going to the place where the ethnography was collected, and see what further questions you would like to ask . . .

References

Appadurai, Arjun (1986) *The Social Life of Things: Commodities in Cultural Perspective* (Cambridge University Press).

Asquith Pamela and Arne Kalland (1997) *Japanese Images of Nature: Cultural Perspectives* (London: Curzon).

Barnard, Alan and James Woodburn (1988) 'Property, power and ideology in hunter-gathering societies: an introduction', in Ingold *et al.*, *Hunter-Gatherers* (Oxford: Berg) pp. 4–31.

Barnes, R. H. (1996) *Sea Hunters of Indonesia: Fishers and Weavers of Lamalera* (Oxford: Clarendon).

Campbell, J. K. (1964) *Honour, Family and Patronage* (Oxford: Clarendon).

Douglas, Mary and Baron Isherwood (1979) *The World of Goods: towards an Anthropology of Consumption* (London and New York: Routledge).

Einarrson, Niels (1993) 'All animals are equal, but some are cetaceans: conservation and culture conflict', in Kay Milton (ed.), *Environmentalism: The View from Anthropology* (London: Routledge) pp. 73–84.

Foster, George (1965) 'Peasant Society and the Image of Limited Good',*American Anthropologist*, **67**: 293–315.

Goldstein Gidoni, Ofra (1997) *Packaged Japaneseness: Weddings, Business and Brides* (London: Curzon).

Ingold, Tim (1993) 'Globes and Spheres: the Topology of Environmentalism', in Kay Milton (ed.), *Environmentalism: The View from Anthropology* (London: Routledge) pp. 31–42.

Ingold, Tim, David Riches and James Woodburn (eds) (1988) *Hunter-Gatherers* (Oxford: Berg).

Leeds, Anthony (1969) 'Ecological Determinants of Chieftanship Among the Yaruro Indians of Venezuela', in Andrew P. Vayda,*Environment and Cultural Behaviour* (Austin and London: Universiy of Texas Press) pp. 377–94.

Milton, Kay (ed.) (1993) *Environmentalism: The View from Anthropology* (London: Routledge).

Sahlins, Marshall (1974) *Stone Age Economics* (London: Tavistock).

Tambiah, Stanley Jeyaraja (1990) *Magic, science, religion, and the scope of rationality* (Cambridge University Press).

Further Reading

Firth, Raymond (ed.) (1967) *Themes in Economic Anthropology* (London: Tavistock).

Forde, Daryll (1934) *Habitat, Economy and Society* (London: Methuen).

Humphrey, Caroline and Stephen Hugh-Jones (1992) *Barter, Exchange and Value: An Anthropological Approach* (Cambridge University Press).
Leach, Edmund (1961) *Pul Eliya* (Cambridge University Press).
Mauss, Marcel (1979) *Seasonal Variations of the Eskimo* (London: Routledge & Kegan Paul).
Piddocke, Stuart (1969) 'The Potlatch System of the Southern Kwakiutl: A New Perspective', in Andrew P. Vayda (ed.), pp. 130–56.
Vayda, Andrew P. (1969) *Environment and Cultural Behaviour* (Austin and London: University of Texas Press).

Novels

Høeg, Peter, *Miss Smilla's Feeling for Snow* (London: Fontana, 1994).
Ondaatje, Michael, *The English Patient* (London: Picador, 1992).

Films

Bushmen of the Kalahari (John Marshall and Robert Young, 1974), a National Geographic film, is the personal account of film-maker John Marshall, son of the anthropologist Lorna Marshall, when he returns to find the people of the Kalahari among whom he lived 20 years earlier. He has since made several other films about these people.
The Emerald Forest (John Boorman, 1986) is another feature film about industrial threats to the life of an imaginary indigenous people of the Amazonian tropical rain forest in which the young son of the chief engineer is captured and reared by the Indians.
The Gods must be Crazy is a somewhat overly dramatic feature film about the same Bushmen of the Kalahari and the encounter of one of them with life in a neighbouring African war.
Nanook of the North (Robert Flaherty), one of the earliest ethnographic films, depicts the life of an Inuit man and his family.

Filmography

See below for explanation of abbreviations; the running time is given in parentheses after the name of film.

Granada 'Disappearing World' Series (GL, NLA, PMI, RAI-H)

Azande, The (52")
Dervishes of Kurdistan, The (52")
Kalasha: Rites of Spring, The (60")
Kataragama, A God for All Seasons (50")
Kawelka: Ongka's Big Moka, The (52")
Kayapo: Out of the Forest, The (55")
Kirghiz of Afghanistan, The (51")
Lau of Malaita, The (52")
Masai Manhood (DER) (53")
Masai Women (DER) (53")
Mehinacu, The (52")
Mursi: Relations with the Kwegu, The (50")
Mursi: War with the Bodi, The (52")
Some Women of Marrakesh (53")
Trobriand Islanders, The (50")
Wodaabe, The (51")

'Strangers Abroad' Series (RAI-S)

Everything is Relatives (55")
Fieldwork (50")
Off the Verandah (55")
Strange Beliefs (55")

General List

Bushmen of the Kalahari (National Geographic film) (DER) (50")
Caste at Birth, a Sered film made for British television (50")
Emerald Forest, The (commercial feature film) (113")
Feast, The (DER, NLA, RAI-H) (28")
Gods must be Crazy, The (commercial feature film)

227

Life Chances: Four Families in a Greek Cypriot Village (NLA, RAI-H-S) (43")
Nanook of the North (NLA, RAI-H)
Osôshiki [*Funeral, Japanese-style*] (commercial feature film) (NLA)
Secrets and Lies (commercial feature film)
Trobriand Cricket (EMC, NLA, RAI-H)
Under the Sun: The Dragon Bride (National Geographic film) (55")

Abbreviations

DER – available for sale or rental on VHS and VHS PAL format from:
Documentary Educational Resources
101 Morse Street
Watertown
Massachusetts, 02171, USA
Tel. 617–926–0491
Fax. 617–926–9519
E-mail: cclose@delphi.com
Web catalogue: http://der.org/docued

EMC:
Extension Media Center
2176 Shattuck Avenue
University of California
Berkeley, CA 94720, USA

GL – available for purchase in the UK from:
Granada Learning
1 Broadbent Road
Watersheddings
Oldham OL1 4LB, UK
Tel. 0161–627–4469

NLA – available sometimes VHS, sometimes 16 mm to educational institutions and others in Australia.
National Library of Australia
Film and Video Lending Service
c/o Cinemedia
222 Park Street
South Melbourne
Victoria 3205
Australia
Tel. 03–9929–7044
Fax. 03–9929–7027
E-mail: nfvlsbookings@cinemedia.net
Website: www.cinemedia.net/NLA

PMI – available in the USA from:
Public Media Incorporated
5547 North Ravenswood Avenue
Chicago
Illinois 60640, USA
Tel. 773–878–2600
Fax. 773–878–2895

RAI-H – available for hire, on video, within the UK
RAI-S – available for purchase worldwide for non-commercial use in PAL and NTSC format. Contact:
Film Officer
Royal Anthropological Institute
50 Fitzroy Street
London W1P 5HS
Tel. 44–171–387–0455
Fax. 44–171–383–4235
Email: rai@cix.compulink.co.uk

Index of Authors and Film-Makers

230

Index of Peoples and Places

This list is made up of categories which may be used to identify groups of people who share ideas by virtue of membership in those groups. The world map, on p. 249, gives the approximate locations of peoples and places which may be defined geographically, but national boundaries, anyway less relevant sometimes than a notion of shared identity, have not been marked. However, further geographical information is included below.

233

General Index

Note: Anthropological and other technical terms which appear in **bold** in the index are discussed particularly at the page numbers which also appear in bold.

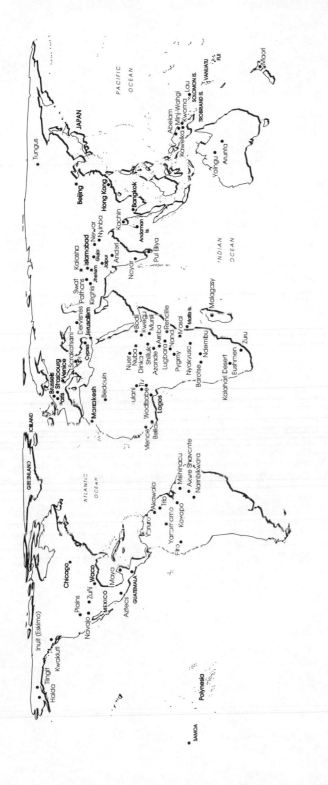

Peoples and places mentioned in this book